Developing Literacy
in the Primary Classroom

Education at SAGE

SAGE is a leading international publisher of journals, books, and electronic media for academic, educational, and professional markets.

Our education publishing includes:

- accessible and comprehensive texts for aspiring education professionals and practitioners looking to further their careers through continuing professional development

- inspirational advice and guidance for the classroom

- authoritative state of the art reference from the leading authors in the field

Find out more at: **www.sagepub.co.uk/education**

Developing Literacy
in the Primary Classroom

Gary Woolley

Los Angeles | London | New Delhi
Singapore | Washington DC

SAGE Publications Ltd
1 Oliver's Yard
55 City Road
London EC1Y 1SP

SAGE Publications Inc.
2455 Teller Road
Thousand Oaks, California 91320

SAGE Publications India Pvt Ltd
B 1/I 1 Mohan Cooperative Industrial Area
Mathura Road
New Delhi 110 044

SAGE Publications Asia-Pacific Pte Ltd
3 Church Street
#10-04 Samsung Hub
Singapore 049483

Editor: James Clark
Editorial assistant: Rachael Plant
Project manager: Jeanette Graham
Production editor: Thea Watson
Copyeditor: Sharon Cawood
Proofreader: Isabel Kirkwood
Indexer: Anne Solomito
Marketing manager: Catherine Slinn
Cover designer: Naomi Robinson
Typeset by: C&M Digitals (P) Ltd, Chennai, India
Printed in India by: Replika Press Pvt Ltd

Library of Congress Control Number: 2013951865

British Library Cataloguing in Publication data

A catalogue record for this book is available from the British Library

ISBN 978-1-4462-6728-8
ISBN 978-1-4462-6729-5 (pbk)

CONTENTS

ACKNOWLEDGEMENTS

This book acknowledges the support that I received from my wife, Helen Woolley, Griffith University and the University of the Sunshine Coast. I would also like to thank Independent Schools Queensland, particularly Dr Janelle Wills; and I would like to thank Faith Lutheran College, Eloise Beveridge (Junior School Principal), Glenda des David, Tracey Underhill, Caroline Hay and Rachael Nociforo for actively supporting my research.

Publisher's acknowledgements

SAGE and the author would like to thank the following reviewers whose comments on the proposal helped shape this book:

Christine Allan, Leeds Metropolitan University

Howard Cotton, Plymouth University

Susan Feez, University of New England

Eileen Hyder, University of Reading

Lesley Lancaster, Marchester Metropolitan University

Noella McKenzie, Charles Sturt University

ABOUT THE AUTHOR

Dr Gary Woolley is a senior lecturer in Inclusion and Diversity at the University of the Sunshine Coast. Gary's particular professional interests include reading comprehension difficulties, memory, cognition, learning engagement and English as a second language. He has had a broad primary school teaching experience in public and private school systems for over 30 years. He has published widely and taken part in several national research projects in literacy and inclusive education. In recognition of a significant contribution in the field of literacy and learning difficulties, Gary was awarded the Tertiary Student Award for 2007 by Learning Difficulties Australia (LDA). In 2008, he developed the COR Literacy Framework as a professional development programme for primary school teachers and has an ongoing involvement in its implementation. In 2010 and 2011, he was awarded the Outstanding Early Career Researcher Award for his contribution to the research activities of Griffith University.

Author's Blog: http://reading4meaning.blogspot.com.au

LIST OF FIGURES
AND TABLES

Figures

Tables

INTRODUCTION

Literacy is not only important for the prosperity and development of individuals but also for the cultural, social and economic health of nations. It is fundamental to a basic education for all, and as such is essential for the eradication of poverty and in addressing many other social problems such as the reduction of child mortality, reduction in population growth, achieving gender equality and fostering sustainable development, peace and democracy. Thus, literacy is a tool of personal empowerment and also a means for social and human development (UNGA, 2002).

Literacy is not something confined to classrooms during school time but continues throughout the individual's life span in a range of social contexts. As a teacher, you will be the crucial factor for effective literacy learning and student literacy engagement. While there is no single instructional method that has been found to be the most effective, it is generally recognised that a balanced approach to teaching literacy using evidence-based practices that draw on a number of theoretical perspectives is often the most desirable (Gambrell et al., 2007). Your relationship with your students can have a powerful influence on them. You will be able to engage them more effectively if you seek to know your students by smiling and talking to them face-to-face in class and on a casual basis outside the classroom. Whenever possible, take the opportunity to ask them about their interests and experiences and also share aspects of your own life experience.

Emphasise collaboration and cooperation with others in the knowledge that literacy is a social enterprise. Offer support where needed but in such a way that it develops student autonomy. Differentiate instruction to support diverse learners by using appropriate adjustments and adaptations to the curriculum. The support provided for your students should provide realistic challenges and focus on authentic learning tasks. You should integrate new technologies wherever possible into classroom activities and regard everyone as a learner and teacher. Finally, you should develop key competences, and your teaching emphasis should promote critical thinking, creativity, initiative, problem solving, risk taking, decision making and the constructive management of feelings and attitudes (Rose, 2009).

There are, however, considerable challenges for literacy teachers in contemporary classrooms. These challenges can be met effectively by building the children's capacity to use a range of literacy practices in authentic environments (Walsh, 2011). As teachers, you will constantly need to bring together your understandings about literacy, pedagogy and curriculum, your subject area, and what you intend for your students to achieve within the learning community (Beavis, 2007). Effective teachers of literacy are teachers who possess the following types of knowledge:

- declarative knowledge – knowing effective, evidence-based best practices for effective literacy instruction
- procedural knowledge – knowing best practices and how they are implemented
- conditional knowledge – knowing when a particular practice is preferable to another
- reflective knowledge – knowing whether or not a particular teaching practice is working effectively
- adaptive knowledge – knowing how to combine or adapt practices or techniques to meet the diverse needs of students.
  (*Source:* Brown, 1978; see also Paris et al., 1984)

Social networking has the potential not only to enhance your own knowledge but also to connect you to a community of teacher-researchers from different parts of the world. Social networking sites, such as Twitter, Facebook and Pinterest, are examples of these. There are a plethora of other Web 2.0 networking sites that are also specifically designed to inform the teaching community.

Teachers as researchers

You should also consider yourself as a teacher-researcher. Teacher research is about empowering you as a teacher, and has the power to enrich your professional life as it involves selecting areas of interest and participating in research activities that will enhance your professional development and teaching practice. It is essentially about inquiry and asking questions such as:

- What are the essential things to be learned?
- When and where is literacy learning taking place?
- How supportive is the specific learning context?
- What social factors will influence the students' approach to learning?
- What research-based best teaching practices will enhance learning?
- What are the outcomes and how will you know when your students have achieved them?
- How will you know when your literacy teaching has been effective?

Action research is an example of research in an educational context. It is an example of reflective, evidence-based inquiry that requires teachers to identify a problem, collect appropriate information about that problem, and design a solution and collect data to support the effectiveness of the solution. The benefits of doing action research in the classroom are that you will be able to tell your own stories and share your findings with other practitioners (Honan, 2012). One possibility is to identify a problem or issue and to partner with another teacher, mentor or academic to provide appropriate support for investigation and research. The important thing is that you become a reflective teacher-researcher or co-researcher and think of yourself as a knowledge builder.

You should also view learning theory as playing an important role in how your literacy curriculum is delivered to the children in your care. This type of knowledge will empower you as a teacher because it will give you more options and a framework in which to build a greater repertoire of appropriate evidence-based strategies (Grant and Walsh, 2003).

There will be many other ways for you to update your theoretical and practical knowledge in teaching. One of the most useful ways is through professional development where, for example, academics or expert teachers are invited to a school to share their research with you and your colleagues. Another option is to network with like-minded educators and form a collaborative network. For example, you may be able to join a literacy network of teachers from different schools in a particular domain of interest so that you can share ideas and practices and discuss issues.

Staff meetings and informal sharing sessions can also be opportunities to create a community of literacy educators. Another important way to keep abreast of trends in education is to join a university library. Professional associations also provide information on their websites, in their journals and newsletters and at conferences. These professional activities not only have the potential to empower you as a teacher and enrich your professional life but will flow on to enhance the literacy enjoyment and learning of your students (Gambrell et al., 2007).

References

Beavis, C. (2007). Critical engagement: ICTs, literacy and curriculum. In *Australian Literacy Educators Association: The Best of Practically Primary* (pp. 17–21). Norwood, SA: ALEA.

Brown, A. L. (1978). Knowing when, where, and how to remember: A problem of metacognition. In R. Glaser (ed.), *Advances in Educational Psychology*. Hillsdale, NJ: Erlbaum.

Gambrell, L. B., Malloy, J. A. and Mazzoni, S. A. (2007). Evidence-based best practice for comprehensive literacy instruction. In L. B. Gambrell, L. M. Morrow and M. Pressley (eds), *Best Practices in Literacy Instruction* (3rd edn) (pp. 11–29). New York: The Guilford Press.

Grant, H. and Walsh, C. (2003). Teacher research: What's it all about? *Practically Primary*, 8(2), 4–7.

Honan, E. (2012). *Teachers as Researchers*. PETAA paper 187. Newtown, NSW: Primary English Teaching Association Australia.

Paris, S. G., Cross, D. R. and Lipson, M. Y. (1984). Informed strategies for learning: A program to improve children's reading awareness and comprehension. *Journal of Educational Psychology*, 76(6), 1239–1252.

Rose, J. (2009). *Independent Review of the Primary Curriculum: Final Report*. Nottingham: DCSF Publications.

United Nations General Assembly (UNGA) (2002). United Nations literacy decade: Education for all; International plan of action; Implementation of the General Assembly Resolution 56/116. Available at: www.unesco.org/education/pdf/un_decade_literacy/un_resolution.pdf

Walsh, M. (2011). *Multimodal Literacy: Researching Classroom Practice*. Primary Newtown, NSW: English Teaching Association Australia.

CHAPTER 1

WHAT IS LITERACY IN TODAY'S WORLD?

Chapter objectives

- To understand what literacy is.
- To develop appropriate instructional approaches to literacy learning.
- To develop a repertoire of strategies to foster literacy engagement.

Key questions

1. How does the social context affect literacy learning?
2. How do literacy learners use literacy to construct meaning?
3. How do literacy users regulate their own learning?

Key words: best practice, context, literacy, new literacies, practice, process.

Introduction

This chapter begins with a discussion about what is meant by literacy in a changing multi-literate world. The discussion is designed to discover a number of dimensions of literacy practices that are appropriate in the contemporary classroom. This theoretical perspective will establish a foundation for teaching methodology, pedagogy and learning within a socio-cultural context. It examines the contemporary ideas and theoretical understandings of what literacy is and what is meant by literacy best practices.

> It is no longer possible to think about literacy in isolation from a vast array of social, technological and economic factors. Two distinct yet related factors deserve to be particularly highlighted. These are, on the one hand, the broad move from the now centuries-long dominance of writing to the new dominance of the image and, on the other hand, the move from the dominance of the medium of the book to the dominance of the medium of the screen. These two together are producing a revolution in the uses and effects of literacy and of associated means for representing and communicating at every level and in every domain. Together they raised two questions: what is the likely future of literacy, and what are the likely larger-level social and cultural effects of that change? (Kress, 2003: 1)

Literacy: a changing landscape

Globalisation has had a distinct influence on the pace of change in our culture and language. The pace of change in society has been given impetus by the proliferation of multimedia and information technologies (Kalantzis et al., 2002). In the above quote, Kress (2003) gives us an insight into the big questions that are associated with literacy in contemporary society. These changes have affected everyone – for example, children are now able to participate in twittering, wikis, blogs or in various social networking sites (e.g. MySpace, Facebook, YouTube, Flickr); obtain instant information from the web; or participate in a virtual environment through gaming or in a virtual world such as 'Second Life' (Walsh, 2011).

According to the UNESCO World Education Report, *Teachers and Teaching in a Changing World*: 'the young generation is entering a world that is changing in all spheres: scientific and technological, political, economic, social and cultural. The emergence of a "knowledge-based" society is changing the global economy and the status of education' (UNESCO, 1998:16). The challenge for you, as a teacher, is how to effectively design a curriculum to provide your children with the necessary skills to function in a rapidly changing technological landscape. This is particularly important since the new technological and social developments have been accompanied by rapid social, cultural, economic, political and educational changes. In this electronic, mediated world that we live in, 'being literate involves the understanding of how different modalities are combined in complex ways to create meaning' (Snyder, 2002: 3). New national language curriculums in the UK and Australasia are based on the notion that language is a socially situated practice, and a purposeful literacy curriculum needs to be implemented in classrooms (Karantzola and Intzidis, 2001).

Traditional print-based texts have taken on new forms and combinations that involve a more integrated approach to words and text in the post-modern environment (see Chapter 6). You will need to draw students' attention to images in texts, discuss how the images and texts relate to each other and identify any new meanings that might arise from the interaction. Thus, new technologies have positioned the learner so that there are many more choices and systems to navigate. In our contemporary society, children are not only reading from and viewing these technologies but responding to them by producing their own diverse, multimodal and digital text formats (Walsh, 2011).

There are two broad perspectives that have been identified within these changes and which will be discussed in this chapter. The first perspective is the effect of the technological changes that are inherent in reading, writing and producing on-screen compared with reading and writing print-based texts. The second perspective relates to the changes that are occurring in the social practices of literacy, which have changed and expanded exponentially with the development of Web 2.0 technology.

Print and technological changes

Literacy is a cultural practice and is also associated with personal identity and belonging in society. For many years, literacy has been regarded as a form of communication, a mere matter of developing a skill set and the ability to communicate effectively in the context in which the individual is situated. However, over the last few decades the social foundations of literacy, as observed in everyday environments such as schools, workplaces, and in broader cultural settings, have broadened contemporary thinking about what literacy is and how it can empower people in various circumstances. Your challenge is to understand how the varied needs of students within diverse communities and with wide-ranging multimodal forms of expression in which they communicate can be addressed in classrooms (Luke et al., 2003).

The literacy research has identified five factors that impact on reading within the socio-cultural context of the classroom (see Figure 1.1). This model recognises that literacy is the product of a complex combination of factors, and each of these factors, either individually or in combination, needs to be considered when designing the literacy curriculum (Snow, 2002).

Learners

Today's literacy learners bring a large repertoire of knowledge and abilities to learning tasks and texts of all kinds. To some degree, this will depend on their own background experiences, socio-cultural circumstances and opportunities to use various literacies at home, at school and within the community in which they live. Unfortunately, this is not a level playing field as some children have

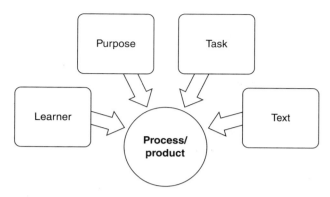

Figure 1.1   Factors that impact on literacy

had a much richer exposure to good literature of all kinds and ample opportunities to explore them. Learners are also limited by other internal facets such
as: the breadth of their background knowledge, the efficiency of their working
memory and their thinking processes.

Purpose

Learning is enhanced when the content is embedded in situations that are
meaningful and valued by the learner. The chances of learning being meaningful and valued are maximised when there is a clear purpose for the task
and the participants are aware of that purpose.

Task

Rich learning tasks are purposeful and meaningful activities that can be as
diverse as creating a web page or designing a school garden landscape. Out
of the task should come the need to develop a range of skills, which are
necessary to the achievement of that task. A number of important strategies
will be involved in the development of these skills, depending on the types
of texts or resources used (Green, 2003). The nature of the task is also
dependent on the role that the viewer, reader, writer, actor or designer
assumed in completing the task (a discussion about roles and resources will
be developed further later on in our discussion).

Text

Texts are what we construct or are constructed when we speak, listen, write
or read. They are usually part of a discourse that is embedded in social

communicative acts that are situated in particular social institutions such as classrooms, libraries, friendship groups, clubs and homes. These institutions most often favour various artefacts such as books, magazines, videos, blogs, plays and myriad other products that support them and are situated within a much broader social discourse. In other words, when we write, read, speak or listen on particular occasions, we use specific forms of language and various objects, tools, technologies, sites and organisational genres to engage with others (Gee, 2003).

Process/Product

Literacy learning has often focused on certain products or cultural artefacts. For example, reading a book is an act of engaging with a cultural artefact, while typing a text message on a smartphone is an act of producing digital artefacts. In today's world, the act of sending a message is often just as important as the product itself. The process is concerned with social engagement while products are concerned with artefacts.

Table 1.1 provides examples of texts of various types and shows how these five elements interact in any literature-based activity.

Table 1.1 Examples of pedagogical practice and the factors that impact on literacy

Text	Task	Learner	Purpose	Process/Product
Examples of letters	Write a letter to the council to make comments related to a proposed development of a park next-door to the school	Knowledge about why people write letters and the particular features of the genre	To make comments and recommendations as future park users	Process: the processes that are used (including cooperative writing skills) to construct a letter; Product: a letter for a specific purpose
Audio podcast of the interesting features of the school and its surroundings	Identify and describe favourite places within the school environment	Knowledge of podcasts and the features of the genre; awareness of their surroundings	To create pride in the environment in which they are placed	Process: to develop planning and speaking skills to inform parents
A movie trailer depicting a science fiction event taking place in the playground	Engage with the science fiction genre using artefacts within the playground	Knowledge about the science fiction genre and science fiction films; knowledge about how films are made	To entertain and to develop an appreciation for the things that we use every day	Process: to develop basic filming and editing skills; Product: a two-minute film trailer that can be placed on YouTube

Vignette 1.1

In the following chapters, we will be looking at vignettes utilising practices that you may find in some typical classrooms. This first vignette is one about you and your own literacy endeavours.

Brainstorm and list the types of literacy practices that you might have engaged in over the past week. Choose one of those activities and copy the chart below (Table 1.2). Write your comments in each of the columns. After you finish, add this to what others have done so that a more comprehensive list can be constructed.

Table 1.2 Literacy practices

Text	Task	Learner	Purpose	Process/Product

Questions

1 How do you use texts in everyday life?
2 How does the notion of purpose affect the other three components of the model?
3 What are the differences between process, product and purpose?

Debates in the teaching of literacy

There has been a somewhat heated debate that has been raging in literacy education for several decades concerning how reading should be taught. Back in 1955, Flesch published a book, which was one of the bestselling books in literacy education at the time, entitled *Why Johnny Can't Read*, and claimed that the 'look-say approach' was responsible for the crisis in teaching reading. Later, he published another book (Flesch, 1981) in which the blame was placed on the 'whole language' method of literacy instruction in conjunction with a lack of explicit teaching of phonics.

Chall (1967) coined it the 'Great Debate'. More recently, this debate has reached such intensity that public confidence in literacy teachers has been undermined and many believe we have a literacy crisis n our schools (Snyder, 2008). Over this period of time, the 'debate' has taken on the form of polarised and very dogmatic points of view. In many circles, including the popular media, this debate has sometimes been referred to as the 'Literacy Wars' (Coles, 2003). Green, Hodgens and Luke (1997) claimed that this battle has become a permanent feature of the continuing educational dialogue and policy (p. 7). However, the debate has changed somewhat over this period from 'whole word' versus 'phonics' to 'phonics' versus 'whole language' (Cambourne, 2008).

One of the main literacy clashes concerns the very definition of literacy. This is because there are different views on how literacy can be defined and how it should be taught. In essence, these disputes focus on either a bottom-up (surface feature driven) or top-down (or conceptually driven) approach. The intensity of the debate may be due to a polarisation of opinion that has been fuelled by a narrow and very static understanding of what literacy entails. More often than not, these discussions focus on whether phonics should or shouldn't be taught, or whether the 'right' English grammar is also being taught. Newspapers have capitalised on this debate because it captures the public's attention and sells newspapers (Snyder, 2010). Publishers also tend to promote and market books to practise basic skills, so that teachers can teach to increase children's scores in high stakes testing.

In response to this controversy, the Australian and UK governments have advocated a 'return to basics' that includes the teaching of grammar and phonics (Le et al., 2011; Rose, 2009). The current call to 'return to basics' in language and literacy education shows a strong influence of ideology, public opinion and politics in literacy education (Le et al., 2011). Cambourne (2008) believed that just ignoring these 'debates' or 'wars' disempowers teachers and leaves them at the mercy of those who may be driven by their own political or financial agendas.

Fortunately, in more recent times, researchers have called for a more balanced approach that incorporates a combination of methods utilising a range of evidence-based pedagogies (Farris et al., 2004; Pressley, 1998, 2006). This balanced approach would seek to firmly develop students' skills and knowledge by teaching them to be able to transfer their abilities across a range of contexts. However, what must be emphasised is the essential social and contextual nature of literacy. Thus, your curriculum design should focus on providing a range of authentic cognitive, social and multi-modal dimensions and contexts for literacy acquisition and creation for students of all ages and stages of development (Kell, 2001). In the next section, you will be introduced to a number of dimensions of literacy practice.

Cognitive dimensions

According to Woolley (2011), there are three cognitive processes that operate simultaneously at different levels: (a) perceptual, (b) cognitive and (c) metacognitive. At the surface level, the learner is concerned with perceptual features such as signs and symbols. In terms of reading, the learner directs his/her attention to the graphic, phonic and linguistic features of the text. Essentially, at this level, the learner is concerned with the learning task and is guided by a bottom-up or surface-level process.

At the cognitive level, the learner uses a deeper level of processing that requires the learner to note the underlying ideas and to construct new knowledge by combining or altering the new knowledge in light of their existing background knowledge. This is a type of transactional process that is guided by what is often referred to as a top-down approach.

At the third level, the literacy practitioner steps back from the learning situation to consider his/her actual thinking processes. This is a process of thinking about thinking. It is essentially a self-regulating process that is concerned with setting appropriate goals, monitoring progress, making decisions about appropriate strategies and reflecting on the adequacy of the learning task (Zimmerman, 2002).

In terms of the 'great' literacy debate, these processes are executed at different levels but are interdependent and often happen simultaneously. The third level is an executive function that coordinates the top-down and bottom-up functions of the first two levels. It is not a matter of one approach or the other but is an orchestration of all three.

Socio-cultural dimension

In the information age, there is much more of a blending of literacy practices. There is no longer a clear distinction between reading and writing, listening and viewing. Particularly with new electronic literacies, there is more of a combination of forms and literacy practices are defined more by the roles of the literacy user in contemporary contexts.

Freebody and Luke (1990) sought to incorporate the cognitive and social aspects of literacy by viewing the literacy learner as taking on particular roles in any literacy activity within their 'Four Roles' model. The role of 'code breaker' was mainly concerned with coding competence; the 'meaning maker' involved the learner with semantic competence; the 'text user' focused on pragmatic competence; and the 'text critic' was concerned with critical competence. More recently, Luke and Freebody (1999) revised their earlier model to consider 'practices' rather than 'roles' and referred to it as the 'Four Resources' model with the emphasis on: (1) breaking the code; (2) participating in understanding the texts; (3) using texts; and (4) analysing texts. Thus, literacy may be considered in a much broader context (Tindale, 2005). The basic proposition of the 'Four Roles' model is that effective literacy in complex print and multi-mediated societies requires a broad and flexible repertoire of practices. This repertoire is characterised as a set of roles that participants in literacy events are able to assume (Freebody and Luke, 2003).

Engagement with texts of all kinds positions the learner in different roles. Each of these roles will develop a range of competencies according to how learners interact with different technologies. Rather than treating competencies in terms of reading, writing, listening and viewing, literacy today is much more concerned with positioning the literacy learner as a participant rather than an inactive recipient of information. As an actor on the literacy stage, these distinctions become somewhat blended, particularly when using multi-media. Even when using print-based media during writing, the writer becomes a reader, a listener and a viewer as well, depending on the role the student assumes moment by moment.

New technologies: Web 2.0 applications

Information technology can make a unique contribution to strengthening learning across the curriculum, including literacy and numeracy (Unsworth, 2001). It will become even more important to develop ICT skills to prepare for the technologies of the future. The increasing digitisation of information worldwide requires all children to develop digital literacy to enable full participation in society. Information required for work, finance, communication, leisure and citizenship will be mediated electronically. New technologies and Web 2.0 applications will be an essential part of all vocations and children not only need to learn to use specific technologies and applications, they will also need to understand how to use them safely and wisely. Therefore, the foundations for this digital engagement are best formed in primary school, where children's enthusiasm for ICT is most evident (Rose, 2009). The challenge is that educators must avoid creating a population divided on the basis of ICT haves and have-nots because this would pose a considerable danger to both economic wellbeing and social cohesion (Rose, 2009).

In a very short space of time, schools have progressed far beyond what used to be called computer-assisted learning, in which computers were seen as mere pedagogical aids or tools to assist conventional print-based learning. However, more and more children are becoming increasingly independent and are developing technological expertise beyond that of classroom teachers, and are using electronic media to share, socialise, collaborate and create. For example, they use mobile technology such as smartphones, PDAs, tablets and laptops to exchange messages and information via SMS and through online networking sites such as MySpace, Facebook and Twitter (Alexander, 2010). Many of these 'tech savvy' children also locate information using Google and Wikipedia, and download music, DVDs, games and other material by using their mobile phones, PCs and laptops. Many of these children also routinely take photos, record videos and post them on Facebook.

Design

With increasing cultural and linguistic diversity in the world today and the multiplicity of communication systems there is a need for a much broader view of literacy than has been portrayed by traditional language-based approaches. The process of learning through literacy and the creation of literacy products are the results of the designs or structures of complex systems of people, environments, technology, beliefs and texts (The New London Group, 1996). Design is important for blogs and will need to be carefully developed to reflect the author/producer and to engage an audience who can respond with text and images. While considering these differences, it is not possible to completely separate the processes of reading or writing on-screen from the social practices that accompany them (Walsh, 2011).

As reading and viewing are often interchangeable processes, reading should include aspects such as analysing, browsing, decoding, hyperlinking, interpreting, navigating, responding and searching (Walsh, 2011). As designers of meaning, we are designers of social futures, workplace futures, public futures and community futures. At the same time, it is the unique product of human agency: a transformed meaning. And, in its turn, the redesigned becomes a new available design and a new meaning-making resource (The New London Group, 1996).

Writing has moved towards a digital product that often contains quite sophisticated layout, graphics, photographs and images (Walsh, 2011). The theory of multi-modality (Kress, 2003; Kress and Van Leeuwen, 2006) contends that the simultaneous processing of different modes of text, image, sound and gesture in visual, media or digital text is a different function from the linear, sequential reading of traditional print-based texts (see Chapter 5).

Dimensions of literacies

Social practices of literacy have also changed and expanded exponentially through the development of Web 2.0 technology. For example, readers now have wireless access to Wikipedia, which is the world's most up-to-date encyclopaedia of the New Oxford and American dictionaries. Simply by placing the cursor before an unknown word, the dictionary meaning will appear at the bottom of the page for the reader. The search function on the Kindle, for example, enables readers to search for words, phrases and character names in an eBook.

The overwhelming concern for researchers and educators is whether literacy itself, as a social practice, will continue to change and need redefining as further online and mobile technology devices evolve and establish new ways of communicating. Literacy has enabled different forms of communication and communities to develop over a very short period of time. However, there would appear to be a current discrepancy involving the quality of different types of literacy practices students engage in at home on a daily basis. The types of texts students are exposed to and engage with at school need to be expanded to bridge this growing digital divide or gap between many poorer homes and the schools they attend (McKenna et al., 2011).

Rapid changes in digital communication have enabled reading and writing to combine quite complex relational aspects – images, music, sound, graphics, photography and film (Walsh, 2011). Responding to animated icons, hypertext, sound effects and the continuous pathways between and within screens for Web 2.0 and the intranet, we have only just begun to understand the process of navigating hypermedia. Kress (2003) argues that the shift from page to screen, from word to image as the dominant communicative mode, has profound implications not just for the ways in which we understand what is seen, but also for the kinds of relationships readers have with texts (Beavis, 2008). Reading and viewing are now regarded as much more interchangeable and fluid processes – for example, reading must now include other aspects such as analysing, browsing, decoding, hyperlinking, interpreting, navigating, responding and searching.

Durrant and Green's (2000) 3D model (see Table 1.3) proposes that there are three dimensions of electronic forms of literacy that you should consider when you are designing your curriculum: operational, cultural and critical. The operational dimension includes technical competence such as the 'how-to' of dealing with technology. This includes the basics of how to turn the computer on, knowing how to use a word processor or finding information on Web 2.0. The cultural dimension focuses on the meaning-making process within the technological and cultural contexts. It is the process of going beyond just knowing how to use technology to doing things in the world for specific practices and purposes. The critical dimension taps into aspects of history, context and power. It assumes that someone's story is a partial representation of reality and is usually connected with particular interests and cultural perspectives.

Table 1.3 Dimensions of literate practice

Dimension	Durrant & Green, 2000	Freebody and Luke, 1990	Woolley, 2011
Representational	Operational	Code-breaker	Factual (Task)
Cognitive	Cultural	Text participant Text user	Conceptual (Cognitive)
Reflective	Critical	Text analyst	Metacognitive

Vignette 1.2

Not only are people introduced to new forms of techno-literacy but technology has changed the way that we work and conduct our day-to-day affairs. It would not be uncommon to walk into your teenage son or daughter's room and see them multi-tasking in ways that you would not have dreamed about.

(Continued)

(Continued)

A typical example is Jessica (see Figure 1.2), who, while doing her homework, could be seen with an earphone connected to her iPod in one ear while asking her friend about a maths problem with a mobile phone held to her other ear. All of this is happening while Jessica is sitting in front of the computer typing a message on her email and to her Facebook page. Jessica's behaviour illustrates the point that literacy today comes in many forms and often these are presented simultaneously.

Figure 1.2   Jessica multi-tasking while doing her homework

Questions

1   How do you like to do your work at home?
2   Do individuals engage with literacy for different reasons than in the past? If so, what are these differences?
3   How would you as a teacher organise your classroom to cater for the learning preferences of your students?

What should you do as a teacher?

With the expansion of the World Wide Web and other multimedia technologies, students must now acquire new skills that allow them to effectively evaluate the quality of screen-based sources of information and the potential bias of the material (Education and Training Committee, 2006). New digital technologies will only transform classrooms if teachers are interested in and comfortable with using them. However, there are dangers in using Web 2.0 technologies without some form of external or internal control mechanism. For children, the main issue is one of trust – who and what can be believed on Web 2.0 (Alexander, 2010). The challenge that you will be confronted with is knowing how to discriminate between and utilise the new technologies efficiently, ethically and responsibly, with a view to exploiting their educational possibilities (Lankshear et al., 2000). One way for you to do this is to collaborate with other teachers by locating and using Web 2.0 resources and sharing useful websites that offer free or inexpensive material. It is clear, however, that the social environment of the classroom will always play a central role in determining how your students use an electronic tool.

In the recent past, teachers have tended to use technology as a helpful tool for developing print-based literacy, such as using a word processor. However, technology in education has evolved to create new types of literacy. There has also been a greater emphasis on evidence-based best practices in literacy education. However, by the time research studies are published, the technology used in the classroom will have moved on and these studies may quickly become outdated soon after publication, so you will need to be constantly updating your knowledge and skills.

Conclusion

Globalisation has had a distinct influence on the pace of change in our culture, language, modes of communication and the way in which we think and interact. Scientific and technological advances have given rise to a proliferation of multimedia and information technologies. Although print-based materials will possibly never be completely replaced, the same factors of learner, purpose, text and task determine the quality of the literacy engagement and the literate futures of individuals.

Whatever form a literacy endeavour takes, it will reflect the socio-cultural preferences that influence individuals in the context in which they live. When teaching children, you need to focus not only on the products of literacy endeavours but also on the actual learning processes that give rise to and support them. While engaging with literacy, you should also consider three broad dimensions that consider the representational, cognitive and reflective aspects of literacy engagement. The differences will reflect whether or not the emphasis is related to cognition, socio-cultural or technological context. An examination of these perspectives should lead to a more balanced view of learning and teaching in literate contexts.

Discussion questions and activities

 Points for discussion

1 List the various types of literacies that you would engage in in everyday life.
2 What sort of literacies would you imagine that someone your age would have engaged with 100 years ago?
3 How does our social context determine what type of literacy we will engage in?

 Group activities

1 What do you understand by levels of engagement?
2 The Luke and Freebody (1999) model has had a name change from the Four Roles to the Four Resources model. What do you think is the difference and why do you think that this shift was made?
3 How would the Four Resources model promote a balanced approach to literacy learning?
4 Use a black bag to cover an unseen object and describe it so that others have to guess what it is. Discuss, 'How does this develop language?' and 'How does this develop visualising skills?'
5 Divide into groups of two. Provide each group with a picture of someone engaging in a literate activity. List the purposes that could be achieved using the particular technology or system. Make another list of other ways in which the same purpose could be achieved using another medium. Are there any differences? List these.

Whole-class activity

Obtain the book *The Arrival* by Shaun Tan (2007), divide into groups of about eight and simulate a literacy circle in the primary classroom.
   Ask:

1 Why doesn't the author use words in the book?
2 What colours are used in the book?
3 Why do you think that the author used these colours?
4 What sort of city is depicted in the book? Is it similar to your nearest city? Is it a modern city or is it placed in another period of time?
5 What is a visual metaphor? How is it used in this graphic novel?
6 What are the giant vacuum cleaners meant to represent? Why do you think that the author used them in the story?
7 Why do you think the main character left his homeland?

References

Alexander, R. (ed.) (2010). *Children, their World, their Education: Final Report and Recommendations of the Alexander 2010 Primary Review*. Oxon: Routledge.

Beavis, C. (2008). Paying attention to texts: Literacy, culture and curriculum. *English in Australia*, 43(1), 23–31.

Cambourne, B. (2008). What can teachers do about the current debates in reading? *Practically Primary*, 13(2), 4–5.

Chall, J. S. (1967). *Learning to Read: The Great Debate*. New York: Harcourt-Brace.

Coles, G. (2003). *Reading the Naked Truth: Literacy, Legislation and Lies*. Portsmouth, NH: Heinemann.

Durrant, C. and Green, B. (2000). Literacy and the new technologies in school education: Meeting the l(IT)eracy challenge? *The Australian Journal of Language and Literacy*, 23(2), 89–108.

Education and Training Committee (2006). *Education in the Net Age: New Needs and New Tools – Report on the Inquiry into the Effects of Television and Multimedia on Education in Victoria*. Melbourne: Victorian Government Printer.

Farris, P. J., Fuhler, C. J. and Walther, M. P. (2004). *Teaching Reading: A Balanced Approach for Today's Classrooms*. Boston: McGraw-Hill.

Flesch, R. (1955). *Why Johnny Can't Read and What You Can Do about It*. New York: Harper & Row.

Flesch, R. (1981). *Why Johnny Still Can't Read: A New Look at the Scandal of Our Schools*. New York: Harper & Row.

Freebody, P. and Luke, A. (1990). 'Literacies' programs: Debates and demands in cultural context. *Prospect*, 5, 7–16.

Freebody, P. and Luke, A. (2003). Literacy as engaging with new forms of life: The 'four roles' model. In G. Bull and M. Anstey (eds), *The Literacy Lexicon* (2nd edn) (pp. 51–66). Frenchs Forest, NSW: Pearson Education Australia.

Gee, J. P. (2003). Literacy and social minds. In G. Bull and M. Anstey (eds), *The Literacy Lexicon* (2nd edn) (pp. 3–14). Frenchs Forest, NSW: Pearson Education Australia.

Green, D. (2003). So what should my classroom look like? In D. Green and R. Campbell, (eds), *Literacies and Learners: Current Perspectives* (2nd edn) (pp. 197–208). Frenchs Forest, NSW: Pearson Education Australia.

Green, B., Hodgens, J. and Luke, A. (1997). Debating literacy in Australia: History lessons and popular fictions. *Australian Journal of Language and Literacy*, 20(1), 6–24.

Kalantzis, M., Cope, B. and Fehring, H. (2002). Multiliteracies: Teaching and Learning in the New Communications Environment. Primary English Teaching Association Australia, *Pen* 133.

Karantzola, E. and Intzidis, E. (2001). Multimodality across the curriculum. In M. Kalantzis (ed.), *Languages of Learning: Changing Communication and Changing Literacy Teaching* (pp. 9–21). Melbourne: Common Ground Publishing.

Kell, M. (2001). Literacy and unemployment: Facts and fictions. In M. Kalantzis (ed.), *Languages of Learning: Changing Communication and Changing Literacy Teaching* (pp. 23–38). Melbourne: Common Ground Publishing.

Kress, G. (2003). *Literacy in the New Media Age*. London: Routledge.

Kress, G. R. and Van Leeuwen, T. (2006). *Reading Images: The Grammar of Visual Design* (2nd edn). London: Routledge.

Lankshear, C., Snyder, I. and Green, B. (2000). *Teachers and techno-literacy: Managing literacy, technology and learning in schools.* St Leonards, NSW: Allen & Unwin.

Le, T., Le, Q. and Short, M. (2011). War and peace in language and literacy discourse. In T. Le, Q. Le and M. Short (eds), *Language and Literacy Education in a Challenging World* (pp. 13–21). New York: Nova Science Publishers.

Luke, A. and Freebody, P. (1999). A map of possible practices: Further notes on the four resources model. *Practically Primary*, 4, 5–8.

Luke, A., Comber, B. and Grant, H. (2003). Critical literacies and cultural studies. In G. Bull and M. Anstey (eds), *The Literacy Lexicon* (2nd edn) (pp. 15–35). Frenchs Forest, NSW: Pearson Education Australia.

Mckenna, M. C., Labbo, L. D., Conradi, K. and Baxter, J. (2011). Effective uses of technology in literacy instruction. In L. M. Morrow and L. Gambrell (eds.). *Best Practices in Literacy Instruction* (4th edn) (pp. 361–394.). New York: Guilford.

Pressley, M. G. (1998). *Reading Instruction that Works: The Case for Balanced Teaching.* New York: The Guilford Press.

Pressley, M. G. (2006). *Reading Instruction that Works: The Case for Balanced Teaching* (3rd edn). New York: The Guilford Press.

Rose, J. (2009). *Independent Review of the Primary Curriculum: Final Report.* Nottingham: DCSF Publications.

Snow, C. E. (2002). *Reading for Understanding: Toward a Research and Development Program in Reading Comprehension.* Santa Monica, CA: Rand Corp. Available at: www.rand.org/publications/MR/MR1465/ (accessed 12 December 2002).

Snyder, I. (2002). Silicon literacies. In I. Snyder (ed.), *Silicon Literacies: Communication, Innovation and Education in the Electronic Age* (pp. 3–12). London: Routledge.

Snyder, I. (2008). Literacy wars cause collateral damage. *The Age*, 14 April, pp. 1–2.

Snyder, I. (2010). *The Literacy Wars: Why Teaching Children to Read and Write is a Battleground in Australia.* Crows Nest, NSW: Allen & Unwin.

Tan, S. (2007). *The Arrival.* London: Hodder Children's Books.

The New London Group (1996). A pedagogy of multiliteracies: Designing social futures. *Harvard Educational Review*, 66(1), 1–25.

Tindale, J. (2005). Reading print and electronic texts. In D.E. Murray and P. McPherson (eds), *Navigating to Read – Reading to Navigate* (pp. 2–15). Sydney: Macquarie University.

UNESCO (1998). *World Education Report: Teachers and Teaching in a Changing World.* Paris: UNESCO. Available at: www.unesco.org/education/information/wer/PDFeng/wholewer98.PDF

Unsworth, B. (2001). *Teaching Multiliteracies across the Curriculum: Changing Contexts of Text and Image in Classroom Practice.* New York: Open University Press.

Walsh, M. (2011). *Multimodal Literacy: Researching Classroom Practice*. Newtown, NSW: Primary English Teaching Association Australia.

Woolley, G. (2011). *Reading Comprehension: Assisting Children with Learning Difficulties*. Dordrecht, The Netherlands: Springer International.

Zimmerman, B. J. (2002). Becoming a self-regulated learner: An overview. *Theory into Practice*, 41, 64–70.

CHAPTER 2

LANGUAGE LEARNING: THE FOUNDATION FOR LITERACY

Chapter objectives

- To understand that language is developed through natural and sociological factors.
- To explore how language is an interplay between text and context.
- To understand that language is about communication and also about making meaning.

Key questions

1. How do most children learn their native language?
2. How should language be further developed in your classroom?
3. What can we learn from Cambourne's conditions of learning?

Key words: approximation, conditions of learning, form, function, grammar, hypotheses, language, language acquisition, meaningful.

Introduction

This chapter will discuss the central role of language in literacy. It will identify how language is acquired and processed by the learner. Language learning is a complex process, however nearly all children develop a good mastery of basic language forms before entering formal schooling. Learning is both a natural and socially mediated process whereby young language learners make successive closer and closer approximations to the adult forms of language. Cambourne's (2002) 'conditions of learning' will provide you with some insight for optimal language learning to occur in your classroom. Language learning should be taught in meaningful contexts and the form and function of language should be taught as a product of language use and real world application. Meaning is constructed when literacy activities have particular purposes that are valued by your students.

> Further, the goal of literacy by the end of [the] primary phase must be more than functional. It is about making and exploring meaning as well as receiving and transmitting it. That is why talking must be part of reading and writing rather than an optional extra. That is why engagement with meanings made by others through literature, and other language through which such meanings [are] conveyed, is no less essential. (Alexander, 2010: 269)

Understanding language and communication enables children to develop their self-awareness and empathy with others, and empowers them to express their own feelings through language. Furthermore, it also provides opportunities to listen to and respond to others, work collaboratively, negotiate and give constructive feedback (Rose, 2009). The above quote conveys the notion that the goals of literacy are about making and exploring meaning as well as receiving and transmitting it. What is certain is that children need to have control over this vital aspect prior to starting the process of reading and writing (Snow et al., 1998).

Natural and social dimensions of language

Nativism was the dominant theoretical perspective for teaching language and literacy in the 1970s and 1980s. It promoted language as an entirely natural and individualistic phenomenon and, thus, relegated language learning to the personal domain. Nativists proposed that language acquisition is innate and is the result of a natural mechanism within the brain. Thus, children were viewed as having inborn mental functions that enable them to make sense of the world around them. These inbuilt mental functions are also used to make sense out of language. In so doing, young children systematically look for similarities, make generalisations, develop hypotheses and form rules that systematise their language. It is their experience of the world that is evaluated and tested. However, this perspective has posed a dilemma for many educators. The problem is: how can language be taught entirely within the private domain?

The socio-linguistic view, on the other hand, proposed that the ability to produce language is an entirely social function. It was thought that, like other abilities, language is learned through experience. While individuals produce language, the shape and structure of language is determined by various social conventions, such as genre, text and grammar (Knapp and Watkins, 2005). For example, when young children enter into play-based activities, this involves sustained symbolic thinking, the use of narrative structure and the use of oral language to inform, hypothesise and imagine (Hill, 2010). In particular, phonology, vocabulary, syntax, discourse and pragmatics are important aspects of oral language that children gain from interactions with others.

How much of this language is innate and how much is learned? These views are both extreme and the solution may be found somewhere between the two. In the next section, you will gain an understanding of how these two dynamic processes intertwine and shape children's acquisition of language.

The role of parents

When interacting with young children, parents habitually simplify their speech by slowing down and using short, simple sentences and often repeat their utterances. Thus, children are presented with a type of stylised language as a model. Intuitively, adults, when they talk to children, use what Lindsay and Norman (1977) call 'parentese' or a simplification of language. Thus, a child's introduction to the English language ordinarily comes in the form of simplified, repetitive and idealised utterances (Brown and Bellugi, 1965).

Parents also use attention-getters to attract and hold the infant's attention when conversing with them. For example, they often use the child's name while speaking in a high-pitched voice. Adults often repeat the utterance and exaggerate the intonational ups and downs by pausing between utterances and talking slowly to make it easier for the young child to understand. They also imitate or expand on the child's utterances.

Adults tend to avoid using some words that may be beyond the child's experience. They usually avoid using pronouns, possibly because pronouns are more complex than proper nouns. Moreover, the words parents use in speaking to young children anticipate the nature of the child's world. Adults select the words that seem to have the most immediate relevance to what their children might want to talk about (Clark and Clark, 1977). Very seldom do parents correct what children have to say, but if they do, it is usually related to the truthfulness of the utterance or to correct pronunciation. Children learn by choosing a narrow set of possibilities defined by innate language learning universals.

Infants, however, do play an active role in the acquisition of word meaning when they build 'plausible interpretations of words and utterances from what they know and from cues in the immediate context' (Clark and Clark, 1977: 488). By doing so, children make two assumptions about the function and content of language: (a) language is for communicating, and (b) language makes sense in context. Thus, the young child learns 'a system of meaningful behaviour or a semiotic system' (Halliday, 1975: 15) but it is always within a social context.

This period of early language learning usually coincides with Piaget's sensory-motor stage. Lindsay and Norman (1977) linked this stage of development to the child's concept of their first words. They maintained that children at this stage do not separate actions and events from the concepts of the object. Even if the infant learns the word 'ball', for example, it might initiate a whole host of features and events associated with the concept, including rolling, bouncing and other characteristics of the object. Although the term ball might appear to be applied directly to round, ball-like objects, the child might actually be using it to represent the actions of the item. In this way, a child quickly learns that the surface structure or utterance will have an underlying deep structure or meaning. Children map out meaning structures – which may or may not be similar to the adult meanings – even before they use their first words. In this way, novice language learners are able to understand many of the utterances of the adults around them.

Initially, they form hypotheses about word meanings. In doing so, children rely heavily on the here and now in working out the meanings of words and utterances. Ordinarily, infants learn the definition of a word like 'drink' when they observe their parents drinking and see the glass, as well as hearing the word associated with the action. Often the meanings of words are overgeneralised – for example, the word 'dog' may be applied to any animal with four legs. As the child receives feedback from adults, he/she will develop a series of successive closer and closer approximations to the meanings of words of the adults' language.

Children are immersed in language right from the beginning of life and the language they hear is usually placed in a social context. In order for an infant to make meaning from what an adult is saying, he/she must first decipher the adult's meaning non-verbally. Children will use all the contextual cues available to them – for example, when an adult introduces a new word he/she will use a familiar frame such as 'That is a _____.' or 'Look at the_____.' Apart from clues derived from the syntax, there will be other clues such as intonation, facial expression, pointing and, of course, the object itself. Children often rely on gestures to direct their attention and to do what is most appropriate in context (Clark and Clark, 1977). For example, a parent may glance at a chair and tell the child to sit on the chair. The child's attention is directed to the chair and he infers from the situation the most plausible action.

Ordinarily, one would be tempted to think that children merely copy the language of the adults and older sibling(s) that they frequently engage with. However, young children are much more actively engaged in the actual construction of language rules and conventions. For example, words such as 'came' and 'went' are used very frequently in adult language but are not normally copied or assimilated into the early language structures of the novice language user. Many incorrect verb forms are usually spoken by children and are later dropped. For example, high-frequency words such as 'go' and 'come' are substituted for the child's own 'goed' and 'commed'. Sometimes a parent may attempt to correct the child by modelling the more appropriate form of the verb, but, time after time, the child will say 'goed' instead of 'went'. This is because young children generally look for the more general patterns or systematic occurrences in language. Later, however, they begin to realise that there are exceptions to the rule and drop the incorrect forms of the verbs.

Thus, it can be seen that some aspects of language acquisition are innate and children have an enormous capacity to decipher and make sense of the complex language forms that they are immersed in. It is within the social context that children are able to connect and build meaning and form the rules of grammar. However, the real content of language is the making of meaning. Grammar would have no sense without meaning and, therefore, no communication. Meaning gives substance to grammar and without meaning grammar would have no function. The purpose of grammar is to provide a system of rules through which an indefinite variety of meanings may be expressed as an infinite variety of sentences in various languages.

Active constructors of language

Most children, by the time they enter school, have mastered many of the language patterns of their own community by approximating the speech of the adults around them. When one thinks of the extreme complexity of language and the developing personality of the human infant, then one can see that the task of learning a first language must be an enormous undertaking. Yet most children are able to undertake this complex task without ever having been formally taught. For example, they are often able to understand sentences that they have never even heard before, and children learning to talk show very little imitation of adults. Moreover, young children can usually generate an infinite number of sentences that they have not heard before.

Children must, therefore, develop rules, which permit them to use language in original and creative ways. These rules have never been formally taught to them. Ordinarily, no one sits down and systematically teaches these rules. The child has formed these phonological, syntactic and semantic rules by adopting universal strategies, and forming hypotheses and searching for evidence to confirm or deny them.

Context and text

It is imperative that you understand the role and nature of language in literate environments. This chapter asserts that language is processed and understood in the form of texts. A text can be any form of language used in a meaning-making event. Text should be viewed from two distinct perspectives: as a thing in itself that can be recorded, viewed, analysed and discussed; and as a process that is the outcome of a socially constructed event (Knapp and Watkins, 2005).

Inner language

Vygotsky (1962) proposed that the role of language changes as the infant child matures. In the initial stages, it serves as a social function to express the child's immediate needs and moods. Later, it becomes internalised in the form of inner speech as an instrument of thought. At this point, children can use inner language to express their thoughts without a sound being uttered. Private or inner speech becomes a means of rehearsing, directing attention to important task features and helping the child organise, code and store information in his/her individual memory. The verbalisation of thought processes overtly bridges the gap between external control and self-regulation through inner speech (Vygotsky, 1962). Vollmeyer and Rheinberg (2005) maintained that the verbalising of thought processes raises the efficiency of the learner by instilling a sense of control over their learning. Thus, oral language is inherently related to thinking, understanding and self-regulation.

Holdaway (1980) recognised that parents made a valuable contribution to the development of language in their children by reading to them. Usually this would take the form of a parent reading and talking about a favourite book at bedtime each night before their children went to sleep. Often children would request the same book several nights in a row. Many teachers today try and emulate the richness of this reading and language experience by using 'big books' in their classrooms with the whole class or with groups of children. Big books are larger versions of popular children's books that can be read together because the illustrations and print are enlarged and can be seen and read by all.

Vignette 2.1

Mrs Jones regularly uses 'big books' in her classroom literacy block. Her volunteer parents made big books of popular children's stories. Often the children would request the same book to be read several days in a row. Once the children became familiar with the language of the book and jointly constructed the meanings through whole-group discussions, they were ready to learn more about the language structure of the text. For example, in one lesson Mrs Jones had the familiar big book displayed on her lap while the children sat on the mat in front of her so that they could all clearly see the text. The children had previously read the text several times but this time Mrs Jones covered all the verbs in the text with blank Post-it notes to make a type of cloze activity. The children were required to predict the missing verbs as Mrs Jones flipped over the pages and while the children read the text.

Not only did the children learn about the purpose and function of verbs but they also learned how to use the context to predict, confirm or correct during their attempts at reading. To further their understanding of verbs, Mrs Jones had the children work in groups and make their own innovation of the big book. To do this, they kept the same language pattern of the original text but only changed the verbs to create a slightly different but unique story of their own.

Questions

1　What are some other ways that 'big books' can be used in the classroom to develop grammar?
2　How can an interactive whiteboard be used to emulate a 'big book' experience?
3　What might be the advantages to students of producing their own 'big books'?

Cambourne's conditions of language learning

Cambourne (2002) proposed that children develop oral and written language more easily when certain conditions are present in their immediate environments, at home and at school. According to Cambourne, there are eight conditions of learning: immersion, demonstration, engagement, expectation, responsibility, use, approximation and response.

Examples for each of these conditions are:

- Immersion – children need to be immersed in an environment filled with conversations with high-quality language.
- Demonstration – speaking is regularly modelled for children by their parents, other adults and older siblings.
- Engagement – children become active learners when encouraged to see themselves as active language users.
- Expectation – adults set realistic expectations for language development.

- Responsibility – children are given choices about what they should say and how they should use their spoken language.
- Use – children are encouraged to use functional and meaningful expressions of oral language.
- Approximation – children's mistakes are accepted as approximations when they are learning to talk.
- Response – adults listen to their children, receive their comments and questions, and encourage and extend their use of oral language.

Speech and writing are forms of communication that use the medium of language but they do this quite differently. Writing is not just speech written down. The two operate quite differently. Speech is a time-based medium whereby people exchange information or sequence their descriptions of events or actions over time. Thus, speech can be explained as being temporal, instantaneous and sequential. Writing, on the other hand, is primarily a spatial medium and does not have the same constraints of time. It arranges language hierarchically and with a more formal syntax.

Cambourne's (2002) conditions can be used in the classroom to develop both spoken and written forms of literacy. Table 2.1 on page 26 shows how you may be guided by these conditions to develop effective literacy practices in your classroom.

Language in education

There are two main perspectives in teaching language. On the one hand, language can be seen as a conduit of meaning where meaning is merely transferred from the speaker/writer to the listener/viewer. This implies that the speaker or writer arranges the words and sentences to enable the transmission of ideas and messages to the listener or reader. On the other hand, language can be viewed as a semiotic system that actively constructs meaning rather than merely transmitting meaning. Within this perspective, language is viewed as one of a number of semiotic or meaning-making systems that are shaped by the cultural forms that are generally understood by a society. These may include art, dance, dress, multimodal representations or other forms of expression.

The social semiotic view of language has its foundations built on the work of both Halliday (1975) and Vygotsky (1962) and has become the dominant view of language education in recent times. The implications are that an understanding of the relationship between teaching and learning is one centred on the notion of the construction of shared understandings and shared knowledge. This involves a social constructivist model of teaching and learning (see Chapter 7) in which teachers and students are viewed as being actively engaged in the joint construction of knowledge (Hammond, 2001). Thus, language can no longer be seen as a neutral set of skills but rather as a resource whereby social and cultural values, attitudes and meaning are

Table 2.1 Cambourne's conditions of learning

Conditions	Pedagogical practices
Immersion	Read aloud every day to children, talk to them, play word games with them and use movement and dance to engage them in language, literacy and stories. Make posters, charts, word walls, displays, learning centres, listening posts, etc.
Demonstration	Children need opportunities to observe learning occurring in adult role models. Let them see you writing notes, letters, stories, recipes, poems and lists. Demonstrate reading for pleasure, for information, for directions and for other purposes. Show them how to hold a book, turn the pages and read together. Show demonstrations of different genres and media through report writing, using ICT equipment, tablets, etc.
Engagement	Establish a risk-free environment so the children can experiment with language and literacy. Provide easy access to paper, pencils, crayons, markers, books, iPads, computers and other literacy materials. Engaged learners will naturally take what they are learning and make it meaningful to their lives.
Expectation	Establish a learning environment where realistic but high expectations are communicated. Support and scaffold activities that are developmentally appropriate for the age and stage of learning. Project the expectation that the children will become accomplished readers and writers.
Responsibility	Set up the environment to promote self-direction and self-regulation. Provide the children with choices and give them responsibility for designing their own literacy projects.
Approximation	Reward the children for their accomplishments, even when their efforts are approximations of the adult model. Model the correct forms and encourage self-correction.
Use	Encourage the children to read together with you; ask them to help you write notes, letters, lists, poems, etc. Engage them in discussions, reflections, peer tutoring, and book reviews and editing. Encourage them to use knowledge from their everyday lives by writing, presenting, exploring, experimenting, commenting, etc.
Response	Give appropriate feedback for their efforts but encourage the children to take risks with their learning. Praise should be given in a manner that encourages self-evaluation. Peers should be taught how to give encouragement and feedback.

Source: Cambourne, 2002

constructed. Language in all its forms is not just an artefact of communication but is an ideologically loaded system.

Formal and functional aspects of language

A genre and grammar model of language would require you to become aware of the characteristics language assumes within the social contexts in which texts are commonly used. In order to make language useful, you will also need to use the children's knowledge of grammar as a meta-language to describe how language can be manipulated. Grammatical terms fall into two broad categories: formal and functional. To understand the formal aspects of grammar means that you should give consideration to how the English language is put together. This is often referred to as traditional grammar. The formal category provides us with a way of classifying elements that represent texts. Terms like 'noun' or 'adjective' formerly classify types of words. For example, a noun is the name of a thing, and an adjective is a word that modifies the meaning of the noun. Functional classes, on the other hand, help us to understand what the elements are doing. Words like 'subject', 'object' and 'predicate', for example, are terms that tell us how nouns, adverbs and adjectives are being used in sentences (Knapp and Watkins, 2005).

Forms of language

There is a view that the process of learning to write is similar to the process of learning to speak (Cambourne, 2002). Oral language and written language are both important but each provides different ways of knowing. Grammatical skills can be effectively taught within the context of students' writing rather than being taught in isolation (Black and Bannan, 2010). It is important for students to understand how language works in order to become effective writers. Teaching students how to use the meta-language of speaking and writing will help demystify the process and develop self-confidence (Hamilton, 1998). One way to develop this meta-language is to discuss the form and function of language through writing. The medium of writing provides a tangible way to view how a language operates. Poetry writing is a good example of how children can be made aware of how language functions in short but concentrated forms.

Vignette 2.2

Mr Smith has been doing a series of poetry writing activities with the children in his class. In the first lesson, he focused on adjectives to describe an animal such as a cat. For the first example, Mr Smith created a poem with the class by showing the children a video clip from YouTube and asking them to suggest words that would describe the features of the cat. He then used the letters of the words, such as cuddly, furry, curious, etc., to make the overall shape of the cat. While doing this, he modelled his thinking processes by using a think-aloud technique. After this, the children were required to work in pairs by selecting a picture of a favourite animal and designing a poem of their own.

In subsequent lessons, he had the children make Ezra Pound couplets, rhyming couplets, Haiku and syllable poems while focusing on both the form and function of the words used in the poems.

1   Why did Mr Smith use poetry to promote grammar?
2   In what other ways can poetry be used to promote language skills?
3   How can you promote grammar through other writing activities?

A semiotic system

Literacy has become multimodal and children are now expected to work with texts of all types such as film, CDs, DVDs, the Internet and post-modern picture books. As a result, the grammar of language has been extended to include a broader focus on semiotics or the study of all meaning-making systems within a literate culture (Kress and Van Leeuwen, 2006). This will be discussed further in the following chapters.

Conclusion

It seems that children's language at various points is systematic, governed and generated by rules in the learning strategies appropriate to their stage of development. Rules generated in this way occur in the speech of most children. The acquisition of language develops from the more simple and general to the more complex and specific. However, with time children's language matures and becomes more like the language of the adults around them. Because they are seeking to make sense out of the language they hear, children form hypotheses, which are translated into rules and are in turn tested by gauging the reactions and feedback of the adults around them. Thus, the structure of children's language is the product of the interrelated patterns of experience, social interaction and cognitive processes. Educators can emulate the types of conditions that will promote language learning in their classrooms. However, it should be emphasised that language learning occurs within contexts that are meaningful and communicative.

 ## Discussion questions and activities

 ### Points for discussion

1 Why can children be regarded as active language constructors?
2 List the types of linguistic and social skills children develop during play activities.
3 Make a table using Cambourne's conditions of learning language and list pedagogical practices that would support writing development.

♟♟♟♟ Group activities

1 What can teachers do to develop both natural and social aspects of language development? Make a chart to compare and contrast these two aspects.
2 How would you teach grammar in the classroom?
3 Why do you think that written language seems to take prominence in primary schools?

> ⊞ **Whole-class activities**
>
> 1 Choose a big book and design a set of language activities to develop language skills.
> 2 List the types of activities that you could do with poetry that would promote language and grammar.
> 3 Choose a poetry form and write a short poem. Share this with the whole group and discuss how you could develop language skills.

References

Alexander, R. (ed.) (2010). *Children, their World, their Education: Final Report and Recommendations of the Alexander 2010 Primary Review*. Oxon: Routledge.

Black, A. and Bannan, S. (2010). Functional grammar: A change in writer's self-perception. *Practically Primary*, 15(3), 12–17.

Brown, R. and Bellugi, U. (1965). Three processes in the child's acquisition of syntax. In P. H. Mussen, J. J. Konger and J. Kagan (eds), *Readings in Child Development and Personality* (pp. 211–227). New York: Harper & Row.

Cambourne, B. (2002). Conditions for literacy learning: From conditions of learning to conditions of teaching. *The Reading Teacher*, 55, 358–360.

Clark, H. and Clark, E. (1977). *Psychology and Language: An Introduction to Psycholinguistics*. New York: Harcourt & Brace Jovanovich.

Halliday, M. A. K. (1975). *Learning How to Mean: Explorations in the Development of Language*. London: Edward Arnold.

Hamilton, A. (1998). YAK, YAK, YAK! Teaching functional grammar. *Practically Primary*, 3(2), 19–21.

Hammond, J. (2001). Scaffolding and language. In J. Hammond (ed.), *Scaffolding: Teaching and Learning in Language and Literacy Education* (pp. 15–30). Newtown, NSW: Primary English Teaching Association Australia.

Hill, S. (2010). Oral language, play and learning. *Practically Primary*, 15(2), 4–6.

Holdaway, D. (1980). *Independence in Reading: A Handbook on Individualized Procedures* (2nd edn). Gosford: Ashton Scholastic.

Knapp, P. and Watkins, M. (2005). *Genre, Text, Grammar: Technologies for Teaching and Assessing Writing*. Sydney: University of New South Wales Press.

Kress, G. and Van Leeuwen, T. (2006). *Reading Images: The Grammar of Visual Design* (2nd edn). London and New York: Routledge.

Lindsay, P. H. and Norman, D. A. (1977). *Human Information Processing: An Introduction to Psychology*. New York: Academic Press.

Rose, J. (2009). *Independent Review of the Primary Curriculum: Final Report*. Nottingham: DCSF Publications.

Snow, C. E., Burns, S. and Griffin, P. (1998). *Preventing Reading Difficulties in Young Children*. Washington, DC: National Academy Press.

Vollmeyer, R. and Rheinberg, F. (2005). A surprising effect of feedback on learning. *Learning and Instruction*, 15, 589–602.

Vygotsky, L. S. (1962). *Thought and Language*. Cambridge, MA: Harvard University Press.

CHAPTER 3

READING

Chapter objectives

- To understand the difference between the written and the spoken word.
- To develop an understanding of how reading works.
- To develop appropriate instructional approaches to the teaching of reading.

Key questions

1. How do readers decode text?
2. How do readers engage with print while reading?
3. How do readers use metacognition to regulate their own learning?

Key words: comprehension, decoding, listening, memory, metacognition, phonemic awareness, phonics, reading, written word.

Introduction

The ability to read well is one of the most important factors relating to education in modern western societies. Not only is it important for society as a whole but it is also important in the development of a child's self-concept and self-esteem. Consequently, the teaching of reading has been subject to prolonged debates within education and in wider society. You as a teacher will need to gain a good understanding of the nature of reading and the methods by which reading can be taught, particularly since reading is integral to most areas of the curriculum.

This chapter will discuss the difference between the spoken word and written language. You will gain an appreciation of how readers negotiate and process the written word. It will examine a number of theoretical perspectives and considerations for the teaching of reading. In particular, it will consider three cognitive levels of processing: decoding, comprehension and metacognition. All are essential for effective reading. It will also examine three cueing systems: semantic, syntactic and graphophonic, all cues used to decode print. The central role of reading for meaning and reading for pleasure is also emphasised throughout this chapter.

> Two things are perhaps surprising about the skills and knowledge that a child brings with him when he is about to learn to read: the sheer quantity and complexity of his ability, and the small credit that he is usually given. (Smith, 1971: 223)

Educators have often tried to persuade parents to wait until their children start school before formal reading instruction takes place. However, the above quote by Smith challenges educators to broaden their definition of reading by considering where and when learning to read actually does take place. In the 1970s, research conducted by Clark (1976) reported observations of 32 children in Glasgow who could read by the time they entered school without having received any formal teaching. This and other studies have challenged our notions of reading acquisition and performance.

It follows that reading theory will only be adequate as far as it takes account of children such as these. The following definition takes note of the dynamic role children play in the acquisition of written language. 'Reading is the active process of constructing meaning from language represented by graphic symbols (letters), systematically arranged, just as listening is the active process of constructing meaning from the sound symbols (phonemes) of oral language' (Smith et al., 1970: 265).

Many of the early readers in Clark's (1976) study displayed considerable knowledge about the conventions of print, and often practised writing or writing-like behaviour on a blackboard to role-play themselves as writers. Around this time, Holdaway (1980) also observed that when given the opportunity to role-play as writers, young children would make rapid progress in reading, almost regardless of how they were taught. Thus, given adequate opportunities to experience texts of various types and to experiment with print, children can become beginning readers and writers before entering formal schooling. The implication for you as a teacher is that the children in your classroom will more likely make progress in reading and writing when they are immersed in print and at the same time are provided with ample opportunities to role-play themselves as writers.

In the previous chapter, we discussed how young children acquire spoken language. You will have noted that children are active language learners who regularly make a series of successive closer and closer approximations of the language of the adults around them. However, before we can go any further in this discussion on reading, we must examine the similarities and differences in written and spoken language.

First, it should be understood that print is not merely speech written down, as, for example, spoken language makes use of the ear and the voice while print involves the eye and the hand. Clearly, it is evident that many written transcripts are not suitable to be read aloud; this is because some things are better read than listened to.

Even though it can be seen that print is not merely speech written down, the two do share some basic characteristics. At the surface level of language, both speech and writing share the same lexicon and syntax (see Figure 3.1). The sounds of speech are instantly perishable while writing is preserved over time and distance. Writing is often addressed to an absent person or imaginary persons, whereas speech has an audience present and is often interactive in that it may engage others in conversation.

In contrast, the information and meanings conveyed through oral conversation are often just adequate. Because speakers interact more directly with their listeners, broken sentences are used in conjunction with physical gestures and intonation. In writing, punctuation could arguably be regarded as the equivalent of intonation but the graphic information comes too late for this to be so. Rather, it is the underlying meanings or deep structure which determine the choice of intonation when a reader is orally translating print into sound.

Meaning is constructed using an underlying deep structure of language. However, print must explain the situation or topic entirely in order to be

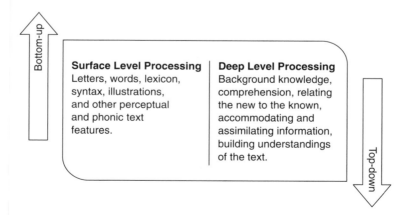

Figure 3.1 Levels of text processing

clearly understood (Vygotsky, 1978). It necessitates the writer supplying much more information than required in all forms of spoken language. In speech, the syntax is often broken and disjointed because there is immediate feedback during conversation. In contrast, the written word has no immediate feedback and so the writer must make sure that the writing will make sense by supplying extra information. The advantage of the written word is that it can be immediately re-read when comprehension fails. In contrast, the aural message is instantly lost due to its temporal nature and cannot be reviewed unless the speaker is asked to repeat the utterance. In essence, the overall differences in written and spoken language are based on their use rather than on their being intrinsic language forms.

Just as print is different from speech, there are also differences in reading and spelling. Reading is a decoding activity whereas spelling is an encoding or writing activity. Spelling also reflects the proposition that print is not just speech written down. In fact, spelling is more consistent with the visual aspects of print. Spelling emphasises the morphological connections between words but often has an inconsistent relationship to sound. For example, the 'c' in the words 'medical' and 'medicine' has different sounds when spoken but looks the same in print. For example, in the spoken word 'medical', the 'c' sounds like a 'k' whereas in the spoken word 'medicine' the 'c' sounds like an 's'. In the written word, the graphic representation does not change and therefore is more consistent.

Many children struggle with spelling because it is different from reading and it requires a constructive orientation. For example, the 'look, cover, write, say and check' technique of spelling is an effective method for learning new words because it makes use of both cognitive modes (visual and verbal). Spelling is also more consistent with its meaning constituents that are called morphemes. Morphemes are the basic units of meaning and words can be made up of one or more of these. They are most often related to their origins; for example, the base word 'port' comes from the Latin word meaning 'journey'. Affixes such as prefixes are also morphemes that carry particular meaning. For example, 're' could be added to the root word 'port' and would convey the meaning 'do again'. When children realise that words can be constructed from common morphemes through word-building activities, it empowers them as learners because they become more active and creative.

Levels of cognitive processing and reading theory

There are a number of interrelated theories that have been put forward to help educators better understand how students learn to read and comprehend text, and these will be briefly reviewed under the headings of: (a) behaviourist theory, (b) cognitive learning theory, and (c) social learning theory.

Behaviourist theory

Behavioural thinking has been part of western thought for centuries and is related to the development of systematic scientific method and the notion that a complex whole can be explained by the sum total of its component parts (Poplin and Stone, 1992). This theoretical orientation focuses on the surface features of texts such as letters, words and sounds. It emphasises external observable behaviours and the manipulation of specific content, procedures and skills to achieve educational goals (Green, 2003). It proposes that student behaviour is learned in a systematic and hierarchical fashion and that undesirable aspects can be unlearned (Gillet and Temple, 1994). Most teachers using traditional behavioural methods have stressed reading readiness and the mastery of basic skills (Samuels, 1978). They assume that by isolating basic elements they can build knowledge and skills through direct and explicit instruction (Lerner, 2003).

Cognitive learning theory

Constructivist theory

Constructivism is a theoretical perspective that belongs to the cognitive tradition and holds that learning is an active cognitive process that occurs as individuals construct understandings in relation to their own prior knowledge (Kroll, 1999; Piaget, 1965; Poplin and Stone, 1992; Symons and Pressley, 1993). Learning is viewed as developing a mental construct that involves both personal and cultural aspects. It is not simply a matter of taking on board external ideas and concepts, but it is part of a continuous construction and reconstruction of knowledge and meanings by the learner. Factors such as interest, motivation, self-concept, trust and expectations (that are often overlooked by behaviourists) are identified as being integral to the learning and reading process (Bernstein, 1955; Farris et al., 2004).

Cognitive theory

Cognitive theorists focus more on children's internal thinking processes, as evidenced by observable behaviours that can be changed using review and reflection techniques. Such an approach involves analysis of the task as well as the planning and thinking processes of the individual (Hareli and Weiner, 2002; Linnenbrink and Pintrich, 2003). This approach focuses on the deeper levels of learning.

Social learning theory

Another important theoretical notion is that learning is developed during social interactions (Bandura, 1978; Vygotsky, 1978). Social learning theory

(Bandura, 1978) has been associated with constructivism and has promoted the idea that learners have some control over their own learning and learn by observing and interacting with others in everyday situations through dialogue (Pressley, 2002; Pressley et al., 1992). This theoretical perspective values the knowledge that learners bring to the task and the way meaning and comprehension are constructed in the social context through the medium of language. The instructional strategy of modelling is often highlighted as an important pedagogical learning strategy in relation to this social learning environment.

Social learning theory supports the notion that the teacher should be the facilitator of meaning-making processes for the child. Thus, effective teaching utilises instructional methods that support language and the socio-cultural context of the home, the classroom and the school environment. The quality of these interactions, the appropriateness of the language of instruction, and the development and phasing out of support as the learner becomes more competent, are essential aspects of learning in the socio-cultural approach (Manset-Williamson and Nelson, 2005; Palincsar and Klenk, 1992).

An important concept in the socio-cultural theory of learning is the central role of the expert in providing temporary support during the student's learning activity. This type of supported instruction is often referred to as scaffolded instruction (Clark and Graves, 2004). The notion of scaffolded instruction relates to the metaphor of using scaffolding as a non-permanent structure to support a building under construction, in the same way that a novice reader can be temporarily supported. Thus, as the child gains skill and confidence in reading, the supports can be dismantled or phased out so that the reader can develop more independence.

Furthermore, Vygotsky (1978) proposed that new learning occurs when cognitive processing takes place just above the level at which the child normally functions independently. This mode of functioning is referred to as the 'zone of proximal development'. It is the condition in which the learner needs the short-term input of expert others, but without this support cannot learn as effectively. This notion recognises the social role of 'more expert others' in providing input to the learner, but emphasises the need to gradually relinquish the control of these 'experts' over the learning process.

Teaching of reading

You will need to be aware of the dynamic and interactive links between children's language, the alphabetic principle, phonics and phonological awareness (Hay and Fielding-Barnsley, 2007). The alphabetic principle is the notion that there are systematic correspondences between the sounds of language and the letters of the alphabet. Phonics stresses the knowledge of sound–letter relationships and their use in reading and writing. Phonological awareness is the ability to recognise the sound units of language and their manipulation, such as recognising that there are three phonemes in the word 'tree', and that the words 'scat' and 'hat' rhyme, while also understanding that 'can' starts with the same sound as 'car' (Rohl, 2006). For children to progress in reading, they need to be able to understand these basic concepts.

In Australia, the National Inquiry into the Teaching of Literacy (DEST, 2005) stressed the importance of direct systematic instruction in phonics during the early years of schooling as an essential component that lays a solid foundation for teaching children to read. Furthermore, in the USA there was considerable evidence (NRP, 2000) to support the notion that children learn best when teachers use an integrated approach that incorporates phonemic awareness, phonics, fluency, vocabulary knowledge and comprehension. This report also suggested that there is often a false dichotomy between phonics and whole-language approaches to the teaching of reading. It was emphasised that teachers need to draw on a wide repertoire of techniques and teaching strategies that can provide a balanced approach to the diverse educational needs of learners.

The Simple View of Reading is a model of reading in which reading consists of two elements: word decoding and listening comprehension (Gough and Tunmer, 1986). The model suggests that phonics, although essential for progress in reading, is, by itself, insufficient (Fielding-Barnsley et al., 2005). Normally, word reading and reading comprehension are highly correlated and one reason for less skilled readers' initial failure may be that they focus more on word reading accuracy rather than comprehension (Cain and Oakhill, 1999).

This model conceptualises reading as the product of the two dimensions: listening comprehension and word decoding. The model proposes that children might differ in relation to the two specific dimensions and this, therefore, necessitates different teaching approaches to support their reading progress (Joshi and Aaron, 2000; Kirby and Savage, 2008). However, when teachers focus on word-level processing skills as a single indicator of reading performance, the focus may be too restricted and may lead to an inadequate assessment of reading comprehension difficulties (Bishop and Snowling, 2004). A number of researchers have also noted that younger readers often rely more on word identification skills, whereas reading comprehension skills are more critical for older readers (Ricketts et al., 2007; Velluntino et al., 2007).

Decoding

Many people have supposed that written language has to be decoded into sound by sub-vocalising and that once this has been done the word meanings will become apparent. They suppose that the meaning is implicit in speech and that written language should be decoded into sound so that meaning can be realised (Smith, 1973). However, it is usually harder to read orally and most experienced readers do not sub-vocalise as much as we would expect (Smith, 1971). The problem is that if you listen to see if you sub-vocalise, you will be sure to sub-vocalise. When you are having trouble comprehending, you will most likely vocalise. However, the more you sub-vocalise, the less you will comprehend. Since meaning can be brought directly to print, sub-vocalisation can often be more disabling for the reader.

There is also a severe limit to how much information the brain can handle moment by moment. It takes time for the brain to make decisions; the time taken will be related to the number of alternatives available to the individual. This is because the number of alternatives that must be considered will affect the speed at which the brain can make decisions. For example, if you are flying an aeroplane above your street, you will be able to see the whole suburb. The time it takes to identify your own house will depend on the number of alternatives or significant features. Suppose the houses were very similar or were all built by the same builder – in this situation it would be very difficult to identify your own home. However, if you had a wooden house and all of the other houses in the area were clad in brick, then the alternatives would be far less and recognition would be much easier. Thus, to reduce the amount of information entering working memory, readers must ignore sensations that have no meaning for those that do (Huey, 1908).

Normally, working memory has more work to do when the reading becomes difficult. The harder reading becomes, the more visual information readers need to take in. On the other hand, when reading is easier readers need less visual information for an interpretation (Smith, 1978: 14). For example, if readers are reading a book about a subject they know very little about, then reading will slow down while more and more information is sampled. Thus, comprehension will become more difficult because working-memory capacity is limited and becomes overloaded.

Some methods of reading instruction, such as 'sounding out' individual letters of words while reading, overload working memory, making comprehension more difficult by having to sample more visual information than is necessary. Words and letters are recognised in the same way as dogs and cats are recognised, i.e. on the basis of significant differences while also considering the alternatives. However, phonics works best when the reader is more able to predict what the word is likely to be, thus reducing the amount of information needing to be sampled (Smith, 1978).

Phonological awareness

Phonological awareness is important for reading because it is necessary for children to understand how words in our language are represented. Phonological awareness is commonly defined as 'one's sensitivity to, or explicit awareness of the phonological structure of words in one's language' (Torgesen and Mathes, 2000: 2). Phonological awareness includes phonemic awareness, which involves the ability to recognise and manipulate individual phonemes – for example, knowing the word cat is composed of the three phonemes /c/a/t, that if the middle phoneme is replaced by a 'u' then the word becomes 'cut', and that the word 'pat' can be rearranged to form the new word 'tap'. It is important to structure phonological awareness activities so that children begin with larger units of sound and gradually learn to focus on smaller and smaller units. Activities that focus on single words such as children's names are a good way to start. Throughout the programme, children learn to blend and segment words into syllables, then into onset and rhyme and finally into phonemes. However, some children find it very difficult to identify phonemes and need ample practice and encouragement (Rohl, 2006).

Phonics

Phonics is the cluster of relationships between the sounds in our language and the patterns of letters that can be represented by those sounds (Hornsby and Wilson, 2009). In the English language, there is no single one-to-one correspondence between letters and sounds – for example, there are 44 sounds that can be represented by 26 letters or combinations of those 26 letters in the English alphabet. To add to the complexity, a phoneme is not one sound – it is a set of slightly different sounds. Additionally, English phonemes vary with different dialects – for example, spoken English in London will sound different to spoken English in Sydney.

The Australian Report of the National Inquiry into the Teaching of Literacy (DEST, 2005) gave emphasis to the teaching of phonics within a balanced reading programme (Rohl, 2006). There are many different types of commercially produced reading programmes that seek to systematically develop phonic reading skills. However, there are some serious problems with many commercial phonics programmes. They often teach phonics in a step-by-step manner without considering what children already know or are using in classroom themes or units of work. Moreover, they seldom cater for individual differences and they generally don't build on children's prior knowledge. Phonics, however, is best taught in the context of learning to read and write because it is often more meaningful and purposeful (Hornsby and Wilson, 2009).

Three cueing systems

Readers comprehend what they are reading using what they know about the world. In order to comprehend, the reader must use this prior knowledge to hypothesise and predict in order to eliminate alternative meanings. This economises on the amount of information that working memory needs to process moment by moment. Efficient reading does not involve the precise decoding of letters or whole words but is the process of using a selection of available cues to predict what is to come. This eliminates possible alternatives and lessens the load on working memory with its limited capacity. There are three cueing systems (see Figure 3.2) that readers use to sample the text, hypothesise and predict.

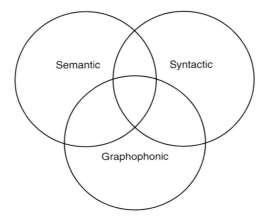

Figure 3.2   Three cueing systems

Automaticity

As readers progress, decoding skills normally become automatised and comprehension increasingly draws on a broader range of different language skills (Perfetti, 2007; Snowling et al., 2001). Thus, reading becomes less about decoding as students rely more on their content knowledge, grammatical structure and higher-level text processing skills, such as inference generation and comprehension monitoring (Cain and Oakhill, 2006, 2007; Woolley, 2011).

Although readers may develop accurate decoding skills, the comprehension of text will not exceed general language ability (Hutchinson et al., 2003). Good readers have the ability to read most words even when there are no semantic context cues available. Many of these words are well known or automatised because they require little or no cognitive effort to decode (LaBerge and Samuels, 1974). Moreover, the active processing of phrases and sentences cannot proceed effortlessly without the ability to automatically recognise individual words (Pressley, 2002).

Vignette 3.1

Ms Jones is a year 2 teacher who makes a habit of listening to every child read during each school term. She collects data from observations, anecdotes and communication with parents, and from teacher aides and volunteer helpers who assist with classroom reading. She also makes sure that the children are working within their zone of proximal development (see page 192) and that the books the children are reading are at the appropriate level without being too easy or too difficult. She does this by recording and scoring each child's reading at regular intervals. After scoring and analysing the running records, she often adjusts the levels of the classroom readers, the take-home readers and the composition of the reading groups within the classroom.

While conducting her running record sessions with individual children, she gains insight into the types of strategies that they are using while decoding print. For example, during one session with Jack it was obvious that he was having some difficulties with reading fluency and accuracy. At times, he would miscue – for example, he would often read a word like 'house' but say the word 'horse' instead. Rather than correcting Jack immediately, Ms Jones allowed Jack to read to the end of the sentence and wait a short while before asking one of two questions: 'Does that sound right?' or 'Does that make sense?' In this case, the word 'horse' sounded right because it was the name of a thing, just as house is the name of a thing. However, he said it did not make sense. Ms Jones asked him to point to where the sentence did not make sense. Jack pointed to the word 'house'. Ms Jones praised Jack by saying, 'It was a good try because the word does look like the correct word and it shares many of the same letters'. Ms Jones asked him to re-read the sentence and self-correct by making the appropriate alteration. This time he said the word 'house' and confirmed that the sentence now made sense.

During sessions with Zoe, Ms Jones had previously noticed that she had difficulties with fluency. Zoe would often inappropriately guess a word as she was reading, and the miscues were often not graphophonically (looking and sounding) similar to the targeted word. However, Ms Jones had noticed that recently Zoe was often self-correcting by repeating and substituting the correct word without any prompting from her, the teacher. She had noted in an earlier running record that Zoe often made miscues that didn't look or sound like the correct word but would not self-correct and so lost meaning during reading. The difference with the present running record was that Zoe was obviously self-monitoring and self-correcting. She was no longer losing meaning during reading and her comprehension had obviously improved. Ms Jones was no longer concerned about Zoe's fluency difficulty because she felt that it would eventually right itself with practice and with growing confidence.

Questions

1   Why is it important for teachers to regularly listen to children read individually?
2   How is teacher feedback and praise given in this scenario?

3 Why was Ms Jones happy with Zoe's reading even though there were problems with fluency?
4 How did Ms Jones use the pause, prompt, praise method to assist her students in reading?

Reading culture

A stimulating reading culture can be created in the classroom by regularly conducting book talks, book reviews, silent reading and sharing sessions where children are given the opportunity to volunteer to share their favourite parts of a story. Generally, however, round robin reading should be avoided wherever possible. This practice is found in many classrooms whereby individual students take turns reading aloud. It usually involves oral reading without any prior practice with the text. The quality of the reading is often diminished because children may be just rehearsing their section of the text before their turn comes and not listening and following on with their peers. Some children may even feel quite threatened or embarrassed because they have much more difficulty in reading than their peers and fear this type of public exposure (Hilden and Jones, 2012a, b).

There are many alternatives that can be used in place of round robin reading, such as readers' theatre which involves the dramatic reading of a script by a number of students. The students usually rehearse by reading the passage during the week and then expressively perform for their peers. The focus is on fluency and expression in order to bring the characters of the story alive. Repeated reading is another instructional strategy which promotes automaticity and fluency by reading and re-reading short passages at appropriate instructional reading levels (90–95% accuracy). Peer-Assisted Learning Strategies (PALS) is another method whereby the teacher pairs the children so that each person takes a turn at being the coach or reader. The pair cycle through reading, re-reading and retelling and the process may include the integration of comprehension strategies such as summarising, predicting and asking questions (Fuchs et al., 1997).

One way to encourage reading practice, reading for enjoyment and reading as a social activity, while increasing parental participation in children's literacy learning, is to develop take-home literacy packs pitched at children's reading levels. The packs may consist of two or three books and any other materials required to carry out the suggested activities. Some packs can be designed to focus on particular themes that children are interested in or that relate to classroom topics. Ideally, specialised school personnel should train parents so that the time they spend with their children is as productive as possible. Above all, home reading time should be enjoyable and relaxed. During this time, children have an opportunity to show their parents their developing command of the reading process (Kavanagh and Caratti, 2006).

Vignette 3.2

Interview

Mr Thomas is an experienced year 5 classroom teacher. He regularly implements 'Sustained Silent Reading' (SSR) for 15 minutes after the lunchtime break each day. It helps to settle the children after play and is commonly used in classrooms to promote reading for pleasure and reading practice, and to provide opportunities to engage with others through shared reading experiences.

Q: Why do you have silent reading sessions in class time?

A: Reading for pleasure is not the only reason for reading but is one aspect that can be very motivating, particularly when children are given opportunities to share their book experiences with others.

Q: Do other teachers have these sessions?

A: No, some teachers at the school are not so keen on this reading method because they feel that some children take advantage of the time to avoid reading by pretending to be engaged. However, I believe that this problem can easily be overcome by building in student accountability and systematically monitoring student progress by way of having regular reading conferences, book-sharing activities, book reviews and project work related to book reading.

Q: How do you motivate students to read during these reading sessions?

A: I have found that one of the best ways to motivate students is to have brief but regular literature sharing circles. These sessions can become more frequent by having others such as older peers, parents, teacher aides or community volunteers lead the discussions or give book reviews. Reading logs are also an effective way for students to keep track of what they have read while being an effective accountability tool. Not only can students be accountable to the teacher or others, but this method can be an effective form of self-assessment, particularly if the children are encouraged to write reflective comments.

Q: I noticed that you allow the students to choose their own books for SSR. Wouldn't it be better to choose the books for them so that you have control over their reading?

A: One of the most important principles of SSR is the notion of choice of books. Obviously, children will be more engaged when they are reading books about topics or themes that they are interested in. Generally, children should be guided to choose books that are not too difficult or too easy. Usually, this means that the ease of reading should require about 95–100% accuracy but many children can go below this level if they are familiar with the topic and particularly interested in reading about it. I provide a large range of books that are colour-coded so that the children have a lot of choice within their ability level.

Questions

1 Why is SSR an important ingredient in the reading programme?
2 How can you make sure that children are reading appropriate books in the classroom?
3 How can teachers provide books that are interesting to children?
4 Should comic books be considered for SSR sessions in the classroom?

Reading and electronic texts

When children engage in digital media, they often multitask between a variety of digital media by simultaneously managing a combination of modes of print, image, movement, animation, video, sound and music (Walsh et al., 2007). This will also involve different ways of viewing from linear print to images that are non-linear and often non-sequential (Kress, 2003). In some situations, electronic texts can make reading easier when the text-to-speech facility is enabled and the reader can listen to the text being read. In some cases, the speed of reading can be adjusted according to the reader's needs. The Kindle also has a paper-like display, which reads just like a real printed book without the glare of a computer screen. Page turning on the Kindle is designed to be effortless, becoming more of an unconscious movement which allows the reader to focus on the story.

It is often the case, however, that electronic texts will present added difficulties for the reader. For example, average readability levels on the Internet may be beyond the grade levels of the intended audience. In most cases, electronic texts are expository in nature and often contain hypertext links. Reading is a complex process and reading from the screen can be much more challenging than reading print-based text. For example, reading from a screen can be substantially slower than reading print-based texts, depending on screen glare, screen resolution and screen size. The screen can be static or dynamic with the ability to scroll manually or automatically at a rate determined by the user. This can cause some problems for the reader. Hypertext can also disorient the reader and increase the cognitive load because it introduces quite complex navigation elements and demands a high degree of metacognitive awareness.

Other challenges include the necessity to evaluate the relevance of additional information, reading texts in non-linear ways and integrating information presented in different media. What is needed is the development of suitable strategies and skills that will enable children to navigate and read digital texts. This will involve the integration of ICT skills with the decoding of words, written dialogue, images and graphics (Walsh et al., 2007). The ability to conduct electronic searches for information and to evaluate electronic references are examples of other specific computer skills that will be required.

Conclusion

Print is not speech written down – there are distinctive differences due to purpose rather than anything else. When processing print, we do not have to interpret print into sound before meaning can be extracted. Rather, as with speech, the surface structure can be directly related to meaning.

The surface structure of written language is sampled by a number of eye fixations, which limit the amount of visual information taken in moment by moment. The brain fills in the missing information, which the eyes do not see. Systematically, the eyes are directed by the brain to fixations where the most significant information is available, sometimes regressing to sample information behind what is being vocalised. Not only is there a severe limit to what the eye can see during the reading process, the brain can only handle a limited amount of information at any one time. The number of alternatives that are available to the reader determines the decisions the brain has to make during reading. Very few items can be held in short-term memory at any one time. For short-term memory to be effective, readers must process large chunks of meaning rather than letters or words. Text sampling is used to avoid an overload of working memory.

 Discussion questions and activities

 Points for discussion

1   What is the difference between deciding what to say and what to write?
2   List the types of readings that you might engage with in a typical week. How are these activities different and how are they the same?
3   In regard to the list that you made for question 2, do you read each one of these in the same way or do you read them differently?

†††† Group activities

1   In your groups, make a list of strategies that you might use to regain meaning when you make an error (miscue) while reading a text.
2   Discuss how you would promote reading for enjoyment in your classroom. Make a list of strategies to share with the whole class.
3   Observe someone in your group research a topic on the Internet using a mobile computing device. List the micro skills that are required to navigate the e-learning environment.

⊞ Whole-class activities

1   Find out how to do a running record or miscue analysis. Record a child reading and make your own running record.
2   How can you explain the child's miscues (recorded reading in whole-class
activity 1) in terms of the three cueing systems as shown in Figure 3.2
above?
3   Connect an iPad to a digital projector and review Profs' Phonics 2 by Doc
Ruth (iTunes store: https://itunes.apple.com/app/profs-phonics/id496793198)
and discuss when and how you would use the app in the primary classroom.

References

Bandura, A. (1978). The self-system in Reciprocal Determinism. *American Psychologist*, 33, 344–358.

Bernstein, M. R. (1955). Relationships between interest and reading comprehension. *Journal of Educational Research*, 49, 283–288.

Bishop, D. V. M. and Snowling, M. J. (2004). Developmental dyslexia and specific language impairment: Same or different? *Psychological Bulletin*, 130, 858–886.

Cain, K. and Oakhill, J. V. (1999). Inference making ability and its relation to comprehension failure in young children. *Reading and Writing: An Interdisciplinary Journal*, 11, 489–503.

Cain, K. and Oakhill, J. (2006). Assessment matters: Issues in the measurement of reading comprehension. *British Journal of Educational Psychology,* 76, 697–708.

Cain, K. and Oakhill, J. (2007). Reading comprehension difficulties: Correlates, causes, and consequences. In K. Cain & J. Oakhill (eds), *Children's Comprehension Problems in Oral and Written Language: A Cognitive Perspective* (pp. 41–75). London: The Guilford Press.

Clark, K. F. and Graves, M. F. (2004). Scaffolding students' comprehension of text. *The Reading Teacher*, 58, 570–580.

Clark, M. M. (1976). *Young Fluent Readers*. London: Heinemann Educational Books.

Department of Education, Science and Training (DEST) (2005). *National Inquiry into the Teaching of Reading*. Canberra: Australian Government.

Ehri, L. C. and McCormick, S. (1998). Phases of word learning: Implications for instruction with delayed and disabled readers. *Reading and Writing Quarterly*, 4(2), 135–163.

Farris, P. J., Fuhler, C. J. and Walther, M. P. (2004). *Teaching Reading: A Balanced Approach for Today's Classrooms*. Boston: McGraw-Hill.

Fielding-Barnsley, R., Hay, I. and Ashman, A. (2005). Phonological awareness: Necessary but not sufficient. *National Conference of the Australian Association of Special Education,* Brisbane, Australia, 23–25 September.

Fuchs, D., Fuchs, L. S., Mathes, P. G. and Simmons, D. C. (1997). Peer-assisted learning strategies: Making classrooms more responsive to diversity. *American Educational Research Journal*, 34, 174–206.

Gillet, J. W. and Temple, C. (1994). *Understanding Reading Problems: Assessment and Instruction* (4th edn) (pp. 13–56). New York: HarperCollins.

Gough, P. B. and Tunmer, W. (1986). Decoding, reading, and reading disability. *Remedial and Special Education*, 7, 6–10.

Green, D. (2003). Children and print: Reading. In D. Green and R. Campbell (eds), *Literacies and Learners* (pp. 113–129). Frenchs Forest, NSW: Prentice Hall.

Hareli, S. and Weiner, B. (2002). Social emotions and personality inferences: A scaffold for a new direction in the study of achievement motivation. *Educational Psychologist*, 37, 183–193.

Hay, I. and Fielding-Barnsley, R. (2007). Facilitating children's emergent literacy using shared reading: A comparison of two models. 30(3), 191–202.

Hilden, K. and Jones, J. (2012a). A literacy spring-cleaning: Sweeping round robin reading out of your classroom. *Reading Today*, 29(5), 23–24.

Hilden, K. and Jones, J. (2012b). Making Sustained Silent Reading really count: Tips on engaging students. *Reading Today*, 30(1), 17–19.

Holdaway, D. (1980). *Independence in Reading: A Handbook on Individualized Procedures* (2nd edn). Gosford: Ashton Scholastic.

Hornsby, D. and Wilson, L. (2009). Early literacy and phonics. *Practically Primary*, 14(3), 4–8.

Huey, E. B. (1908). *The Psychology and Pedagogy of Reading*. Cambridge, MA: The MIT Press.

Hutchinson, J. M., Whiteley, H. E., Smith, C. D. and Connors, L. (2003). The development progression of comprehension-related skills in children learning EAL. *Journal of Research in Reading*, 26(1), 19–32.

Joshi, M. and Aaron, P. G. (2000). The component model of reading: Simple view of reading made a little more complex. *Reading Psychology*, 21, 85–97.

Kavanagh, B. and Caratti, F. (2006). Take-home literacy packs: Connecting school and home through an enjoyable literacy experience. *Practically Primary*, 11(1), 28–32.

Kirby, J. R. and Savage, J. S. (2008). Can the simple view deal with the complexities of reading? *Literacy*, 42(2), 75–82.

Kress, G. (2003). *Literacy in the New Media Age*. London: Routledge.

Kroll, B. (1999). Social constructivist theory and its relationship to effective teaching of students with learning difficulties. In P. Westwood and W. Scott (eds), *Learning Disabilities: Advocacy and Action* (pp. 21–28). Melbourne: Australian Resource Educators' Association.

LaBerge, D. and Samuels, S. J. (1974). Toward a theory of automatic information processing in reading. *Cognitive Psychology*, 6, 293–323.

Lerner, J. W. (2003). *Learning Disabilities: Theories, Diagnosis, and Teaching Strategies* (9th edn). Boston: Houghton Mifflin Co.

Linnenbrink, E. A. and Pintrich, P. R. (2003). The role of self-efficacy beliefs in student engagement in the classroom. *Reading and Writing Quarterly*, 19, 119–137.

Manset-Williamson, G. and Nelson, J. M. (2005). Balanced, strategic reading instruction for upper-elementary and middle school students with reading disabilities: A comparative study of two approaches. *Learning Disability Quarterly*, 28, 59–74.

National Reading Panel (NRP) (2000). *Teaching Children to Read: Report of the Comprehension Instruction Subgroup to the National Institute of Child Health and Development*. Washington, DC: NICD.

Palincsar, A. S. and Klenk, L. (1992). Fostering literacy learning in supportive contexts. *Journal of Learning Difficulties*, 25, 211–225.

Perfetti, C. (2007). Reading ability: Lexical quality to comprehension. *Scientific Studies of Reading*, 11(4), 357–383.

Piaget, J. (1965). The stages of the intellectual development of the child. In P.H. Mussen, J. J. Conger and J. Kagan (eds), *Readings in Child Development and Personality* (2nd edn) (pp. 291–298). New York: Harper & Row.

Poplin, M. S. and Stone, S. (1992). Paradigm shifts in instructional strategies: From reductionism to holistic constructivism. In W. Stainback and S. Stainback (eds), *Controversial Issues Confronting Special Education: Divergent Perspectives* (pp. 153–179). Boston: Allyn & Bacon.

Pressley, M. (2002). Improving comprehension instruction: A path for the future. In C. Collins Block, L. B. Gambrell and M. Pressley (eds), *Improving Comprehension Instruction* (pp. 385–389). San Francisco: Jossey-Bass.

Pressley, M., Wood, E., Woloshin, V. E., Martin, V., King, A. and Menke, D. (1992). Encouraging mindful use of prior knowledge: Attempting to construct explanatory answers facilitates learning. *Educational Psychologist*, 27, 91–109.

Ricketts, J., Nation, K. and Bishop, V. M. (2007). Vocabulary is important for some, but not all reading skills. *Scientific Study of Reading*, 11(3), 235–257.

Rohl, M. (2006). Phonics, phonological awareness and early literacy learning. *Practically Primary*, 11(3), 7–9.

Samuels, S. J. (1978). Why children fail to learn and what to do about it. *Exceptional Children*, 53, 7–16.

Smith, E. B., Goodman, K. S. and Meredith, R. (1970). *Language and Thinking in School*. New York: Holt, Rinehart & Winston.

Smith, F. (1971). *Understanding Reading: A Psycholinguistic Analysis of Reading and Learning to Read*. New York: Holt, Rinehart & Winston.

Smith, F. (1973). *Psycholinguistics and Reading*. New York: Holt, Rinehart & Winston.

Smith, F. (1978). *Reading*. Cambridge: Cambridge University Press.

Snowling, M. J., Adams, J. W., Bishop, D. V. M. and Stothard, S. E. (2001). Educational attainments of school leavers with a preschool history of speech-language impairments. *International Journal of Language and Communication Disorders*, 36, 173–183.

Symons, S. and Pressley, M. (1993). Prior knowledge affects text search success and extraction of information. *Reading Research Quarterly*, 28, 251–259.

Torgesen, J. K. and Mathes, P. G. (2000). *A Basic Guide to Understanding, Assessing, and Teaching Phonological Awareness*. Austin, TX: Pro-ed International.

Velluntino, F. R., Tunmer, W. E., Jaccard, J. J. and Chen, R. (2007). Components of reading ability: Multivariate evidence for a convergent skills model of reading development. *Scientific Study of Reading*, 11(1), 3–32.

Walsh, M., Asha, J. and Sprainger, N. (2007). Reading digital texts. *Australian Journal of Language and Literacy*, 32(1), 40–53.

Woolley, G. (2011). *Reading Comprehension: Assisting Children with Learning Difficulties*. Dordrecht, The Netherlands: Springer International.

Vygotsky, L. S. (1978). *Mind and Society*. Cambridge, MA: The MIT Press.

CHAPTER 4

LISTENING, SPEAKING, VIEWING AND ACTING

Chapter objectives

- To develop an understanding of the importance of listening, speaking, viewing and acting.
- To develop appropriate instructional approaches for the teaching of listening, speaking, viewing and acting skills.
- To develop a solid foundation on which literacy learning can more effectively take place in the classroom.

Key questions

1. Why is it important for children to talk in the classroom?
2. How can teachers encourage their students to develop their listening, speaking, viewing and acting skills in the classroom?
3. How do children develop their imagination and effectively convey their ideas to others?

Key words: acting, dialogic interaction, discussing, elaborating, explaining, listening, memory, questioning, showing, speaking, viewing.

Introduction

When children have a good command of spoken language, they have a powerful means of expressing their own thoughts and intentions. This means that they are able to question, describe, express, speculate, inform, persuade and communicate more effectively. They are more able to express their ideas and feelings and better interact meaningfully with other people by sharing ideas and organising their world, thereby facilitating greater gains in learning across a range of subject domains. As a result, they develop greater confidence within their environment and become more successful in their endeavours. In contrast, children who lack this oral aptitude often have difficulties in the classroom that will impede their learning in other areas such as reading, spelling and writing.

A good literacy education should offer children the means to be successful in their future working lives by being able to organise meetings, hold important discussions, make presentations at conferences or just clarify important decisions and ideas. Teaching children to listen attentively so as to understand what is said and to express themselves intelligibly through well-formed speech, drama and film is crucial to their future success. The entire curriculum should be fully exploited for this purpose because it not only fosters children's intellectual development and enjoyment of learning but also boosts their self-confidence, social and emotional development and continuing motivation to learn.

> Further, the goal of literacy by the end of the primary phase must be more than functional. It is about making and exploring meaning as well as receiving and transmitting it. That is why talking must be part of reading and writing rather than an optional extra. That is why engagement with meanings made by others through literature, and other language through which such meanings are conveyed, is no less essential. (Alexander, 2010: 269)

The importance of talk has been gradually emerging as foundational to children's learning (Smith, 2005). In the above quote, Alexander stresses the idea that talking is fundamental to language and literacy development. This reinforces Vygotsky's (1962) notion that learning more effectively takes place conversationally in social situations. Oral language underpins the development of other literacy activities, such as reading, writing and even viewing.

It has been recognised that when children enter school with impoverished language, it will hamper their literacy development throughout their school life (Rose, 2009). An Ofsted (2011) survey found that a common feature of the most successful schools among those classed as disadvantaged, was the attention teachers gave to developing children's speaking and listening skills. These successful schools recognised the lack of children's initial language skills and their impoverished vocabulary and accommodated the curricula to ensure that they would develop the speaking and listening skills that were considered essential.

Generally, teachers spend a large amount of time explaining and using questions to elicit responses from children, requiring a lower level of cognitive engagement. Most questions are orchestrated to produce responses/answers that do not require higher-order thinking skills and/or elicit a more complex elaboration of ideas. This lack of extended talk and adequate opportunities for children to be able to discuss their ideas can limit their language and speech development. Thus, dialogic interaction in classroom settings has emerged as fundamental to children's literacy development (Rose, 2009; Smith, 2005).

By focusing on the development of oral language, you will help develop skills that enable children to manipulate and control their world. Children should learn to develop and apply their speaking and listening skills to suit a variety of audiences and for different purposes. In doing so, they should listen to and tell stories that explore ideas and opinions in both formal and informal settings (Rose, 2009).

Listening

From a very early age, children enjoy aspects of literacy that combine rhyme, repetition and rhythm and this helps to cement the sounds and forms of language, along with the prerequisite skills for reading such as phonemic awareness. In your classroom or other learning environment, you should, wherever possible, expose children to various listening activities and explore the creative aspects of language through various formats such as expressive book readings, plays, poetry, song and interesting films. As well as being important for language and communication development, listening to good literature can also engender an interest in the appreciation of language as an art form.

Children can easily become distracted by extraneous noises or thoughts; consequently, listening activities need to have clear goals and supports. For example, children may be asked to make notes after they have listened to a documentary podcast or instructional video. KWL (Ogle, 1986) is a useful procedure that can be used to support not only listening comprehension but also self-regulation skills. The KWL procedural framework can be made into a chart and used in the following way:

1. What do I **K**now? List five things that you already know about the topic.
2. What do I **W**ant to know? List three things that you would like to know about the topic.
3. What have I **L**earned? What three things did you learn about the topic?

This gives structure and purpose to the listening activity and develops children's self-regulated learning by enabling students to develop reading goals and reflect on what they have learned. A variation of this procedure is the KWHHL strategy (Know – Want – Head words – Heart words – Learn), which has been developed by Szabo (2006) to specifically develop vocabulary strategy (see Table 4.1). The two 'H' elements (Head words and Heart words) relate to the 'during reading' phase of the procedure and are used to identify low frequency words and words associated with abstract emotions.

Szabo's KWHHL strategy was originally designed for year 8 students to use while reading because it was apparent that the students were having difficulty with content vocabulary while processing text. The first 'H' represented attention to head or hard words (new words) that the students encountered while reading, while the second 'H' related to heart, or feeling, words, that represented emotional word content. Thus, the strategy can also be used to help students to listen and attend to new word meanings and to consider the context clues in which they are embedded.

Listening while stories are read is a particularly valuable means by which children can come to understand the functions and structures of written language (Smith, 1978). As listeners become familiar with the structure of texts, they will be more inclined to anticipate the manner in which things will be said (Smith, 1984). Instruction that accompanies shared reading/listening experiences should include a wide range of literacy elements such as attention to: text features, text structures, vocabulary, comprehension and language appreciation (Topping and Ferguson, 2005).

Good listening skills will also lead to the development of foundational reading skills. In particular, over the past 20 years there has been an abundance of research evidence demonstrating a strong link between phonological awareness and the ability to learn to read and spell. It has been found that there is a strong correlation between children's awareness of phonology, particularly with rhyme and alliteration, and their achievement in learning to read (Bradley and Bryant, 1983). Phonological skills, such as rhyming, are important as they enable children to make comparisons and analogies where there is a pattern of grapheme-to-phoneme relationship (Byrne, 1998: Goswami and Bryant, 1990).

Other aspects of oral language have substantial correlations with decoding and reading comprehension such as: word meanings (semantics), sentence structure (syntax), the architecture of words, word parts (morphology) and sounds (phonology) (Richgels, 2004). Knowledge of how syntax or grammar

Table 4.1 Comparison of the KWL and KWHHL procedural frameworks

KWL	KWHHL
K – What I know	K – What I know
W – What I want to know	W – What I want to know
	H – What are the head words?
	H – What are the heart words?
L – What I learned	L – What I learned

is used in oral language has also been identified as an important element in beginning reading comprehension and vocabulary development (Bowyer-Crane et al., 2008).

Dialogic interaction

With the more recent emphasis on children learning in cooperative groups, there has been an immense need for children to be able to articulate and engage competently in dialogic interaction. Until recently, traditional instructional methods have relied on a transmission model of teaching, in which the teacher assumed control of what was to be learned and did most of the speaking while children passively listened. In contrast, the recent instructional shift asserts that learning will be enhanced when children work collaboratively in small groups. This perception is thought to enable children to use their own language and to formulate their own questions. It enables children to be more engaged and to speculate and hypothesise about the learning materials and topics that they learning about (Mercer, 2003; Smith, 2005).

It is assumed that through dialogic interaction children can recall and review what they have learned about a topic. This type of learning engagement empowers children to develop ideas collaboratively and to learn from each other. It stands to reason that the more children contribute their own ideas, the more likely they will be to engage at much deeper levels of learning. Not only will children develop important language skills by interacting with each other, they will also learn how to take turns and learn when and how to make suggestions and make valuable contributions to group discussions.

This emphasis on interactive and group work, using dialogic interaction, usually requires more sophisticated skills than the children already possess. Thus, they need more suitable speaking and listening skills if they are going to be able to play an effective role as a member of a group. It has been widely recognised that oral language is a consistent predictor of future literacy achievement. Therefore, young children, in particular, need to learn how to take control over many aspects of language (Snow et al., 1998). In endeavouring to do so, there are a number of key principles that should be applied to group work (Dawes and Birrell, 2005):

1. Children need adequate training and preparation to be effectively involved in group work.
2. Children should be expected to develop ideas collaboratively.
3. Children should build meaning from new information combined with what they already know.
4. Children should be provided with social support and encouragement in the dialogical learning process.
5. Group activities must be well structured with each child knowing their role so that ideas and new meanings are clear.

Dialogue and discussion

Good dialogic interaction can be enhanced when children are taught how to ask and answer appropriate questions. A good question is an invitation to think, to act and to become engaged; it is 'good' or productive because it requires a response and will generate further inquiry. A good questioning treatment requires that you facilitate a transition from the basic 'What', 'Who', 'Where' and 'When' questions to higher-order 'Why' and 'How' questions. The former are surface questions that merely elicit factual or explicit information from the text. However, when you consistently ask questions to which only one answer is appropriate, thinking tends to remain at a surface level of engagement. Higher-order questions such as 'Why' and 'How', on the other hand, will require children to think about whether they agree with something or not. These latter types of questions transport children's thinking processes beyond the surface level of understanding, leading them to examine their own deep thoughts and opinions. A good questioning treatment should also require children to elaborate and give examples, or to categorise or organise information. Questions could be posed as either impromptu discussion questions about issues as they arise during a literacy activity or be a prearranged set of thought-provoking questions.

Appropriate questions should direct attention and fine-tune listening skills because they elicit different responses according to the types of questions asked. You should also teach appropriate listening behaviours when children engage with others. For example, taking turns and knowing how to listen and respond to the thoughts and opinions of others are skills that often do not come naturally.

Listening games such as 'I Spy with My Little Eye' or playing a series of recorded 'mystery' sounds and having the students guess what made the sounds can be used to supplement other more formal listening lessons. Other reading/listening/speaking tasks could be routinely organised as short transition activities or as featured activities that are regularly timetabled into the class programme such as:

- readers' theatre
- choral reading
- radio plays with sound effects
- formal drama
- puppet shows
- 'This is Your life' based on story characters
- news items for radio/newspaper based on an incident in a story
- debates
- making a TV advertisement for a book
- writing a poem based on a story character, object or scene.

Oracy

Oracy is the ability to express oneself in speech with fluency and appropriateness, in a variety of settings and audiences (Campbell and Green, 2006). Oracy in the classroom is the principal mode of communication that you, as a teacher, will use to teach ideas, skills and strategies. It is also the principal mode whereby children learn to express themselves and to publicly demonstrate what they have learned. The best way to involve students in developing better oracy skills is to incorporate their experiences and interests wherever possible in the classroom.

A good starting point for incidental opportunities to practise oracy skills is to ask questions such as: 'How do you greet a friend/teacher?' or 'Do you speak differently to a baby or to your friends?' Often, these examples could be an outcome of a story reading. Wherever possible, incorporate the children's own vignettes with a 'What if?' type of focus.

Podcasting

Podcasts are an exciting way for children to learn how to use computers and Web 2.0 technologies, as well as helping them develop the skills of speaking and listening (Kervin, 2009; Travis, 2007). They tend to be approximately 5–15 minutes in length. As a finished product, it is a clear example of oral text. However, there is considerable engagement with writing, drawing, talking and listening.

A podcast is essentially an audio file and is usually encoded as an MP3 file. MP3 files are commonly used by iPods and iPads but there are many other devices that use these files. Podcasting is easy to develop as a learning and teaching tool. The term 'podcasting' is made up from 'pod' which comes from 'iPod' and 'cast' which derives from 'broadcast'. Podcasts are usually audio shows that become part of a series or collection that is published on an Internet site. They can be accessed through iTunes or iPad applications or can be found using a suitable search engine such as Google. There are a growing number of websites that feature podcasts; many of these are dedicated to particular topics of interest.

For a podcast to be done effectively and for it to be useful and interesting, considerable planning and development need to go into it. However, podcasts can be quite easily produced using everyday equipment that is readily accessible to children. An iPod, iPad or smartphone is quite adequate for the task. However, an external microphone will be an advantage and a quiet place to record is essential. The important thing for you to realise is that the process is just as important as the product (see Figure 4.1). When children work in pairs or in triads, they develop many language and social skills, such as negotiating and knowing how to take turns and how to listen to others.

The first stage in developing a podcast is to determine a purpose for the activity and listen to several examples of podcasts that have a similar audience and purpose. The children should then brainstorm to determine what will be similar and what will be different in their own production.

Next comes the planning stage which will determine the length, content and style of presentation. During this time, the children could practise using the equipment by adjusting the tone and pitch of their voices, for example. The children will also need to gather the information or data that they will use as their content. This stage will also require the students to do some brainstorming and note taking and develop a concept map or storyboard to structure their podcast.

The drafting stage may utilise the concept map or storyboard developed in the previous stage to write a suitable script. On completion of the script, the children will need to make one or more podcasts.

The editing stage requires good listening skills and constructive criticism from interested others. It is always a good idea to include the children's peers as much as possible because children often learn from each other. The feedback that is given may also help their peers with their own podcasts.

The creating phase is a polishing phase that may take a number of iterations before the finished product is decided on. This phase is followed by the dissemination of the podcast. This will require uploading to a suitable hosting site on the Internet such as a blog, wiki or iTunes.

Podcasts can be disseminated in a number of ways such as:

- placing them on computers
- putting the audio files on portable MP3 players or iPods
- placing the files in a particular folder on the school intranet
- embedding an RSS feed into an existing website to automatically upload to personal computers.

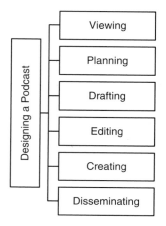

Figure 4.1 A podcast flow chart

Podcasts can take many different forms depending on the purpose and classroom units of work. Such examples are:

- radio talk shows
- news broadcasts
- interviews
- interest articles
- short radio plays
- poems
- show and tells.

Vignette 4.1

Mr Jones, a year 3 teacher, decided to give a book review as a podcast. The children were grouped in pairs and each child in the pair was expected to read the book and to make a diorama of a particular scene from the book. They had earlier developed a class blog that they shared with a class in Australia. A photograph of the diorama showing the book title and author was posted to the blog with a link to their podcasts. The children were excited about this activity because they could easily share the podcast with their parents on their iPad or personal computers. They could also invite friends from other countries to hear their podcasts and to post comments on the site in response. Some of the children had Facebook pages and shared a link to the file with their Facebook friends.

Mr Jones also made a point of including one of his pupils who was on holiday overseas by sending her a link via email.

Questions

1   How important is the process of making a podcast?
2   What skills can be developed while the children are working in groups?
3   Even though this may be a time-consuming process, what are the overall benefits of doing this type of activity?

Viewing

Paivio's (1986) Dual Coding theory has been instrumental in providing some insight into an understanding of how verbal and non-verbal systems interact with each other. Dual Coding theory assumes that all cognition is composed of the activity of two mental codes: a verbal code that uses language and a non-verbal code that uses mental imagery to code objects and events (Sadoski et al., 2000). It was proposed that the two systems function as alternative coding systems or modes of symbolic representation. However, these two systems can function efficiently in a reciprocal relationship (Sadoski,

1983). For example, a concrete object or event may invoke a visual perceptual representation, or be associated with a verbal label or vice versa. In memory, visual information is usually presented holistically while verbally encoded material is presented in a linear and sequential manner (Sadoski et al., 1991). Verbal representations, generally, are more adept in representing abstract information while contributing logic and organisation of thought. Imagery, on the other hand, is much more concrete and holistic (Kosslyn, 1988; Kosslyn et al., 1995; Truscott et al., 1995).

The dynamics of how these two systems function together can be likened to the operation of a movie camera. For example, the viewer can move around a mental image in the same way that a camera can pan from one area to another or, alternatively, it can zoom in on a nested cluster to focus on a single component in more detail. Not only is visual imagery represented as nested clusters, but it can also be linked associatively to elements of verbal memory. Thus, each visual element in each nested cluster can access verbally encoded information by way of an associated link. This, then, enables much greater access to linked information stored in long-term memory. For the skilled reader, this linking process is automatic and does not normally consume large amounts of cognitive attention resources.

Apart from being a fun way to learn, barrier games are a great tool for helping in the development of speaking (composing) and listening (reception/comprehension). Barrier games provide opportunities to develop skills for both speaking (composing) and listening (comprehension). They can promote the development of language skills by giving and receiving instructions in a motivating environment. Furthermore, they require students to listen to instructions and to ask for clarification when they do not understand an instruction or need more information. A common barrier game that many of us will have played is 'battleships': a hit or miss game using coordinates to knock out the opponent's ships that have been placed on a grid but out of the opponent's sight.

Barrier games have been around for many years and require players to give and receive directions while being separated by some kind of visual barrier. A barrier game requires two players to be placed on either side of a table with some kind of screen between them so that they cannot see each other's materials. Almost anything can be used as a barrier such as books, folders or binders. The players take turns, giving the other player very specific instructions or descriptions on how to arrange or manipulate the materials in front of them, without using any visual cues. The goal of the game is to have both players' materials look the same at the end of the activity. For example, one player could build a simple object such as a Lego boat and give instructions for the other player to construct an identical unseen object.

An alternative is to give the participants a map. One player is instructed to place a treasure somewhere on the map and then to give instructions to the other player so that he/she can follow the trail to the hidden treasure.

The maps could be identical pirate maps. A variation of this activity is to photocopy street maps and ask the children to give directions in how to go from point A to point B. This activity requires a great deal of very specific language and the ability to listen carefully. It also requires each participant to visualise the instructions given by the other participant.

An idea to develop the ability to visualise (or to make an imagined picture) is to give one participant a simple picture, such as a colouring-in page. The participant with the picture then describes the scene while the other participant attempts to draw it on a blank piece of paper by following the instructions. This is quite difficult and the children will usually require some hints as to how to give good instructions. For example, the use of words to indicate size, shape, position, direction and perspective could be demonstrated before the beginning of the activity.

Barrier games not only develop language and the ability to imagine, they also develop the ability to link these two modes of thinking in working memory.

Interactive whiteboards: bringing it together

Interactive whiteboards (IWBs) have become a popular device in the classroom and are used to combine aspects of viewing with speaking, acting and writing to engage whole classes or groups, and provide a workspace for individuals (Measday et al., 2007). In some instances, IWBs are merely a substitute for the more traditional chalkboard that is accompanied by teacher-directed approaches to classroom instruction. However, you will be able to use a more dynamic approach to teaching by exploiting the interactivity afforded by IWBs to provide more student-centred pedagogies to enhance their learning (Goodwin, 2011). Moreover, interactive whiteboards have the potential to extend the notion of the big book – for example, by incorporating multimedia elements such as sound, audio, animations and graphics to enhance dialogic interaction and depth of learning engagement. They have the potential to improve student activity and cater for a range of learning styles. Furthermore, they can facilitate the introduction of difficult or abstract concepts through the use of visual or dynamic representations of concepts or ideas. However, it must be emphasised that the use of IWBs should be underpinned by effective teaching strategies.

One advantage that IWBs have over big books is that children's own work can become the focus for group or whole-class discussions. For example, a student's writing composition could be photographed or scanned and displayed on the board and collaboratively edited using the pen tool to add, cross out or make notes. The pen tool can also be used as a highlighter by changing the transparency to annotate text or images. The highlighting feature can also be used to draw attention to spelling or grammatical features in the sample text being studied. The text content could be enhanced by the inclusion of pictures from the Internet or from scanned photos (or directly from a camera or iPad). Hyperlinks could also be added to link the text to video, documentaries or animated demonstrations to illustrate particular concepts. Shapes can also be used as a blind or screen to hide and reveal aspects of the text to focus students' attention and enhance teaching points. Comments and sound effects can be added to student drawings and annotations. A screen-recording tool can be used to replay the activity or part of the lesson for viewing at another time.

More interactivity can be introduced using the 'rub and reveal' technique. A layer of ink the same colour as the background is used to cover the text and the rubber tool is then used to reveal the hidden text. This is particularly useful with cloze activities where a word is covered and the children are asked to predict what the hidden word might be by using the context cues and confirming or correcting as the ink screen is rubbed away. Another way to do this type of cloze activity would be to use a click and reveal technique whereby, as a child clicks on the inked shape, it fades away to reveal the hidden word.

Drag and drop functions can also be used to drag words into a table or as labels in pictures or text. This can consolidate new vocabulary by classifying words into groups and collocations or by developing concept maps by dragging arrow lines and shapes to form links and nodes. Once again, pictures or animations can be dragged to develop the concepts. Hyperlinks can be added. Objects from a clip art collection can also be added and programmed to move, disappear or change in front of selected backgrounds to form an animated sequence. The children's own sound recording can be attached to the animations. This type of interactivity transforms the big book or shared literacy environment into an active speaking, viewing, writing and acting environment where the children can become designers rather than just viewers or passive recipients of teacher-directed talk.

There are many sites on the Internet with stories that can be used on IWBs. A variety of digital tools and templates can be downloaded to build your repertoire of ideas. Interactive games and activities can also be accessed on the Internet and used with the whole class or groups to practise particular skills and enrich their learning experiences. Once you have become familiar with the range of strategies available, the potential of this interactive device cannot be underestimated.

The visual strategies listed below can be used on IWBs or developed as conventional stand-alone items:

- designing a mural
- making an infographic
- making a travel brochure
- making illustrations for a book
- making a comic strip
- creating a timeline

- making a book jacket
- making a wordless, zigzag folded book
- making a diorama of a scene from the story
- making a mural
- doing a painting of a scene from the story
- making a 3D model
- making puppets (using shapes on the screen and animating) and painting or using backdrops (or clip art).

Digital stories

A digital story is a multimodal text created with a digital camera or computer that combines photos, voice and other elements such as movement and music (Kervin and Mantei, 2011; Lowenthal, 2009). Usually, the creator of the digital story selects about 12 images and composes approximately 250 words to accompany each photograph. The finished product is usually about 2–4 minutes in length.

Vignette 4.2

Mrs Garvey divided her year 2 class into groups of three to develop digital stories based on an excursion to the rocky shoreline at the beach near their school. Seven parents and the teacher aide were recruited to accompany the children on the excursion so that they could assist one group. The children were instructed to take one digital camera per group (from a set provided by the school) and to take 10–15 photos of the surrounding area and several photos of an interesting find such as an animal, plant, shell, stone or driftwood. They were also instructed to make a large drawing of an object or organism of interest by using crayons on paper attached to their clipboards and taking a photo of each drawing.

The parents and teacher aide were given instructions to talk to the children about each scene that they were photographing so that the children could recall and reflect on the conversation back in their classroom. After the excursion, each of the parents helped the children select and download the best ten photographs and reflect on each while the helper made some summary notes on a chart. Later, the photographs were arranged in iMovies and the scripts were written from the summary notes to accompany each photo and the children's voices were recorded on the video. One of the photos of the drawings was used for the title frame and the other drawings were inserted in the sequence to highlight the children's impressions of what they had found.

The parents were invited to view the finished film clips and to join the children in a special lunchtime meal.

(Continued)

(Continued)

Questions

1 How could the steps in designing a podcast be used to help the children understand the design process?
2 How would you give a Dual Coding (see above discussion) explanation to this activity?
3 Instead of using crayon and pencil, how could the children use an iPad or Android app?

Variations on this activity include transitions between slides, an added background music soundtrack and the Ken Burns effect (iMovie) to give some movement to the pictures. An alternative could be that the children insert the slides into a PowerPoint sequence and possibly add some video. The PowerPoint could be converted to video using PowerPoint software and uploaded to YouTube or to the class blog.

Acting

Primary schools should make sure that children's spoken communication is developed intensively within all subjects and for learning across the curriculum. In so doing, schools should capitalise on the powerful contributions of the performing and visual arts (Rose, 2009), such as:

- role playing by acting out different endings to a story
- making a movie using an iPad
- interviewing a character from a story
- miming a section from a story – children guess what scene it is
- playing 'Who am I?' and making up a creative dance sequence
- creating a tableau or vignette
- using small figures to create a play
- making a puppet play
- acting out scenes while placing an unexpected problem in the scene – innovating/solving problems
- creating a shadow play.

These activities cut across the curriculum and should not be confined to the 'literacy' hour.

Conclusion

Listening, speaking, viewing and acting are elements that often combine in different ways according to the purposes intended. Traditionally, they have been taught as separate and often isolated activities. However, in the multi-modal and multi-media worlds in which the children are situated, they are exposed to combinations of these elements in many different ways. However, there needs to be a distinction between the process and the product. Too often the product is emphasised while the process is neglected. The process can be just as important as the product. It is not just a means to an end but it is usually situated in a social context and other speaking and listening skills are usually developed along with viewing and acting.

Dual Coding theory emphasises the integration of these aspects of literacy in terms of thinking and understanding. It is when the different modes are combined or linked that memory, comprehension and learning are enhanced.

 Discussion questions and activities

 Points for discussion

1   How might it help children to talk about a task together before attempting it?
2   What are the advantages in children working on ideas together?
3   When is it most appropriate for the teacher to be involved in group discussions?
4   Under what conditions is it more appropriate for teachers not to take part in dialogic interactions during group activities?

†††† Group activities

1   Divide the class into discussion groups and answer the following question by creating a brainstorm chart and writing the group's thoughts on the chart. What are the advantages of having the children contribute their own ideas during group discussion?
2   Choose a topical discussion. Set up a fishbowl activity by nominating a small group discussion and having the rest of the class observe and make notes on the interactions within the focus group. What are the dynamics within the group? What were the positive and negative aspects of the group discussion?
3   Divide the class into groups of about five students and provide used photo-copy paper, tape and paper clips. Ask the groups to make the largest tower possible using the materials given for a competition between groups. Each group will be given 10 minutes to try and build the tallest freestanding paper tower in the time given. The students will be primed to think about the dynamics of the group for a reflective discussion at the end.
4   The same groups (as in group activity 3) will be asked to discuss the notion of assigning roles to individual members as a way of structuring groups. What roles can be given to group members? What are possible barriers to assigning roles to individual group members? How can these be overcome?

(Continued)

(Continued)

 Whole-class activities

1   Read or view a well-known short story, scene or episode and conduct 'This is Your Life' based on some of the story characters.
2   Alternatively, choose one or more of the following in response to a reading/ viewing/listening activity:

- readers' theatre
- choral reading
- radio plays with sound effects
- formal drama
- puppet shows
- news items for radio/newspaper based on an incident in a story
- debates
- a TV advertisement for a book, story or film
- a poem based on a story character, object or scene.

3   Following on from activity 1 or 2, have a discussion about the types of skills that children would need if they were in the role of:

   i   listener
   ii speaker
   iii viewer
   iv actor.

References

Alexander, R. (ed.) (2010). *Children, their World, their Education: Final Report and Recommendations of the Alexander 2010 Primary Review.* Oxon: Routledge.

Bowyer-Crane, C., Snowling, M., Duff, F., Fieldsend, E., Carroll, J., Miles, J., et al. (2008). Improving the early language and literacy skills: Differential effects of an oral language versus a phonology with reading intervention. *Journal of Child Psychology and Psychiatry*, 49(4), 422–432.

Bradley, I. L. and Bryant, P.E. (1983). Categorising sounds and learning to read – a causal connection. *Nature*, 301, 419–421.

Byrne, B. (1998). *The Foundational Literacy: The Child's Acquisition of the Alphabetic Principle.* Hove: Psychology Press.

Campbell, R. and Green, D. (2006) *Literacies and Learners* (3rd edn). Frenchs Forest, Australia: Prentice Hall.

Dawes, L. and Birrell, S. (2005). Developing articulate readers. In E. Grungeon, L. Dawes, C. Smith and L. Hubbard (eds), *Teaching Speaking and Listening in the Primary School* (3rd edn) (pp. 84–102). London: David Fulton.

Goodwin, K. (2011). *Engaging Students in Literacy Learning with Interactive Whiteboards*. E:update 017. Newtown, NSW: Primary English Teaching Association Australia.

Goswami, U. and Bryant, P. E. (1990). *Psychological Skills and Learning to Read*. London: Erlbaum.

Kervin, L. (2009). *Possibilities for Literacy Learning through Podcasting Activities*. E:update 005. Newtown, NSW: Primary English Teaching Association Australia.

Kervin, L. and Mantei, J. (2011). This is me: Children teaching us about themselves through digital storytelling. *Practically Primary*, 16(1), 4–7.

Kosslyn, S. M. (1988). Imagery in learning. In M. S. Gazzaniga (ed.), *Perspectives in Memory Research* (pp. 245–273). London: The MIT Press.

Kosslyn, S. M., Behrmann, M. and Jeannerod, M. (1995). The cognitive neuroscience of mental imagery. *Neuropsychologia*, 33, 1335–1344.

Lowenthal, P. (2009). Digital story telling in education: An emerging institutional technology? In J. Hartley and K. McWilliam (eds), *Story Circle: Digital Storytelling around the World* (pp. 252–259). Chichester, UK: Wiley-Blackwell.

Measday, B., Papas, K., Clark, L., Leatch, M. and Walsh, C. (2007). Interactive whiteboards in the literacy classroom at Ingle Farm Primary. *Practically Primary*, 12(3), 25–29.

Mercer, N. (2003). The educational value of 'dialogic talk' in whole-class dialogue. In *QCA New Perspectives on Spoken English in the Classroom: Discussion Papers*. London: QCA.

Ofsted (2011). Removing Barriers to Literacy. Available at: www.ofsted.gov.uk/publications/090237 (accessed 2 February 2013).

Ogle, D. M. (1986). K-W-L: A teaching model that develops active reading of expository text. *The Reading Teacher*, 39, 564–570.

Paivio, A. (1986). *Mental Representations: A Dual-Coding Approach*. New York: Holt, Rinehart & Winston.

Richgels, D. (2004). Theory and research into practice: Paying attention to language. *Reading Research Quarterly*, 39(4), 470–477.

Rose, J. (2009). *Independent Review of the Primary Curriculum: Final Report*. Nottingham: DCSF Publications.

Sadoski, M. (1983). An exploratory study of the relationship between reported imagery and the comprehension and recall of a story. *Reading Research Quarterly*, 19, 110–123.

Sadoski, M., Goetz, E. T. and Rodriguez, M. (2000). Engaging texts: Effects of concreteness on comprehensibility, interest, and recall in four text types. *Journal of Educational Psychology*, 92, 85–95.

Sadoski, M., Paivio, A. and Goetz, E. T. (1991). A critique of schema theory in reading and a dual coding alternative. *Reading Research Quarterly*, 26, 463–484.

Smith, C. (2005). Developing children's oral skills at key stage 2. In E. Grungeon, L. Dawes, C. Smith and L. Hubbard (eds), *Teaching Speaking and Listening in the Primary School* (3rd edn) (pp. 84–102). London: David Fulton.

Smith, F. (1978). *Reading*. Cambridge: Cambridge University Press.

Smith, F. (1984). The creative achievement of literacy. In H. Coleman, A. Oberg and F. Smith (eds), *Awakening to Literacy* (pp. 143–153). London: Heinemann.

Snow, C. E., Burns, S. and Griffin, P. (1998). *Preventing Reading Difficulties in Young Children*. Washington, DC: National Academy Press.

Szabo, S. (2006). KWHHL: A student-driven evolution of the KWL. *American Secondary Education*, 34(3), 57–67.

Topping, K. and Ferguson, N. (2005). Effective literacy teaching behaviours. *Journal of Research in Reading*, 28(2), 125–143.

Travis, P. (2007). Podcasting. *English Teaching Professional*, 52, 62–64.

Truscott, D. M., Walker, B. J. and Gambrell, L. B. (1995). Poor readers don't image, or do they? Reading research report no.38, National Reading Research Centre.

Vygotsky, L. S. (1962). *Thought and Language*. Cambridge, MA: Harvard University Press.

CHAPTER 5

WRITING, DESIGNING, FILMING AND WEB 2.0 TOOLS

Chapter objectives

- To understand the writing processes that occur in writing composition.
- To develop appropriate instructional approaches to writing.
- To develop a repertoire of strategies to foster writing engagement and writing independence.
- To identify what needs to be taught as part of literacy pedagogy where we will discuss the concept of 'design'.
- To understand what 'Learning by design' is and how it applies to writing, designing, filming and Web 2.0 tools.

Key questions

1. How do writers produce texts?
2. How do writers engage with literacy to construct meaning?
3. How do writers use metacognitive thinking processes to regulate their own writing?

Key words: authentic, collaboration, process, purposeful writing, self-regulation, sharing, writing.

Introduction

Writing compositions are often considered to be the product of a pragmatic activity designed to achieve a specific purpose. For example, narrative texts are usually simple texts that are designed to entertain. They usually describe events through time and are related through a causal or thematic chain; unskilled readers are more comfortable with these simpler and more familiar text structures. The reader's purpose is to read for enjoyment and relaxation. This chapter will discuss the notion of text genre and structure in light of reader and writer purposes.

Writing, however, is essentially a social practice and is linked to oral language. Writing is not just language written down; there are some major differences between language and writing. However, the importance of oral language in learning to write cannot be underestimated. Talk allows children to develop their ideas and ways of thinking by rehearsing their ideas and appropriate language structures.

Multimodal texts have become increasingly prevalent in modern society. They usually combine two or more semiotic systems such as linguistic, visual, audio, gestural or spatial modes. They can be represented in a variety of literacy genres such as comics, graphic novels, electronic books, films, magazines, video and even websites. Multimedia texts can be delivered via a variety of media technologies in the form of live performances, on paper, on film or digitally. A web page can use a variety of elements such as sound effects, oral language, music, a script and still or moving images in the form of video or animation. Each element is usually interwoven and part of a total package. Visual representations, for example in post-modern picture books, are no longer seen as complementing writing but are intertwined in such a way that they can no longer be seen as separate entities.

Our understanding of writing, now more than ever before, involves elements of design and redesign. Our broader experiences of newer forms of multimedia and multimodal texts also shape our understanding of purpose and of the modes that writing now assumes. In our post-modern world, design is being viewed more as a process than a product. Electronic forms of writing, viewing and responding are more spontaneous and non-permanent. For example, Web 2.0 applications such as texting, blogging and communicating via Facebook are forms of writing that are often connected with everyday, moment-by-moment activities. Whatever forms writing takes, nevertheless, it is always a purposeful, communicative and social activity.

If our learners perceive themselves as writers and in particular writers of a certain text, they are going to more likely engage in the language conventions of that text more readily. They will read the text as potential writers of that text. Furthermore, everything our students read, everything we read to them are demonstrations of the written language that they as writers can draw on. (Turnbill and Bean, 2006: 21)

The quote above reminds us of the fact that children model their writing on good examples of high quality writing. Of course, you as a teacher should be aware of what good writing entails so that you will be in a better position to make appropriate decisions about how to teach writing (Cambourne, 1988). How your learners perceive themselves as writers will also be very much influenced by how you perceive yourself as a writer. It is important to examine your own beliefs and attitudes because these will be conveyed incidentally to your students as you engage in writing activities of all kinds.

Obviously, the most important thing is to immerse children in good literature in a wide range of genres. Writing does, however, need to be contextualised. It should be authentic or real writing for a particular purpose and with a particular audience in mind.

Writing

Literacy development does not take place in isolation: children develop simultaneously as readers, listeners, speakers and writers. More recently, the focus on writing has shifted from viewing writing as a perfectly finished product to seeing it as a process that is developed through various stages of self-discovery. A written composition is not normally constructed in a smooth linear process. It happens in stages that may overlap and which reflect a continuing dialogue between the writer and the written composition, often with feedback from a real or imagined audience.

The writing process is no longer a separate process and may not always produce stand-alone written compositions. In today's world, writing is often combined with illustration, pictures, video clips and audio. For example, an edited film will require scripting, story boarding, editing and other processes that cannot be separated from the writing process. This brings with it the notion that all types of literacy activity incorporate active and dynamic practices, whether they are speaking, listening, viewing or acting. Whatever form the writing takes, it usually requires the author to go through a complex process that incorporates elements of design, designing and redesign (Yelland et al., 2008). These three elements of 'literacy by design' align with the representational, cognitive and reflective dimensions of thinking and doing.

Table 5.1 The dimensions of text processing

Dimension	Product (The New London Group, 1996)	Process (Yelland et al., 2008)
Representational	Design	Experiencing
Cognitive	Designer	Conceptualising
Reflective	Redesign	Analysing and Applying

Design: the design element refers to existing designs that are represented by products or grammars of various semiotic systems such as the recorded word, film, photography or gesture. Within any given social context, there are certain conventions associated with the semiotic activity that incorporate certain design elements. For example, a formal speech will incorporate a grammatical structure or convey meaning that can be understood easily by the target audience. On the other hand, film may incorporate a number of different grammars related to speech, visual perception and acting. Often, these conventions are characterised by styles of the particular semiotic elements that make up a particular genre, such as science fiction or drama.

Designing: this is the process of re-representation and recontextualisation. What this means is that meaning is constantly being fashioned and reshaped through various semiotic systems. It transforms knowledge to produce new constructions and representations of reality. It uses available designs in ways that transform them to create new uses of old materials. Therefore, listening, viewing, reading, writing, speaking and acting are all activities that enable new understandings to develop from the various kinds of texts that are encountered in the process of design.

Redesign: this is the process of forming new meanings in different contexts; it is grounded in cultural patterns and shared forms of meaning. Redesign is also the production of new products or resources that are reproduced or transformed (The New London Group, 1996).

Writing is a complex process that involves a number of cognitive and physical operations functioning simultaneously. For example, a high degree of hand–eye coordination and dexterity is required while using handwriting or keyboard skills. The writer must also know the conventions of print such as using correct spelling, grammar and punctuation. The writer must also be aware of genre forms, and write, draw or collate for a particular audience with a specific purpose in mind. Thus, your students will need to have a good repertoire of vocabulary and an understanding and familiarity with words, pictures, film or animations that are associated with particular genres.

Other skills include:

- word-level encoding and decoding such as: inside-the-word strategies, morphemes such as prefixes, suffixes, roots and word families; outside-the-word strategies such as context clues
- text features such as title, headings, captions, illustrations, bold or italic, words, charts, tables, diagrams, glossary, indexes and graphs
- use of other resources: dictionaries, thesaurus, friends or teachers, the Internet and apps
- text structures such as genre, story grammar (plot, setting, character, conflict) and descriptions

- comprehension such as activating background knowledge, inferencing, summarising, predicting, questioning, visualising, monitoring, synthesising, evaluating and relating
- appreciation such as responding to literature that involves reflection and communicating literary ideas
- using appropriate ICT (digital) technologies such as keyboards and skills such as Internet navigation.

However, many children avoid writing and develop poor attitudes towards any writing activity because they may find the writing process demanding even when using electronic forms of text. Creating an engaging approach is one way to overcome negative attitudes to design and to promote a positive and productive environment. Cambourne's (2002) conditions for learning (see Chapter 2) allow children to experiment and to make mistakes in an environment that provides focused and specific feedback, with an expectation of success according to the child's individual developmental level.

Word dictionaries and word journals can personalise the learning of new words and act as a self-measure of progress. Allowing children to select their own, or 'favourite', words increases independent word learning and provides personalised material for use in future creative or descriptive writing sessions. An example of a collaborative creative writing composition could then be placed on an overhead projector or interactive whiteboard, with the class encouraged to discuss interesting words used or suggest other more appropriate ones from words that they have written on the word wall (or in their own word journals) (Woolley, 2011).

A word wall could also be set up in the classroom to specifically promote awareness and interest in words. The idea is that children collect new and interesting words that can be added to the wall and discussed with others in class. A paper 'brick' with the word written or typed on it can be placed on the wall. Word journals can also be used to promote this excitement about new words. As the children encounter new words, they can be added to their journals and used in their creative writing episodes.

Above all, writing by design should be seen as an enjoyable activity in which children learn to develop their own ideas, create novel and original compositions and get involved in a cooperative learning environment. One of the best ways to accomplish this is to provide regular opportunities to write, film, record or illustrate for different purposes and for you, as the teacher, to actively demonstrate the joy of design in its different forms. For example, you may choose to write with the children and share examples of your own writing on the IWB and discuss why you used a particular word to express an idea or feeling. At other times, you may choose to write a cooperative composition with the whole class or with a focused group. While doing this, you may choose to use the technique of think-aloud to make explicit the sort of thinking processes that occur at each stage of the writing process. Whenever possible, you should use the 'think-aloud' method of modelling writing by conducting a shared, or group, writing activity on the IWB or on an overhead projector and ask the children to make contributions as well. You could also invite the children to suggest ideas, words, phrases and endings, for example.

Writing community

This approach reinforces the notion of the classroom as a community of authors/designers. To give momentum to this approach, the teacher may invite children to offer their work for the groups to edit and to share ideas as a community of learners. For this to function well, you will need to create an atmosphere of sharing and demonstrating respect for the ideas of others. This will not happen naturally but will need to be developed over time.

Currently, writing is considered to be a process that evolves through a number of distinct stages and usually over a number of writing sessions, whereas in past practice children were expected to complete a composition based on a given set of topics within a given period of time. Writing does not necessarily follow a set pattern but individuals may stop, start, restart and go through various iterations before completing a piece of work. While engaging in this process, the children may be required to help others or to seek help. What is important is that writing is a work in progress and that writing skills are developed during a purposeful and authentic activity.

The writing process should involve choice, with children progressively taking control of their own writing activity. For this self-regulating process to take place, the children need to become metacognitively aware so that they are able to make informed choices during the writing process (Graham and Harris, 1997). Good writers should be able to explain the process they go through when developing their writing skills as part of this self-regulating process (Cambourne, 1988).

The process approach for teaching writing

When young writers are encouraged to view themselves as readers as well as writers, they can see their writing from a different, but more critical, perspective (Cambourne, 1988). Whether or not the writing is meant to be a free writing activity, there will be times when you will need to explicitly teach the skills and processes of writing. It is asserted that a more structured framework will enable better skill development through a guided sequence of clearly defined stages. This can routinely be developed in the classroom and conducted on a regular basis. Most writing skills can take an extended period of time to develop and should not be viewed as a one-off activity (Holliday,

2010). However, there are a number of discrete stages that all writers go through and it is important that children see this as a thinking process that takes place over time.

The writing stages, as outlined below (see Figure 5.1), should be viewed as a guide rather than seen as inflexible fixed stages. Writers do not necessarily go from one stage to the next but often go back and forth and then back again as they review and make changes while their thoughts galvanise throughout the writing process.

Pre-writing stage

The pre-writing stage involves the setting of a specific purpose. Setting a purpose requires writers to also envisage an audience for their work. However, it should be an authentic piece of writing in that it has a real-life purpose and will communicate real-life products, whether they are fiction or non-fiction texts. At this stage, the writer should consider appropriate forms to suitably communicate with his/her audience such as genre, style and media. Once the purpose and audience have been considered, the writer needs to view samples of the type of writing that will be required (Cruickshank, 2011).

Drafting stage

The drafting stage requires the writer to plan the structure of the composition. This, again, will depend on the audience and the purpose of the writing. For example, if the genre is a narrative then the story plot will follow a particular structure. Moreover, most forms of writing are organised according to the way we think. Top-level structure is the plan or organisation used to pattern and structure expository text. Often, a graphic organiser can be used to plan the composition by jotting down ideas according to where they would be situated in the narrative. Alternatively, the writer may decide to do a series of drawings to organise his/her ideas. It is important for the child to think like a writer in order to go through the same process that real-world authors go through.

Revising stage

The revising stage can alternate between drafting, revising and redrafting. It is a process whereby the writer takes a step back and revisits his/her ideas and looks at them from the standpoint of the intended audience. The writer may also seek information from peers or teachers as to how the ideas are flowing.

Editing stage

Editing is the polishing stage that looks at the conventions of print or other media. Spelling, punctuation and grammar are corrected and vocabulary and language expression are improved for publication.

Post-writing stage

This is the publishing stage whereby the author seeks to engage an audience either by producing a story, blog, exposition or set of instructions. Also to be considered is whether illustrations, film clips or sound media will be included. This could involve others in the publication process providing expertise related to illustration and media production.

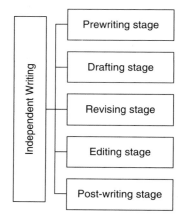

Figure 5.1   Stages of writing

How to self-edit

One of the best ways for you to teach editing is to choose a class- or group-created text to edit on the IWB. This is a particularly good method of demonstrating how to edit because it uses real texts in real-life situations. There is also a sense of shared responsibility and shared learning so that all children can learn from each other. Class or group editing sessions will tend to focus on the development of particular skills, such as using adjectives and choosing words to convey exact meaning.

   Put simply, the process of editing requires the opportunity to add words, change words and move words around. It may also require the author to consider punctuation and expression. What is important is that each and every word in a sentence should play a specific role. Children should be taught how to use a thesaurus to find synonyms that can develop a more precise meaning. What is important is that student writers are made aware that words like 'bad' are vague whereas words such as 'disdainful' or 'pathetic' are much more exact (Bates, 2011). Some adjectives, on the other hand, are often overused, like 'little', 'pretty', 'big', as are conjunctions like 'and' and 'but'. As far as possible, such words should be reconsidered and replaced by words that are less frequently used but more expressive.

Writing conferences

One of the best ways to promote interest and excitement about writing is to regularly conduct writing conferences with individual children or with small groups. The purpose of this is to find out about students' beliefs about writing, about their attitudes and interests, and to assess and refine their writing skills.

Ten tips for writing conferences

1. Preview and read the work.
2. Focus on ideas and content first.
3. Use very specific feedback.
4. Always make positive comments and give encouragement.
5. Even when the child has made an error, they have usually done more things correctly that can be praised.
6. Don't try and correct everything but target particular problems that seem to reoccur.
7. Ask questions rather than point out errors.
8. Ask the child how they like their work so far: are there any changes that need to happen?
9. Ask the child to write down what they have achieved since the last conference.
10. Ask the child to indicate what skill they think they need to develop next.

Open-ended tasks

Open-ended tasks have the potential to develop children's knowledge, skills and understandings (see Figure. 5.2) by providing them with opportunities to engage in authentic writing with a purpose and particular audience in mind. This is because children generally learn better in classrooms that are connected with the real world (Campbell and Green, 2006). Open-ended tasks are real-world tasks that involve process and outcomes (Glass and Pearce, 2010). The idea is that children work to address an issue such as recording a school event or writing a letter to the editor of the local newspaper about the need for an environmental park near the local pond. However, writing/designing tasks should be constructed so that the writing journey and the destination are very clear.

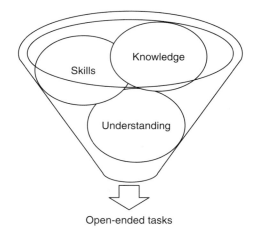

Figure 5.2 Model for embedding open-ended writing tasks

Source: Glass and Pearce, 2010

Spelling

Reading and spelling are quite different and employ quite different mental processes (Westwood, 2005). Learning to spell is thought to be a natural developmental process reflecting the child's current knowledge about letters and units of meaning within words. The developmental stages of spelling can be traced to a study conducted by Reed (1971) who investigated preschool children's knowledge of English orthography by examining their invented spellings; he found that the children generated common and systematic spellings at a number of distinct stages. Thus, it is assumed that children's attempts at invented spelling are not random but can be classified into identifiable orthographic stages, which normally advance at varying rates (Westwood, 2005; Young, 2007).

Identifiable orthographic stages:

1. random symbols represent words
2. some sounds in words represented
3. all sounds in words represented
4. awareness of orthographic patterns
5. application of syllable rules
6. application of derivational/meaning knowledge
7. generally accurate spelling.

Westwood (2005) concluded that Dual Coding theory is particularly relevant for the development of orthographic awareness. According to this theory, the orthographic elements of words are stored in the visual memory while the sound elements are stored in the phonological store of working memory.

An examination of the child's unaided writing will give insight into the child's level of development. The think-aloud methodology can further provide insight into children's cognitive processes when spelling both known and unknown words. Having children think aloud (see Chapter 2) while they engage in spelling-related activities is very useful in this regard and should also form part of children's spelling programmes. Using the strategy with both novice and expert spellers can be valuable in making instructional decisions. This method could also prove useful as a peer-tutoring strategy.

One of the best ways of checking one's own spelling is to look carefully at the word by asking, 'Does it look right?' Most good spellers have good memory storage to retain commonly occurring letter strings and the visual impressions of high-frequency words. One of the problems with spelling in the English language is that sounds or phonemes can be represented in a number of ways orthographically. However, the orthographic representations of words tend to be much more consistent (see Chapter 3).

One of the best methods for learning spelling words incorporates both visual and sound elements and is known as the look-cover-write-check method – it involves the following steps:

1. Look carefully at the targeted word and carefully note the graphic features of the word.
2. Cover the word and try and see the word in the mind's eye.
3. Write and say the word.
4. Check that the word is the same as the original targeted word.

A fifth and sixth step could be added to consolidate word learning and to connect with background knowledge. These are:

5. Think about the meaning of the word or find a word meaning in the dictionary, and use the word in a new sentence.
6. Identify morphemes that are present within the word and add other morphemes such as prefixes and suffixes as a word-building exercise.

A common problem with children who find it difficult to spell consistently is their unwillingness to risk-take for fear of making a mistake. The habit of teachers putting a red mark through spelling errors on children's writing will tend to make them resistant to experimenting with writing. There is, however, a difference between putting your ideas down on paper and editing. You should consider allowing children to use invented spellings and encouraging them to edit by identifying words that do not look right and using a dictionary, either a standard English dictionary, a personal dictionary with topical words, or a class vocabulary chart using a themed list of words.

Vignette 5.1

Ms Baker has a year 3 class and implements a spelling programme that reflects elements of formal word study and skill-oriented lessons. Her lessons are also supplemented with open-ended activities so that students are able to practise and use their skills in creative ways. Each child has their own spelling loose-leaf folder that has space for a spelling word list that usually conforms to particular spelling patterns. Another section of the page is devoted to word building or word study that focuses on syllables, morphemes, word roots and affixes such as prefixes and suffixes. In another section of the page, there is space for children to paste in an individualised spelling word list to supplement the whole-class spelling list. This list will be based on each child's independent writing activities such as daily diary, journal, email, blog and process writing activities.

Each term Ms Baker has the children participate in a free or open-ended writing task. For example, the diary activity operates each day with the expectation that the children will record events or write about something of interest to them such as an excursion or after-school activity.

Once a week, the children select a diary entry to illustrate and write an appropriate caption for. While the children are writing, Ms Baker moves around the room and endeavours to write a comment on at least half of the diaries. The remaining diaries are collected at the end of the lesson and she replies to them before the next session. When she writes a reply, she always endeavours to remodel the correct spellings, grammar and punctuation. She prefers to remodel rather than put a red mark through incorrect spelling so that the children are more inclined to experiment and to risk-take by using remodelled words in their writing. While writing in the diaries, she also notes the incorrect spellings and writes them on a strip of paper (one for each student) that will be pasted onto their loose-leaf weekly spelling page. Each child will have an individual quota according to ability level and any overflow words will be put in the following week's list.

Ms Baker also has class sets of game-boards that she has made for the children to use in pairs to practise their individual word lists. Each pair of students swaps their individual lists and after they throw the dice they ask each other to spell a word. During reading/writing group activities, they play practice games to reinforce the word-building focus for the week.

Questions

1   Why do you think that Ms Baker has opted to use a part-individual spelling list?
2   What are the advantages of using a diary as a source of individual spelling lists?
3   What apps (for mobile devices) can be used to support this type of activity?

Handwriting

Handwriting and spelling are closely linked. Not only do good spellers remember phonic and orthographic elements of words, but they also remember the sequential hand movements that are associated with handwriting. According to Dual Coding theory, these elements are encoded and stored in long-term memory. Therefore, it is most important that children are able to write letters and words with some precision because it not only aids legibility but it also enhances the production of correct spelling patterns. Typing spelling words on the keyboard may help spelling due to memorisation of the movement of each finger and the position of the letters on the keyboard.

Poetry

The process of writing and designing in general is about bringing together the jumbled life experiences of the writer and focusing their thoughts by narrowing the focus of their attention (Powell, 1967). The process of writing poetry enables feelings to surface that may never be expressed in any other way. Young poetry writers should be made aware that poetry is a form of expression that is concise and more structured than most forms of prose. Thus, poetry writing not only provides a means of expression but it also enables the writer/designer to become familiar with the way in which words are used. Poetry can be used to make children aware of how words can take on different grammatical functions (see Chapter 1).

Top-level structuring

Top-level structuring refers to a method of scaffolding children's writing. Normally, graphic organisers are used as a visual map of how a particular genre is constructed (see Chapter 8 for examples of graphic organisers). They help children to chunk information in order to plan and construct written dialogue. Graphic organisers can take many forms, from simple Venn diagrams to more detailed graphic organisers that can be constructed using software such as 'Kidspiration' or 'Inspiration'. They help children to organise and to apply their thinking skills to construct a logical and coherent piece of writing. Teachers may provide extra scaffolding in the form of clues or sections of text, providing children with a starting point to connect to their own writing. Graphic organisers are extremely useful for teachers to model and introduce new concepts or text types. They allow the teacher to break the topic down into various elements so that particular features can be discussed and modelled. The typical vocabulary of various genres can also be used in conjunction with graphic organisers (see Chapter 8).

Using a word processor

Many children now have access to word processors and in most western countries children have their own computers. Most homes will have several computers, tablets and smartphones. Those that do not have these new forms of technology may have access through their local library. Many word processing and other Web 2.0 skills are picked up incidentally by many children but there is what has often been referred to as the digital divide whereby many students from disadvantaged communities and homes do not have the same opportunities to explore these digital technologies (see Chapter 9).

You will need to be proactive in reducing this digital divide by providing the necessary keyboard and navigation skills so that children are not handicapped in writing tasks. For example, some students may be unfamiliar with some of the formatting features of word processors or may not be aware of the most efficient ways to use the on-board thesaurus or spell-checker when they are writing. You will also need to become familiar with the literacy practices taking place outside of school such as texting, using Facebook and blogging so that you can take advantage of children's existing knowledge and common literacy practices.

Video

YouTube has become a popular phenomenon among young people. With the proliferation of smartphones and tablets, youngsters are easily able to make their own films using iMovie or other editing programmes. Students also have easy access to online video tutorials that show them how to film, edit and load video to YouTube.

One way to encourage children to explore the world of video is to use video in the classroom wherever possible. When developing lessons, you could do a search on YouTube or iTunes U for interesting videos about a topic; this would appeal to children who have been raised in an environment of TV and multimedia. You might also want an archive of activities or assignments that children have completed to show as examples to future students. Another way teachers can use the media is to film highlights from an excursion or even do a film excursion to a place that is not normally accessible to the class. Alternatively, students could film their own weekend excursions and present them to the class as an introduction to a unit of work or new topic. There is no reason why this type of digital literacy should be confined to the classroom.

Blogs

The word blog is a shortened combination of the words web and log. A blog is a website that is a type of interactive diary. It is usually composed of three parts: a header, posts and comments. The blog is a Web 2.0 writing tool that has the power to motivate students to write (Constanti, 2010). It appeals to children because it has a worldwide audience. Students' literacy is improved because the blog is an authentic platform to enable them to communicate with each other and to others outside the classroom for a particular purpose. The purpose of using a blog will be different depending on the needs of the children at the time. The purpose may be to set up a forum for a particular issue raised in class. For example, after reading a newspaper article about creating wind farms in populated areas, a blog could be set up to discuss the pros and cons. A summary of the main points of the article could be posted as a blog entry and students could be invited to post their comments in response. Arguments for and against can then be posted as comments.

A blog is an example of a written conversation and is a contemporary example of communicating to a wider audience (Kervin, 2009). A blog can easily be set up to provide a platform for a collaborative project. Some teachers might be hesitant about using blogs because they are open to a worldwide audience. However, incoming posts can be monitored and screened before being posted. The initial proposal, such as starting a vegetable garden, could be posted as a blog. Other students could be invited to post their comments about the design of the garden or to make suggestions as to what should go into the garden and the roles each person should have. Another way in which a blog could be used is to post students' own compositions or artwork to the blog to enable other children to comment.

Vignette 5.2

Mr Henderson, a year 6 teacher, developed a class blog using 'Blog Spot' to record weekly class activities, news and highlights. Initially, he contacted another class in the USA with the intention of using it as a form of whole-class penpal correspondence. Each week, the teacher assigned a small group to work on a draft article of a class project for their blog and to take a photograph of the activity using an iPad. The draft was edited with Mr Henderson's help and the blog entry was posted and opened for other people to comment on. The partner school also had its own blog and the students there were encouraged to make comments as well. The posts were checked before being allowed to be published.

Sometimes short video clips were uploaded to YouTube and included via a hyperlink to the blog. On one occasion, the children selected a creative writing composition and decided to write a film script using a storyboard app that they

(Continued)

(Continued)

had downloaded from the iTunes store so that they could make a short film to be included in their blog. They used their iPads and the iMovie software to film and edit before publishing to their blog. The partner class in the USA was invited to do the same. At one stage, one of the students went on a holiday with her parents during term time and was able to keep in contact via the blog.

Questions

1   What are the advantages of operating a class blog?
2   How could this be organised during the weekly programme?
3   What are some ways in which the blog could be expanded using mobile devices?

Visiting authors/film-makers/bloggers

Inviting an author to visit the school is a good way to inspire writers. This could be organised for Book Week or by arranging an excursion to the local library when staff there are hosting a special event. A typical author visit may involve a talk or 'show and tell' session and may include topics such as: how they became a writer; where their ideas come from; how they write; and how they work through the writing process. This may be accompanied by a display of drafts, manuscripts and different editions. Having the author read aloud sections of a book and answering questions may also be featured. Often, writers who reside in the community may offer their services for little or no cost to the school. If the sessions are open to parents attending, it may be a good opportunity for the author to sell some of their work. A display could be set up in the library or classroom to display the author's books, with drafts and other things that have inspired the writer's work.

The children should also be regarded as authors and their own publications should be displayed in the classroom or library; special events such as open days and community show days could be organised. The children could also give talks or present their work by giving a slide presentation or showing edited video, demonstrating progress through the various writing stages.

Conclusion

Writing is a process that progresses through a number of stages and takes time regardless of what form it assumes. Today, the forms of writing are diverse and cannot always be separated out from other forms of expression such as illustration, filming, poetry writing, etc.

Discussion questions and activities

 Points for discussion

1 How can the joy of writing be developed in the classroom?
2 What instructional approaches are needed to enhance creative writing?
3 How do you foster writing engagement and writing independence?

 Group activities

1 Discuss the importance of setting a purpose for a writing activity.
2 Write a composition to be shared in a small group.
3 In pairs, discuss each other's composition and edit.
4 Design a folder in which children can keep their work. Use an A3-sized sheet of paper and fold it so that it can contain one or more compositions. What can you include in the folder to promote the development of writing skills and independence?

Whole-class activity

1 Choose a pair to simulate a writing conference. Use the writing activity above (group activity 2) for focus in the interview. Also, use the writing folder as a way to record important points from the interview.

References

Bates, D. (2011). How to self edit (to improve writing). *Practically Primary*, 16(3), 13–15.

Cambourne, B. (1988). *The Whole Story*. Wellington, NZ: Ashton Scholastic.

Cambourne, B. (2002). Conditions for literacy learning: From conditions of learning to conditions of teaching. *The Reading Teacher*, 55, 358–360.

Campbell, R. and Green, D. (2006). *Literacies and Learners: Current Perspectives*. Sydney: Pearson Education Australia.

Constanti, G. (2010). *Why Bother Blogging?* E:update 015. Newtown, NSW: Primary English Teaching Association Australia.

Cruickshank, B. (2011). Supporting children during the prewriting stage: Developing an author's understanding of purpose and audience using interviews. *Practically Primary*, 16(3), 25–28.

Glass, C. and Pearce, J. (2010). Coming to grips with planning for literacy learning: A template for designing open-ended tasks. *Practically Primary*, 15(1), 31–34.

Graham, S. and Harris, K. R. (1997). Self-regulation and writing: Where do we go from here? *Contemporary Educational Psychology*, 22(1), 102–114.

Holliday, M. (2010). *Strategies for Writing Success*. Newtown, NSW: Primary English Teaching Association Australia.

Kervin, L. (2009). *Possibilities for Literacy Learning through Podcasting Activities.* E:update 005. Newtown, NSW: Primary English Teaching Association Australia.

Powell, B. (1967). *English Through Poetry Writing: A Creative Approach for Schools.* Sydney: Ian Novak.

Reed, C. (1971). Pre-school children's knowledge of English phonology. *Harvard Educational Review*, 41(1), 1–34.

The New London Group (1996). A pedagogy of multiliteracies: Designing social futures. *Harvard Educational Review*, 66(1), 1–25.

Turnbill, J. and Bean, W. (2006). *Writing Instruction K-6: Understanding Process, Purpose, Audience.* Katonah, NY: Richard C. Owen Publishers.

Westwood, P. (2005). *Spelling: Approaches to Teaching and Assessment* (2nd edn). Melbourne: Australian Council for Educational Research.

Woolley, G. (2011). *Reading Comprehension: Assisting Children with Learning Difficulties.* Dordrecht, The Netherlands: Springer International.

Yelland, N., Cope, B. and Kalantzis, M. (2008). Learning by design: Creating pedagogical frameworks for knowledge building in the twenty-first century. *Asia-Pacific Journal of Teacher Education*, 36(3), 197–213.

Young, K. (2007). Developmental stage theory of spelling: Analysis of consistency across four spelling-related activities. *Australian Journal of Language and Literacy*, 30(3), 203–220.

CHAPTER 6

CHILDREN'S LITERATURE

Chapter objectives
- To understand the role and function of children's literacy.
- To develop appropriate instructional approaches to the appreciation of children's literacy.
- To develop a suitable pedagogy to foster engagement with good literature and to develop dialogic inquiry.

Key questions
1. How do readers engage with children's literacy to understand their world?
2. How do readers/viewers engage with multimodal and post-modern picture books?
3. How can readers develop higher-order thinking and apply it to what they read?

Key words: children's literature, critical literacy, dialogic inquiry, graphica, inquiry, multimodal texts, questioning.

Introduction

This chapter introduces the reader to children's literature in its various forms. While fairytales, folk tales, novels and other traditional forms of text continue to have a wide appeal, there are newer forms that have the power not only to entertain children but to evoke emotional responses and thoughtful consideration of the important issues of the world in which they live. In recent times, visual literacy has become just as important as textual literacy. The newer forms of graphic representation go beyond mere illustrations of story content to incorporate their own visual grammar or symbolic language that conveys the thoughts and intentions of the artist. Often, graphic representations interact and merge with the text so that there is a blending of semiotic systems. Sometimes the graphics step out of their frames to interact directly with the reader so that meaning is intentionally a product of the author's thoughts and those of the reader. This chapter will explore these issues and develop some pedagogical approaches through children's inquiry and dialogic interaction.

> The lessons we learn from studying pictures and stories are best applied to a similar study of life in general – people, places, objects, emotions, ideas and the relationships between them all. At its most successful, fiction offers us devices for interpreting reality, and appreciating the extent to which it can actually be re-imagined; the realisation that 'normal' is a relative concept. (Tan, 2006: 6)

The above quote by Shaun Tan shows us that children's literacy, while entertaining, deals with some of the big issues in life. It has the potential to make readers aware of the thoughts and motivations of others without them having to experience the kinds of problems others may have to deal with. Stories enable children to explore human emotion in all its manifestations and to value qualities such as courage, valour, integrity, honesty, kindness and forgiveness by empathising with story characters. There is the capacity to explore important life issues such as hunger, war, discrimination, segregation and cruelty by viewing them through the eyes of story characters that sometimes live through quite extraordinary circumstances. Often, human virtue is able to blossom and flourish when problems arise and children are immersed in situations where they are more likely to understand the feelings of loss, separation or even anger that others are confronted with. It gives them the opportunity to experience the private thoughts and motivations of those achieving extraordinary feats of endurance or heroism.

Values, cultural understanding and literature

Narrative has the power to engage the reader's curiosity, fears, expectations, excitement and sense of order. Story plays a vital role in many aspects of our lives – we dream, remember and plan in narrative, we make up stories about ourselves and others and we relate the narratives of others to ourselves by relating to their worlds in time and place. There is more than one way to tell a story and differences in storytelling and the structure of narratives should be recognised and appreciated through discussion in class (Pantaleo, 2009). However, narratives vary within and between communities, societies and cultures. Storytelling operates at many levels and ways of fictionalising events to relate directly to real life but with a certain kind of distancing. For example, fantasies have the power to lead readers to a kind of imaginative understanding necessary for the solving of social difficulties at different levels. Thus, stories are a way of making sense of human experience. To be enriching, fantasy must be rooted in a firm grasp of reality and a firm belief in one's own individuality and experience (Berg, 1977).

Theoretical foundations

There are three main theoretical approaches that underpin the teaching of literacy in modern classrooms: author-centred, child-centred and transactional. The author-centred approach is founded on cognitive, information-processing theories that assume discrete skills can be learned and mastered. It presupposes that some skills should be mastered before learning other higher-level skills. This approach assumes that the meaning, as put forward by the author, is fixed and is found only within the text. Teachers who use this approach tend to teach using direct instruction and teach hierarchical component skills which build on one another. These skills are usually taught in isolation and often with texts that have been artificially constructed to support individual skill learning. More complex reading and writing skills usually follow on after the foundational skills have been mastered. The teacher assumes the role of instructor and the children often work together as a whole class and respond directly to their teacher's instruction.

The child-centred approach is based on Piagetian/naturalist theories that tend to have an environmental focus, with the expectation that the child's literacy development will unfold naturally when children are immersed in literacy-enriched contexts. This is largely dependent on the notion that language develops naturally and that children have an innate ability to learn their native language within their social and cultural context (see Chapter 1). Instruction takes place in a classroom environment that is saturated with literature of all kinds, and exposure to good literature is frequent and regularly supported. The focus is usually student-centred and often pitched at the children's interests. Strategies and skills are taught in conjunction with natural book-sharing situations in the classroom that seek to replicate reading at home, particularly the home bedtime reading situation. The teacher assumes the role of a facilitator by encouraging the children to read books that are authentic texts, which connect with real-life topics that the children are familiar with. Often, instruction takes place in whole-class shared book experiences, small group and peer groupings or in individualised reading settings. Moreover, teachers generally encourage children to experiment with and use speech and to express, write and respond to the book language in a variety of ways. An emphasis is usually placed on open-ended questioning and student discussion with the student actively discovering and constructing meaning. The teacher activates the background knowledge of students through brainstorming and discussion. Children are encouraged to make decisions and to explore the use of language in an environment that accepts the ideas and thoughts of others.

The social-constructivist approach is modelled on the work of Vygotsky (1962: 78) who promoted the idea that knowledge is formed from language and social interactions. Thus, it is a transactional approach that engages young learners with literature in the form of an interaction between the author, the child and the child's peers. Meaning is viewed as a product of this social negotiation. Teachers model and encourage independent learning activity by providing appropriate scaffolding, while, at the same time, progressively reducing the need for continuing overt support. Objectives are usually based on the present needs of students who often work in pairs or in small groups to explore the pragmatic and social aspects of language. The teacher assumes the role of a facilitator and encourages students to pursue their interests and experiment with new language forms that are encountered. The students are immersed in a literature-rich environment that encourages them to select and respond to language in a similar way to the Piagetian/naturalist approach.

The big question is, 'How do today's teachers introduce the study of language with literary texts?' What is certain is that there is a fine balance between learning about good quality literacy and engaging with the various forms and modalities of literate practices. What is needed is a balance between: (a) learning about structure and forms, (b) appreciation of those forms and (c) creating literate products by using the knowledge of those forms in new and novel ways (Simpson, 2012). In the following sections, we will discuss these three aspects in more detail.

Literary genres

Literary texts are organised according to form and structure: prose, poetry and drama. Authors also arrange literary compositions in terms of structure, which can be fiction or non-fiction based. The quality of the literature is often related to theme, plot, characterisation, writing style, setting and point of view.

Myths are usually about gods, and about the creation of all things, about the origin of evil, and man's soul. Legends are generally about heroes and the events in relation to kings and peoples in the period before history.

Fairytales, folk tales and fables are about human behaviour in a world of magic. Fantasy tends not to be realistic and does not take place in a particular time but does reflect some of the big issues in life.

Non-fiction texts are designed to inform and instruct the reader. The writers of these usually try to objectively describe people, places, events and things. They may present these as poetry or prose in the form of autobiographies, biographies and information texts. Writers gain authentic information from extensive research that examines historic material from journals, letters, archives and other sources. Biographies are similar to novels in that they develop narrative-linked events with an embedded overall theme. They are concerned with accuracy and authenticity and often this type of literary material will include an appendix, glossary, index and bibliography of sources used and a list of recommended reading for exploring further.

Background experiences

A child's background experiences will influence their interest in literature. Their level of language and social development and their experiences with shared books will affect their appreciation of good literature. By exploring literature, the child is exposed to the ideas, opinions, motivations and views of other people and other cultures. They are also learning social skills through the interactions of the characters within a story. Through their encounters with plots, themes and interactions, the reader can experience, through their imagination, thought-provoking situations and see how others resolve typical problems. These encounters can facilitate an appreciation and respect for others (Goforth, 1998).

In a literature-rich classroom environment, children are immersed in an atmosphere of discovery and adventure. They are part of a community of learners that share their book experiences and ideas. The physical arrangement of the room will also support the types of activities that children will engage in (see Chapter 10).

Multimodal texts

Picture books are examples of multimodal texts that use more than one semiotic system to convey meaning (Ansty and Bull, 2012). They form meaning when image and text work together in what may be an intricate juxtaposition of text and images (Callow, 2011). Picture books are ideal for shared reading treatments as they appeal to different modes of learning. Researchers and theoreticians have generally underestimated the impact of images in books used in school (Freebody and Bin, 2008). Pictures should not be considered as merely an add-on to add interest to books. Texts can no longer be thought of as print only, particularly in a culture where there is increasingly more visual information required. Consequently, no longer will older ways of interpreting meaning be adequate for an analysis of books. This is because visual texts require new ways of interpreting and comprehending (Ansty and Bull, 2006).

Picture books have been around for a long time. In 1484 William Caxton printed *Aesop's Fables*, which contained both words and pictures and became the forerunner of the modern picture book. The underlying meanings in picture books are not always apparent to young children as there may be several sophisticated layers of meaning (Torr, 2008). However, very little attention has been paid to educating children about the language of pictures. Furthermore, more recent styles of the picture book may be referred to as post-modern and are usually comprised of a picture narrative with words intertwined.

Newer forms of the novel can be found in electronic form and employ computers, TVs and other devices such as tablets and even smartphones (electronic modes will be discussed later in this chapter) to convey a story or message. However, conventional paper forms of linear texts are expected to continue to co-exist with electronic hypertext for some time, and old and new literacy technologies are likely to have complementary roles in a wide range of contexts (Unsworth, 2001).

Electronic texts position the reader not only as a viewer and reader of post-modern texts, but also as a participant. The viewer/reader is often expected to make decisions by interacting and making choices on the screen. Often, the text complements and interacts with the illustrations, but in some cases the pictures may be set in contrast to the text to present multiple viewpoints. Some of these viewpoints may contain different perspectives and require the reader/viewer to supply their own ending. Authors often employ new literary devices to affect the way in which the viewer/reader interacts with the text. It is important that the viewer/reader is aware of these devices and can appreciate how they are being used. In post-modern picture books, the reader and author interact in different ways to create meanings. These books are no longer intended just for children but are more sophisticated and may convey layers of meaning depending on the age and experience of the reader/viewer – for example, *Where the Wild Things Are* (Sendak, 1963) and *The Rabbits* (Marsden and Tan, 1998). They require multiple readings and multiple ways of viewing and urge the reader to read them in different ways. What is important is that they require a critical approach to reading/viewing.

Contemporary picture books are produced and bought by adults who are largely guided by what they have grown up with a generation or two earlier. Many of these post-modern texts make reference to these earlier works and this gives them an intertextual quality by combining meaning into new juxtaposed forms. In other words, they draw on multiple traditions that reflect the changing contemporary, multicultural and multimodal literate landscape.

Pictures, sculptures and relief sculptures were used in medieval churches to enlighten a largely illiterate population. However, the emergence of the printing press and recent painting techniques promoted more realistic artworks, leading to a clear separation of words and pictures (De Silva Joyce and Gaudin, 2011). The classic manuscript used illustration as decoration or as an alternative to reading for those that were illiterate. In today's classrooms, there has been a shift from focusing on text only to valuing both text and pictures. However, the images can often be more complex than the verbal texts associated with them.

Kress and Van Leeuwen (2006) have argued for the use of the term 'grammar' to describe and interpret the visual design elements of graphic illustration in literacy. For example, the same meta-language that can be used to describe written text can also be used to analyse pictures, such as metaphor, allusion, plot and setting. Literary elements can be used to discuss the congruence between visual and verbal texts so that children can experience synergy between the two. In Table 6.1, the various elements

Table 6.1 Visual elements

Feature	Description
Narrator	The person telling the story
Characters	Type casting, dress and facial expressions
Action	What characters appear to be doing to further their motives
Form	Graphic features
Colour	Are the colours harmonious or are they contrasting?
Illumination	Refers to the way in which an element is lit, but is distinct from the brightness of colours, e.g. shadows
Texture	Smooth or rough can indicate mood
Line	Straight or jagged
Shape	Regular or irregular, angular or round
Relationships	Relative positioning of characters and objects
Perspective	Shows how a point of view is constructed, e.g. convey depth of field and integrate foreground and background
Space	Refers to the amount of space taken up by the character – long-shot, medium-shot, close-up-shot – can indicate familiarity or empathy
Focus	Sharp or blurred, e.g. central character may be sharp while the unimportant elements are blurred
Setting	The scene where the incident is happening – will give an indication of mood
Lighting	Brightness and contrast
Editing	Gestalt
Font	Style, colour, size – used to create mood, phrasing, intonation
Vectors	An element within a picture frame that gives an indication of direction of movement

are shown so that students can use traditional story descriptors such as characterisation, setting, plot, action, problem and resolution to discuss the reasons why the illustrator has used certain design elements to elicit the viewer's reactions to them. This can also be used for children, not only to appreciate the skill of the illustrator but also so that they will be enabled to design and develop their own picture books, graphic novels or comics. Kress and Van Leeuwen (2006) maintain that there is no universal grammar but that many of the design elements are culturally based. For example, western books often show red as symbolising death, sacrifice, movement and passion. In contrast, eastern cultures may use red to symbolise good fortune, luck, prosperity and happiness.

Picture books

Picture books have traditionally focused on a younger audience, however many picture books have become quite sophisticated and are increasingly targeting an older audience. Picture books such as Maurice Sendak's (1963) *Where the Wild Things Are* can be regarded as works of art in themselves. Picture books that have been written for younger audiences can also be used with older students to examine how writers and illustrators use various illustrative and literary devices to convey meaning in pictorial and verbal forms.

Computer games

Computer games such as narrative role-playing games, for example, are another form of communicative expression that uses many elements of traditional print-based texts while engaging in more interactive screen-centred multimedia devices. The computer game is, essentially, a reworking of old and new literary forms that includes media such as television or film, elements of fantasy and three-dimensional graphics, while locating itself within the tradition of realistic perspective painting. The use of electronic games in the classroom is becoming an accepted pedagogical practice that can provide opportunities for deeper engagement with the curriculum. The integration of various types of games into the classroom-learning environment may have the added benefit of linking to the children's outside world of everyday experience. By building these links, you will foster an enriched understanding of the literacy classroom in ways that do not exclude many groups (Beavis, 2000, 2007).

One framework (see Table 6.2 opposite) that has been developed to explore the way multimodal texts use images to construct meaning is based on functional linguistics (Halliday and Matthiessen, 2004; Kress and Van Leeuwen, 2006).

Table 6.2 Framework for analysis of annotated responses

Stage	Skills
Perceptual level (experiential): Who, what, when, where? Interpersonal (relationships)	Labelling Describing Questioning Speculating Relationship to author Adding voices/characters' thoughts Relating to own experience (cultural, as a reader, as immigrant) Questioning
Conceptual level (textual): How?	Questioning and speculating based on colour and shade, perspective, direction of movement, gaze design of framing, etc. (see Table 6.3 for other examples)
Metacognitive level: Why? What does this mean?	Hypothesising and predicting (based on prediction story evidence and causality) In view of the whole image or the whole text

Source: Woolley, 2011

Vignette 6.1

Ms Smith introduced her year 2 class to a picture book that has fascinated children for the last couple of decades – *Where the Wild Things Are* (Sendak, 1963) is the story of a little boy named Max who was banished to his bedroom without having any supper. While in his bedroom, he set out on an enchanting journey to where the wild things are and then returned to his room. Initially, Ms Smith had four copies of the book for the children to share in pairs while sitting in a circle on a mat in a group of eight. The rest of the class were engaged in other group activities related to the theme of fantasy.

At first, Ms Smith familiarised the children with the book by asking them to glance through their copies and used Table 6.2 to generate particular questions. The first questions were labelling and describing questions such as: 'What can you see in the first picture?' and 'Describe what Max is doing in the picture.' She then gave each pair a cue card with the question cue stems 'Who...?', 'What...?', 'When...?' and 'Where...?' so that each pair could make up their own questions to ask when they returned to the group session. During the whole-group session, Ms Smith went on to the interpersonal style of questioning, such as 'Have you had any similar experiences?' and 'What do you think will happen in the story?' The children's ideas were written on a whiteboard as examples of their predictions. 'Let's read the story and see if your predictions are correct.' Ms Smith read the story out loud while the children followed along in pairs.

At the conceptual level of questioning, Ms Smith asked the children what they noticed about the pictures as she flicked through the pages. At first, the children noticed that Max was making mischief. The initial illustration is framed

(Continued)

(Continued)

on the right-hand side of the page and the images become bigger and the frame smaller until they fill the entire right-hand page. They also noticed that when Max begins his journey to 'where the wild things are', the images edge across into the left-hand side of the page. When he arrives, the images extend fully across the double-page spread and are framed by the edges of the page with only a small amount of white space at the bottom of the double-page spread for the print. During the wild rumpus, the images completely take over all of the space on the double-page spreads with no room for the text. The children then discovered that the images gradually recede to the right-hand side of the page. The final image of Max in his bedroom takes up the entire right-hand page. This is in contrast to the first image of Max in his bedroom. The children also noticed that Max moved in a right-hand direction at the beginning and changed to the opposite direction in the second half of the book. The children were asked to speculate about why the illustrator might have done this.

Prior to his fantastic journey, Max was sent to bed without any food, and when he returned to his bedroom he found his supper waiting for him and it was still hot. At the beginning of his journey, 'Max sailed off through night and day in and out of weeks and almost over a year to where the wild things are'. On the return journey, he 'sailed back over a year and in and out of weeks and through a day and into the night of his very own room'.

Questions

1   Why do you think Ms Smith familiarised the children with the story before reading the text?
2   How else did she engage readers with the book to construct meaning?
3   Why did Ms Smith encourage the children to predict how the story might progress?
4   What questions did Ms Smith use to address the three cognitive levels in Table 6.2?
5   Why do you think that it is important to discuss the visual grammar in picture books? Why or why not? Can you give examples of other picture books that convey meaning through their illustrations?

Graphica

Graphic novels and comics have been around for a long time but it is only recently that they have been considered acceptable for children to read in class. In earlier times, it was assumed that the graphic representation simplified the literacy elements and the quality was thought to have been inferior to that of the standard text-based novel. Rather than simplifying the literary element, they are now considered to be somewhat more complex due to other elements, such as interpreting a character's facial expressions or non-verbal gestures, making inferences from visual cues such as colour, perspective and line (see Table 6.3). The

Table 6.3   Forms of graphica

Format	Characteristic	Example
Cartoons	One or more panels	Newspaper cartoons
Comic strip	Three to eight panels	Peanuts
	Newspaper funnies	
Comic book	Periodical issues	Spiderman
	Thin durability – similar to magazines	
	Often in a series	
Graphic novel	Book length	Maus
	Sturdier durability	
	Storyline starts and ends within the same text	
	Can be an anthology of previously printed comic books	
Trade paperback	Anthology of previously printed comic books or storylines	Spiderman Team-up
Manga	Japanese-style graphic novels	Dragon Ball Z
	Stylised drawings	
	Simplified features and outlines	
	Some read from back to front	
Anime	Japanese animated productions featuring handdrawn or computer animation	Spirited Away

brain has to process a complex mix of verbal and non-verbal semiotic codes simultaneously. Until recently, there were also concerns that graphic novels were morally bad for children because in some cases the themes were considered violent, sexy or banal. It is true that some comics and graphic novels are more suitable for an adult audience but this is no different to selecting good quality text-based novels for the classroom. Responsible teachers normally vet the kinds of books that they introduce into the classroom. Another genre that integrates pictures and words to tell a story or convey information is presented in comic-strip form: also known as the comic (Thompson, 2008).

There are two broad classifications for graphica: fiction and non-fiction, and each of these classifications can be further subdivided into a number of genres. For example, fiction graphica can be realistic, historical science fiction, fantasy, superhero, romance, humour, mystery, western, horror and adventure. Non-fiction genres include biography, history, social issues, human interest, memoir, information, true crime, reality, content areas and satire.

Graphic novels

It has been widely acknowledged that graphic novels appeal to a range of learners such as boys, girls, reluctant readers, disabled readers, English-as-second-language learners and those that have difficulty visualising story events or scenes (Thompson, 2008). Graphic novels don't just appeal to popular culture but can be just as powerful as some of the classics. For example, *The Arrival* by Shaun Tan (2007) is an award-winning graphic novel that depicts an archetypal story of a man who travels to a strange land. Tan presents the images in the story to the viewer like a photo album looking over the actual life story of an immigrant. The expert use of colour, texture and page composition develop a mood and place the events in time. Tan's story evokes empathy for others that have a different experience in life, giving the reader/viewer an understanding and empathy for the subject. Other social and moral issues have been dealt with in *Maus 1* and *Persepolis*, for example.

Graphic novels tend to be longer than comics, have elaborate illustrations on high-quality glossy paper and are usually bound well. They not only have artistic merit in themselves but are also uniquely suited to capitalise on student interest and share common literary conventions with mobile phones, tablets and laptops where text and imagery are intertwined. Hollywood has recently produced screen versions of 'Superman', 'Spiderman', 'the Fantastic Four' and 'Hell Boy' that give familiarity and relevance to reading and connect students to popular culture where they can see how people lived in another time and place. Many graphic novels are increasingly being produced as digital versions that can be downloaded onto tablets and computers. Some of these electronic versions include animations, which tend to blur the distinction between comic and cartoon.

Artists must convey as much information as possible in the available space, so graphic elements are seldom accidental (see Table 6.4). If a character has

Table 6.4 Graphic elements

Feature	Description
Narrator	The person telling the story within the text
Narrative boxes	Contains the narration text
Directionality	The arrangement of the panels can indicate the direction and time sequence; the size of the panels can also determine the pace of the viewer/reader
Speech bubbles	The boundaries that contain the words – different shapes to indicate spoken words or thoughts; also show the order of speaking/thinking
Panels	The frames that contain the pictures and words
Layout	The way in which the page is organised
Gutter	The space between the panels
Framing	A device used to separate, connect or confine elements within pictures and help interpret meaning
Interpersonal function	Establishing a relationship between the reader and the character
Symbolism	Something that stands for or represents something else
Speech and thought processes	Speech and thinking bubbles
Composition	The arrangement of elements in the picture to give a sense of what is happening; salience – the way in which the creator of the picture gives prominence to one element over another; left-to-right orientation – a western device to indicate movement or growth, with good on the right and evil on the left

dark glasses, then ask why. If there is a picture on the wall, then it may be an important element. A panel refers to the box or unit that depicts a scene in a storyline. Some panels have definite borders with each panel arranged in an orderly fashion. Others are not so clearly defined and some characters may reach out into other panels and scenes may mesh into others. The gutter is the space between panels and this represents a shift in time and space. It also gives the reader time to fill in the action by creating an impression of movement and action. The time between panels could represent a split second or it could represent a week or a month. Sometimes smaller panels can read more quickly than larger panels with more graphic and text information; this is often done deliberately to alter the pace and mood of the narrative.

Vignette 6.2

Mr Jones began a series of lessons on graphica for his year 6 class. In the classroom, he introduced comics and graphic novels in the same way as he introduced legends, drama, poetry anthologies and other text types, and by allowing students to explore and experience reading various genres using bulk borrowing from the library. He also asked the students to lend their own comics and books to the class collection and created some displays and posters to promote particular books/comics. Next, he carefully selected students to form pairs and choose three comics or books to explore. He gave each pair of students a card with a list of questions that were listed according to the ability levels of each pair.

One of the cue cards had the following questions:

1   What did you notice?
2   How is it organised?
3   How is it similar to other books?
4   How is it different from other books?
5   What did you like about it?
6   What did you not like about it?

The students were instructed to paste a copy of the questions into their Literacy exercise book and to record their answers so that they would be ready to share their responses with a larger group. Typical responses were: 'It doesn't look real' and 'Some are in black and white but some others are in colour.' These responses were meant to develop an awareness of some of the features and differences in relation to other texts.

When the children had finished this exploration stage, Mr Jones formed several groups by putting five pairs of students into each rotation group and systematically worked with each group while the other groups were doing independent activities. The focus group shared their findings and then Mr Jones introduced the graphic novel *The Rabbits* by Marsden and Tan (1998), and each pair within

(Continued)

(Continued)

the group was given a strip of paper divided into equal sections related to 'Convention', 'What does it look like?' and 'What is it for?' For example, one group looked at the convention speech of bubbles while others studied narrative boxes, lettering, gutters and pictures. The responses were pasted onto a poster board so that the three sections lined up in rows and columns in chart form. Some space was made available for the rest of the group to add their own comments. Each pair once again gave a report and the children added their comments. Each of the three groups had a turn according to the rotation of normal group work.

In another session, Mr Jones used the regular group organisation to further investigate *The Rabbits* by Marsden and Tan (1998). Mr Jones had a set of six books so that each pair of students had a copy between them. He used the KWL strategy (see Table 6.5) and set this out on a chart to guide the students' discussions.

Table 6.5   KWL strategy

What do I Know?	What do I Want to know?	What have I Learned?

Source: Ogle, 1986

Before the reading of the book, Mr Jones asked the children to look at the front cover of the book and to note any interesting features. He asked what they could remember about the conventions of graphica and referred to their charts. He then proceeded to ask them what they knew about rabbits and their characteristics. He also asked them what they understood about colonisation and the benefits of machines and industry. The students' responses were written up on the chart under 'What do I know?' Next, Mr Jones gave the students a preview of the sequence of pictures in the book and asked them to predict what the story was about and to suggest what they wanted to know about the theme. This was written on the chart and Mr Jones then proceeded to read through the story with the students following along with their shared copies. After they had finished, Mr Jones led a discussion about the themes of the story and listed their comments relating what they had learned. He then proceeded to go through the pages, discussed how Marsden and Tan used these conventions to support the story plot and noted the children's responses on the chart under 'What have I learned?'

Mr Jones asked how emotion was portrayed in the book. He deconstructed the graphic novel by examining the creators' intention, characters and context, as well as the relationship between the choice of design, images and style.

A number of activities were introduced to give students an understanding of the various ways that the emotions and qualities of the characters were portrayed in the graphics. The students were asked to note the different facial expressions, body language, words, colours and metaphors. The students were then asked to discuss how the characters were able to show movement and what effect different angles produced. The students were then led to discover how the passage of time was shown in the sequence of panels.

In a follow-up series of lessons, the students were asked to do a 'show-and-tell' to give encouragement and to create interest by showing their favourite comics and to highlight the particular visual features that had impressed them the most. At first, the students were quite reluctant to use their drawing skills but Mr Jones showed them examples of many different illustrations and it was noted that some of the most effective comics were quite simple in drawing style and design. The children were instructed to design their own books by making a first draft with rough sketches. The art specialist teacher also showed them how to make ink drawings and use coloured dyes to add depth and interest to their work. As they worked in pairs, it was obvious that they learned from each other. When the children displayed their work to the class, the teachers were amazed by the quality of the words and phrases they had used in the text.

1   Why did Mr Jones give cue cards to the children in their pairs?
2   How does this relate to metacognition?
3   Why do you think Mr Jones used the KWL strategy for brainstorming?
4   Why is brainstorming a useful activity in a literacy appreciation lesson?
5   Discuss why it might be important for children to make their own books.

Literature circles

Literature circles are student-led small groups or clubs where students take responsibility for their own learning. Effective literature circles assign roles to each of the participants such as: discussion director, word master, connector, illustrator, passage picker, timekeeper and questioner. This enables the session to be structured and predictable and allows each child to take ownership. Literature circles can operate using different formats and usually comprise 4–8 participants in a group, depending on ability and maturity. Participants usually read the same story or novel and ideally the students should have some say in the selection of the text. If possible, the school librarian should be involved in the selection of books and possibly during the first phase of reading (Sanders-Brunner, 2004).

During the session, the students read the text individually or in pairs and fill in their particular role sheets. After this preparation phase, they come together for a group discussion led by the discussion director while the others use their assignment sheets to guide them in their discussion roles. The discussion director opens the meeting by asking some general discussion questions and then directs others to share their role. All members are asked to contribute to the discussion according to the leading of those with assigned roles.

It is helpful to have group rules for discussion, allowing the children to take ownership of those rules or guidelines. The rules could be initialled and agreed on by the whole group. For example, the following could be considered: listen to others; do not interrupt while others are talking; respect the opinions of others; stay on topic; everyone needs to share. To begin, the teacher might work with a capable group and model how the group should function in a type of 'fishbowl' situation where the other class members observe and enter into a discussion about their observations at the end of the demonstration (Cameron et al., 2012).

Literature circles help students to generate ideas and to form and communicate their opinions. The scaffolds that are provided enable the students to break away from the discourse patterns that are typical of most classrooms and to initiate more complex levels of thought and appreciation of good literature (Brabham and Villaume, 2000).

Critical literacy

Stories usually convey the author's particular points of view while downplaying others in an attempt to influence the reader's thinking. Texts may also have multiple meanings and these meanings may change over time or from one location to another. The text meanings may conflict with one another and may rely on reference to other texts. An analysis of a particular text will not always reveal the purposes of the message and will often be open to interpretation. Being a text analyst is about being an active and informed citizen. Callow (2008) asserts that reflecting critically allows learners the space to step back and consider the points of view presented. Another important aspect of being a text analyst is what the reader should do in response to an engagement with texts.

The critical literacy approach is aligned to Luke and Freebody's (1999) Four Resources model and the Text Analysis role of the learner. Essentially, it is about empowering students as consumers and producers of literate forms, enabling them to consider a wide range of texts, purposes and responses with a critical awareness and understanding (Statkus, 2007). Empowerment comes from:

- being aware that literate texts of all kinds come from a range of modalities and genres
- being aware of the way language is used to establish power
- identifying bias and stereotyping
- determining the point of view of the author and forming opinions based on the consideration of various arguments
- knowing that opinions expressed in literate forms reflect the world view of the author and their culture.

A key issue in any critical literacy lesson is related to the kinds of questions that teachers model. Obviously, the quality of the discussions that ensue will be related to the quality of the questions. Open-ended questions are better than questions that seek a specific right or wrong answer because they promote discussion and higher-order thinking skills. Brown (1997) found that when she began her group discussion sessions she used the following questions as a starting point:

- Has anything that happened in the book ever happened to you?
- Were there any patterns or connections that you noticed?
- Was there anything that puzzled you?
- When you first saw the book, what kind of book did you expect it to be?

These questions should be seen as a springboard for children to construct their own questions based on the types of inferences that they can draw from the book. The questions that the teacher asks will strategically model the types of questions that children should be asking themselves (see Chapter 7 for more about self-questioning).

Philosophy for children in the classroom

Who generally asks most of the questions in the classroom? Who usually gives answers to those questions? The answers to these questions will most likely reveal the power relationships that operate in most classrooms. Empowerment can be related to opportunities to ask appropriate questions at the right time and in the right context. In the author's research (see Troegger, 2011), it was found that most primary-aged children were often unsure of what questions to ask and how to go beyond forming basic literal or factual types of questions. Byrne (2011: 13) expressed it this way: 'But like so many teachers, I wondered how I was going to encourage my students to seek deeper understanding of complex ideas through thoughtful dialogue, not to mention where this might fit into my busy classroom program.'

Philosophical inquiry is a metacognitive process that develops higher-order thinking skills that favour inquiry and self-questioning. It develops a reasoning mindset towards literacy, by fostering giving reasons, developing self-reflections, open-mindedness and the seeking of truth. It essentially prepares students for active engagement in a democratic society. It does this by developing an open community of thoughtful inquiry. It is structured on a student-centred model that fosters listening to others, independent thought and the development of ethical values (Lynch and Learney, 2008). Furthermore, it develops co-inquiry with cooperative learning outcomes and promotes a positive attitude towards others in a non-judgemental environment.

C. S. Lewis's book, *The Lion, the Witch, and the Wardrobe* (1955), for example, develops a number of universal themes such as beauty, love and faith. Values, such as honesty, faithfulness, loyalty and honour, can be openly explored through discussion and follow-up activities such as re-writing a story ending. Questions can be formulated in terms of three levels of thinking: perceptual, conceptual and metacognitive (Woolley, 2014) to promote an inquiry perspective. Sample questions are listed below.

Perceptual level – inferring and clarifying what has been suggested, making a distinction, asking an appropriate question, making an assumption, generalising and asking for a reason:

- What is the author saying?
- Do you think these points are the most important?
- What reasons do you think the author has for saying that?
- Is the author saying that...?
- Correct me if I am wrong, but isn't he/she saying...?
- What do you think the author means by...?
- Aren't you thinking that...?
- Could you give me an example from your own experience of...?

Conceptual level – forming an opinion, clarifying, justifying, giving a reason, inferring, giving counter examples and using criteria:

- In light of what the story was about, do you think that...?
- Why do you believe that what you said is correct?
- Can you tell us why you think that?
- Does anyone else have any questions for...?
- Do you agree with his/her reasons?
- Is that evidence good enough?
- What evidence are you using to make that statement?
- Is it possible that you and the other person are contradicting each other?
- Can you try to see the issue from someone else's point of view?

Metacognitive level – personal reflection and evaluation, and also evaluation of the responsiveness of the group:

- Did we listen to each other well?
- Did we respect each other's opinions and ideas?
- What have we learned from this discussion?
- Did we use good reasons for what we said?
- What has it changed? (Self-correction, concepts, experience, attitude)
- How did you feel about the discussion?
- Is what you just said consistent with what you said before?

Conclusion

Students in primary schools should be introduced to a wide repertoire of genre types, styles of writing and illustration. Literacy appreciation is a two-way constructive process: readers/viewers use their own prior knowledge together with their understanding of the message conveyed by the print to develop an interpretation. There are many different genres that children will encounter and often meaning is conveyed by text, by pictures or by a combination of both.

Reading instruction should engage learners as active constructors rather than passive receptors of information. However, understanding and appreciating good literature requires an understanding of genre and message mode and the skilful use of language or pictorial conventions. All of this is influenced by the socio-cultural context in which the stories are situated. Thus, good literature, in its various forms, can be appreciated on a number of levels.

Literature circles and philosophical discussions will position the reader/viewer as a critical analyst who will look for and interpret meanings not just at the surface level but at deeper levels of cognition and metacognition.

 ## Discussion questions and activities

 ### Points for discussion

1 What are the thinking processes that occur in literacy circles?
2 What instructions are needed to enhance reading group discussion?
3 How do you foster the sharing of ideas and opinions in group discussions?

🕴🕴🕴🕴 Group activities

1 Why do you think that children's literature is an important area of the curriculum?
2 Tell the group about a book that you read as a child and the impact it had on your life.
3 Think of a fairytale and discuss why you think it is important to promote such stories in the classroom.
4 Divide into two groups with two-thirds of the students in one group and one-third in the other. The smaller group sits in a circle while the larger group forms an outer circle. After *The Rabbits* by Marsden and Tan (1998) is read aloud, the inner circle is asked to discuss the visual features of the graphics using the charts that have been presented in this book. The students in the outer circle should listen to the discussion and note down ideas about how to improve future sessions by suggesting ways to structure the discussion.

(Continued)

(Continued)

5 Form four groups and use the discussion questions presented in this chapter, together with the ideas about group structure (raised in activity 4), to conduct a reading of *John Brown, Rose and the Midnight Cat* (Wagner and Brooks, 1980) (or another suitable picture book).

▦ Whole-class activity

Obtain the book *The Arrival* by Shaun Tan (2007). Divide into groups of about eight and simulate a literacy circle in the primary classroom.
Ask:

1 Why doesn't the author use words in the book?
2 What colours are used in the book?
3 Why do you think that the author used these colours?
4 What sort of city is depicted in the book? Is it similar to your nearest city? Is it a modern city or is it placed in another period of time?
5 What is a visual metaphor? How is it used in this graphic novel?
6 What are the giant vacuum cleaners meant to represent? Why do you think that the author used these in the story?
7 Why do you think the main character left his homeland?

References

Ansty, M. and Bull, G. (2006). *Teaching and Learning Multiliteracies*. Newark, DE: International Reading Association.

Ansty, M. and Bull, G. (2012). *Using Multimodal Factual Texts during the Inquiry Process*. PETAA paper 184. Newtown, NSW: Primary English Teaching Association Australia.

Beavis, C. (2000). Reading, writing and role-playing computer games. In I. Snyder (ed.), *Silicon Literacies: Communication, Innovation and Education in the Electronic Age* (pp. 47–61). London: Routledge.

Beavis, C. (2007). Critical engagement: ICTs, literacy and curriculum. In *Australian Literacy Educators Association: The Best of Practically Primary* (pp. 17–21). Norwood, SA: ALEA.

Berg, L. (1977). *Reading and Loving*. London: Routledge & Kegan Paul.

Brabham, E. G. and Villaume, S. K. (2000). Questions and answers: Continuing conversations about literature circles. *The Reading Teacher*, 54(3), 278–280.

Brown, A. L. (1997). Transforming schools into communities of thinking and learning about serious matters. *American Psychologist*, 52, 399–413.

Byrne, G. (2011). Using Socratic circles to develop critical thinking skills. *Practically Primary*, 16(2), 13–15.

Callow, J. (2008). Show me: Principles for assessing students' visual literacy. *The Reading Teacher*, 61(8), 616–626.

Callow, J. (2011). *When Image and Text Meet: Teaching with Visual and Multimodal Texts*. PETAA paper 181. Newtown, NSW: Primary English Teaching Association Australia.

Cameron, S., Murray, M., Hull, K. and Cameron, J. (2012). Engaging fluent readers using literature circles. *Literacy Learning: the Middle Years*, 20(1), 1–8.

De Silva Joyce, H. and Gaudin, J. (2011). *Words and Pictures: A Multimodal Approach to Picture Books*. Putney, NSW: Phoenix Education.

Freebody, P. and Bin, B. Z. (2008). The designs of culture, knowledge, and interaction in the reading of language and image. In L. Unsworth (ed.), *New Literacies and the English Curriculum: Multimodal Perspectives* (pp. 23–46). London: Continuum.

Goforth, F. S. (1998). *Literature and the Learner.* Washington, DC: Wadsworth Publishing Co.

Halliday, M. A. K. and Matthiessen, C. (2004). *An Introduction to Functional Grammar* (3rd edn). London: Edward Arnold.

Kress, G. and Van Leeuwen, T. (2006). *Reading Images: A Grammar of Visual Design* (2nd edn). London: Routledge.

Lewis, C. S. (1955). *The Lion, the Witch and the Wardrobe*. London: The Bodley Head.

Luke, A. and Freebody, P. (1999). A map of possible practices: Further notes on the four resources model. *Practically Primary*, 4, 5–8.

Lynch, S. and Learney, G. (2008). *Strategies for a Thinking Classroom*. e:lit 003. Newtown, NSW: Primary English Teaching Association Australia.

Marsden, J. and Tan, S. (1998). *The Rabbits*. Sydney: Lothian Children's Books.

Ogle, D.M. (1986). K-W-L: A teaching model that develops active reading of expository text. *The Reading Teacher*, 39, 564–570.

Pantaleo, S. (2009). The influence of postmodern picture books on three boys' narrative competence. *Australian Journal of Language and Literacy*, 32(3), 191–210.

Sanders-Brunner, M. (2004). Key words in instruction: Literature circles. *School Library Media Activities Monthly*, 20(7), 39–43.

Satrapi, M. (2003). *Persepolis: The Story of a Childhood*. New York: Pantheon Books.

Sendak, M. (1963). *Where the Wild Things Are*. London: Random House.

Simpson, A. (2012). Language and children's literature: Sorting through the puzzle pieces. *Practically Primary*, 17(1), 9–13.

Spiegelman, A. (1986). *Maus, Volume 1*. N.Y.: Pantheon Books.

Statkus, S. (2007). What is critical literacy (and how do I use it)? *Practically Primary*, 12(3), 10–12.

Tan, S. (2006). *Picture Books: Who Are They For?* Occasional paper 2. Newtown, NSW: Primary English Teaching Association Australia.

Tan, S. (2007). *The Arrival*. London: Hodder Children's Books.

Thompson, T. (2008). *Adventures in Graphica: Using Comics and Graphic Novels to Teach Comprehension, 2–6*. Portland, ME: Stenhouse Publishers.

Torr, J. (2008). Multimodal texts and emergent literacy in early childhood. In L. Unsworth (ed.), *New Literacies and the English Curriculum: Multimodal Perspectives* (pp. 47–66). London: Continuum.

Troegger, D. (2011). Teaching reading strategies by using a comprehension framework. *Practically Primary*, 16(1), 10–13.

Unsworth, B. (2001). *Teaching Multiliteracies across the Curriculum: Changing Contexts of Text and Image in Classroom Practice*. New York: Open University Press.

Vygotsky, L. S. (1962). *Thought and Language*. Cambridge, MA: Harvard University Press.

Wagner, J. and Brooks, R. (1980) *John Brown, Rose and the Midnight Cat*. London: Puffin Books.

Woolley, G. (2011). *Reading Comprehension: Assisting Children with Learning Difficulties*. Dordrecht, The Netherlands: Springer International.

Woolley, G. (2014). Students with Literacy Difficulties. In M. Hyde, L. Carpenter and R. Conway (eds.) *Diversity, Inclusion and Engagement* (2nd edn) (pp. 109–128). Melbourne: Oxford University Press.

CHAPTER 7

READING COMPREHENSION

Chapter objectives

- To understand the thinking processes that occur in reading comprehension.
- To develop appropriate instructional approaches to reading comprehension.
- To develop a repertoire of strategies to foster reading engagement and reading independence.

Key questions

1. How do readers process text?
2. How do readers engage with literacy to construct meaning?
3. How do readers use metacognition to regulate their own learning?

Key words: comprehension, context, fluency, language, memory, questioning, reading, strategies, vocabulary.

Introduction

Reading comprehension is a constructive, cognitive practice that is influenced by factors within the learner and by external factors such as text readability, task difficulty and socio-cultural purposes and practices. This chapter explores the notion that readers are actively engaged in constructing a meaningful interpretation. The meaning-making process is enhanced when readers actively engage in an interaction between what the reader already knows and the new knowledge that is extracted from the text. This two-way process is both a top-down and bottom-up activity, where learners create a situation model of text-based information. Comprehension is not only concerned with word forms and meanings but it requires the reader to process text information simultaneously at a number of levels. This requires readers to be involved with texts in such a way that the reader develops a repertoire of self-regulating strategies.

> 'Just look down the road and tell me if you can see either of them.'
>
> 'I see nobody on the road,' said Alice.
>
> 'I only wish I had such eyes,' the King remarked in a fretful tone. 'To be able to see Nobody! And at such a distance too!' (Lewis Carroll, 1866)

Here, the king interpreted Alice's statement differently from what Alice intended. Even though their understandings may have been different, they both seem logical. However, words and combinations of words by themselves do not convey the whole meaning. There are other contextual and inferential factors such as tone of voice, hand and facial expression and the context in which the people find themselves that contribute to the meaning-making process. Thus, comprehension is an active process in which the learner constructs meaning from a range of spoken or written contextual cues.

How do readers process text?

Reading comprehension is defined as the process of simultaneously extracting and constructing meaning (Snow and Sweet, 2003). This definition recognises that reading comprehension involves a two-way process that is data-driven (print-directed) and at the same time conceptually driven (or directed by knowledge that the reader supplies). It involves extracting meaning from text-based clues and building and integrating new meanings from a combination of new knowledge and the learner's own prior knowledge. Reading comprehension is similar to listening comprehension in that it builds on the spoken word. However, as mentioned above there are some fundamental differences that can make reading comprehension a considerable challenge for some readers as they engage in a type of interaction with the text. Normally, readers extract some meaning from the text (bottom-up), while simultaneously contributing meaning from their own background knowledge (top-down) and prior experiences related to the reading activity. This constructive mental engagement requires readers to actively utilise bottom-up/top-down processes. Consequently, each reader constructs a slightly different interpretation of a read text because it is largely dependent on the reader's own prior world experiences and understanding.

Educators need to recognise and foster this dynamic meaning-making process by choosing appropriate learning experiences that will encourage and enhance the application of the learner's own background knowledge to the meaning-making process. As reading is largely dependent on individual engagement, comprehension instruction should enable children to develop appropriate strategies to self-monitor and self-regulate their learning activity. Moreover, readers need to be encouraged to ask questions and form opinions about the author's intended message as they read. This active and critical reading process can be facilitated when readers interact with others by developing questions, giving explanations and elaborating on their ideas about the content of their reading. This can only take place within a learning environment that encourages respect for the opinions of others, supports risk taking and provides respectful and constructive feedback from teachers and peers.

At the most basic level, effective comprehension of print or multi-media text involves the reader being able to do three activities simultaneously: (1) decode print; (2) construct the meaning around words, sentences and longer discourse; and (3) be able to reason about the content of the text. Therefore, reading comprehension should be considered as a complex and multidimensional process that readers individually develop in the context of a purposeful social engagement.

Theoretical underpinnings

Early reading theorists viewed reading comprehension as a passive cognitive activity that was largely governed by bottom-up or memory-based processes (Greene, McKoon and Ratcliff, 1992). For example, earlier last century it was thought that a student's memory recall of information extracted from text was the best indication of learning. Thorndike (1917), on the other hand, maintained that the role of the reader was not one of simply recording the knowledge contained in a text passage but that of an active participant and problem solver. This led to the notion of a flexible knowledge structure known as a schema to describe the active and fluid organisation of past experiences that can then be used to structure and organise newer information (Bartlett, 1932). Thus, the child was seen to be an active operator, who developed his/her own individual knowledge structures. Schema are flexible knowledge structures that enable readers to interpret new experiences, which may, in turn, lead to adjustments being made to existing knowledge schema. More recently, Anderson (2000) proposed that a schema could be directly applied to the reading process because 'schemas represent categorical knowledge according to a slot structure, where slots specify values that members of a category have on various attributes' (2000: 155).

A constructivist approach to reading comprehension proposed that the construction of meaning was a top-down process that could be made easier by the application of the reader's own schema as an organisation of knowledge that economised on the amount of information that the learner needed to process (Graesser et al., 1994). Others viewed this construction of meaning as both top-down and bottom-up processes that operate simultaneously (Stanovich, 1986). This view proposes that an interpretation of a text message relies on information contained within the mind of the learner and within the text itself. Thus, comprehension is likened to a dialogue or negotiation between the reader and the author. The author limits the amount of information supplied to the reader and assumes that the reader brings a certain amount of prior knowledge to the reading task. If this wasn't so, the author would need to supply all the information and the reader would be overloaded with too much detail to process all at once.

Van Dijk and Kintsch (1983) developed the idea that comprehension could be perceived as operating simultaneously at three different levels of interpretation: the surface level, the text base and the situation model. The surface-level interpretation relies on the reader processing text in terms of phonic and syntactic constructions. At another level, the text-base model was viewed as a type of mental representation of text ideas in the form of propositions (or small units of meaning). At the third level, situation models are formed that incorporate elaborative inferences, as well as imagery, that integrate the child's background knowledge with information from the text being read. The construction of a situation model is a dynamic and ongoing constructive process, which is jointly determined by the interaction of the reader's prior knowledge, text structures and semantic (or meaning) text content. For example, when important information is not explicitly stated in the text, the reader will often make the necessary inferences by incorporating relevant background knowledge to fill in the information gaps (Pearson and Johnson, 1978; Snow, 2002; Stull and Mayer, 2007). Thus, the situation model is a cohesive representation of the perceived meaning of the text's content (Kintsch, 1998).

Mental models do not normally retain the verbatim or exact word-by-word text information but support more flexible knowledge structures that can integrate both visual and verbal representations. Mental models are flexible structures that are often moulded by the predictions that readers make about upcoming story events or content. Predictions are forward inferences that enable readers to think ahead and anticipate likely scenarios and the type of knowledge that the reader will need to bring to the task. However, predictions are sometimes in error and the mental model needs to be fluid enough to be able to be adjusted when readers encounter unexpected information as the story or instructions unfold (Catts, 2009).

Comprehension is not only influenced by text ideas and text structures and by the prior knowledge and schema of the reader. It is also influenced by the socio-cultural context in which learners are situated (Vygotsky, 1962) and by the purpose and type of instructional activity that the learner is required to engage with (see the Introduction). Thus, reading comprehension is influenced by factors within the learner, within the text and by the learning activity within a socio-cultural context (Snow, 2002).

Vocabulary instruction

Comprehending the written form of a language is significantly related to students' vocabulary knowledge in that language (Ricketts et al., 2007). The successful comprehension of a read text is highly dependent on both fluent word recognition skills and vocabulary (their knowledge of word meanings) (Kintsch, 1998; Neal and Kelly, 2002; Paris, 2005; Stanovich, 1986; Swanborn and de Glopper, 2002). As readers become more experienced and skilled, they tend to learn new words from the context as they read and with greater efficiency than do less able readers (Anderson and Freebody, 1981; Stanovich, 1986; Wharton-McDonald, 2002). This frequent exposure to the volume of print facilitates their ability to decode and derive meanings from unknown words (Jenkins et al., 1989; Worthy et al., 2002). The effect of reading volume and frequency on children's vocabulary growth, combined with large differences in reading skills, creates a cumulative advantage for those children who are successful readers (Stanovich, 1986). Those children who struggle with reading tend to read less, have less exposure to new words and, as a consequence, fall further behind their more experienced peers. Thus, teachers should provide ample opportunities for all children to practise their reading in class and encourage reading in other settings.

Vocabulary instruction should ideally occur within the framework of a passage or text being studied (Woolley, 2011). One way to develop intentional word learning during a literacy activity is when teachers explicitly teach new words around a theme or content area. This may include the explicit teaching of selected words, as well as providing background information associated with the text being explored. The emphasis should be on the promotion of word awareness and intentional lexical encoding (word learning). Other words may also be taught incidentally as they are encountered during whole-class or group sessions.

Vignette 7.1

Very strong research evidence suggests that students benefit from word-rich classrooms where teachers capitalise on incidental learning opportunities by pausing during the planned lesson and discussing new words. For example, Mr Jones, the classroom teacher, is reading *The Magician's Nephew* by C. S. Lewis (1955) to his year 5 class. During reading, he stops at the end of a sentence to model the use of context clues to determine the meaning of a word. He says to the children, 'I wonder what the word rigid means? I will read the last two sentences again to see if I can find a clue as to its meaning; please follow me.' He reads, 'The Queen let go of his hand and raised her arm. She drew herself up to her full height and stood rigid' (Lewis, 1955: 57). He pauses and says, 'Hmm … I wonder what rigid means. Can you see anything in these two sentences that can give us an idea of the meaning? What about when it says, she drew herself up to her full height. Hmm … I think this gives us a clue.'

By this stage, the children should have been able to associate the context clues with the targeted word. Alternatively, Mr Jones could have asked the children, 'What else could we do to find the meaning of the word rigid?' This gives the children an opportunity to see that they often need a number of strategies in case one strategy fails. It also gives them the opportunity to learn from each other.

(Excerpt from Woolley, 2011)

Questions

1   How do readers process text?
2   How do readers engage with literacy to construct meaning?
3   How do readers use metacognition to regulate their own learning?

In this encounter with the word 'rigid', Mr Jones then went on to ask the children to imagine how the Queen was standing and describe, role-play or draw her as she stood rigid. Then Mr Jones said, 'Let's read the rest of the paragraph and we will discuss how she might be feeling.' By doing this, the children were more able to develop a depth of meaning around the word 'rigid' and to make links with other words in their mental lexicons. This type of activity not only develops a richness in lexical encoding but also enhances the children's ability to form appropriate inferences (Gambrell et al., 1987).

Word-level learning strategies

Strategic use of outside references, such as a dictionary or thesaurus, can help students check for meaning, spelling, pronunciation and examples of common usage. Some online electronic resources provide other opportunities to increase independent word learning. Figure 7.1 shows the online thesaurus, 'Visuwords', which incorporates colour, size and various connecting lines to show how word meanings are related. This can also be a good model for developing children's word concept maps to show how word meanings are interconnected.

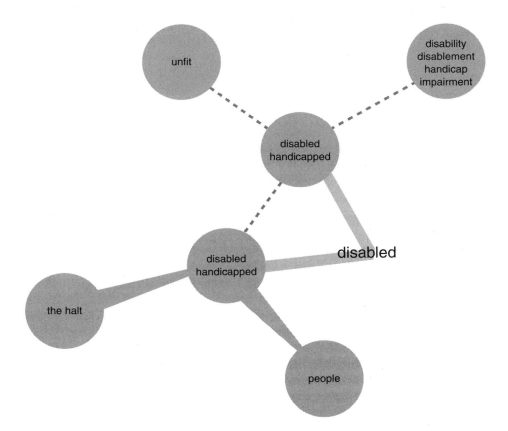

Figure 7.1 Online thesaurus 'Visuwords'

A concept map is a graphic device used to organise words and to graphically represent word relationships. It is a network in which the nodes signify concepts, the lines linking the nodes denote relationships and the labels on the lines (or style of the lines) represent the nature of the relationships. Making a concept map enables learners to become aware of their own understanding because it facilitates their meaning-making and metacognitive thinking skills. Moreover, group concept mapping can also encourage discussion and negotiation of meanings at deeper levels. This negotiation process should be characterised by asking and answering questions, resolving disagreements and co-constructing meanings. Children can develop an awareness of their new words, knowledge gaps and inconsistent reasoning through focused dialogue in cooperative group settings.

Although frequent reading provides momentum for vocabulary development, if the text contains too many unfamiliar words it will place heavy demands on the reader's memory during a slow and tedious word-decoding process that requires the reader to decode each succeeding word (Nation and Norbury, 2005). It is more efficient for this new incoming reading information to be linked with other prior information (or experiences) relevant to the topic being read. Unless the teacher is able to adapt his/her teaching approach and encourage the students to read words fluently, comprehension of any text will be adversely affected when a reader's memory capacity is over-extended. Typically, by the time these readers reach the end of a sentence or passage, they have little or no understanding of the text information that they recognised earlier and are unable to answer correctly the comprehension questions that may have been related to that text.

As children move from the lower primary grades, the texts that they encounter will become increasingly complex. For example, comprehending a science text is often difficult for many children because a new topic in science typically involves a number of unknown concepts and new vocabulary. Thus, each curriculum subject in the middle and upper years of primary schooling becomes differentiated by different traditions and orientations of knowledge involving written, spoken and symbolic forms. Thus, the reading of science texts is often in contrast to English story texts because the words in non-fiction texts become more phonologically and morphologically complex. Furthermore, older and more experienced readers are expected by their teachers to be more accurate in their reading and there is a greater need for them to decode written information much more rapidly with less assistance and support (Horner and Shwery, 2002; Leach et al., 2003; Snow, 2002).

Word building

Teachers can encourage children to collect root words or morphemes. However, children do not always have a good awareness of morphemes. Morphemes are important because the meanings of new words can be understood if the component morphemes are already known. For example, the word untidiness is composed of three morphemes: un – tidy – ness (Bryant and Nunes, 2006).

Root words usually share some aspect of meaning, for example farm and farmer are related in that they share the morpheme 'farm' whereas 'corn' and 'corner' do not. True or false sentences can be included as an extension activity such as, 'A person who makes dolls is a dollar. Is this true or false?' Students can use these to build new words by attaching morphological units such as prefixes and suffixes or Latin and Greek roots.

Children can develop their creativity and interest in words when they construct new words that they have never actually seen before. A word feature analysis chart can visually display the component morphemes that build words such as the word 'disabled', which is composed of three morphemes (see Table 7.1). Morphological knowledge can also be developed by the use of sentence completion tasks, requiring students to generate morphological changes in given words, e.g. *bake* to complete a sentence such as 'My uncle is a *baker*'. A variation of this activity may reduce the demands of this task by allowing children to choose among a selection of possible words from a list. The difficulty level may be increased when children are directed to generate an entire sentence containing specific multi-morpheme words. The most important thing is to foster the notion that word learning is not only useful but can be a creative and fun activity.

Table 7.1   Word feature analysis

Word	Interesting features	Base word	Word building	Sentence
disabled	Starts and ends with a 'd'	able	dis ed ing	The boy in the wheelchair could not run in the race because he was disabled.

Source: Woolley, 2011

Global text structures

The level of reading comprehension is not just confined to a familiarity with words and word segments, such as morphemes or word roots – there are many other factors that will affect the ease of reading and the understanding of written dialogue. For example, readers who have a clear knowledge of narrative story schema and other types of genre are more likely to be successful in their comprehension (Pearson and Raphael, 1990). This is because various genres, such as adventure novels, detective stories or plays, carry with them predictable language and text structures that make reading more negotiable. The global structure of a narrative, for example, might include the overall plot and organisation of the story, the development of the plot and the resolution of the conflict. Introductory paragraphs, for example, may introduce themes, characters and storylines. This enables the reader to relate the story information to their own prior knowledge, making it easier to form links with pre-existing ideas about the story. Within the narrative framework, there may also be several sub-plots or vignettes that form the foundations of the larger story. The inter-relationships of the main characters may also provide story coherence by providing an interlinking story thread. Coherence within the text and the theme of the story are, therefore, critical factors in the readability of narrative text (Harris and Pressley, 1991; Zhang and Hoosain, 2001).

Cloze

The context of sentences or paragraphs will help the reader to 'read ahead'. Obviously, if you can predict what is likely to be encountered, it is much easier to interpret what is in front of you. For example, suppose you are talking to a friend while driving a car. Usually, you are able to concentrate on the conversation without having to focus conscious attention on the skills required to drive the car. Normally, driving is highly predictable, for example drivers usually don't slow down when they come to a hill because they can't see the road on the other side. This is because they expect that the road will continue on the other side of the hill unless there is a road sign that says otherwise. Imagine what happens when suddenly a dog runs out onto the road in front of the car. The driver no longer attends to the conversation, even though it may have been very interesting, but instead focuses all his attention on the road ahead to avoid a possible accident. This scenario demonstrates one's ability to drive without using focused attention simply because the driver can predict what is coming up. In situations where something unexpected happens, it forces the driver to use focused attention. Focused attention is demanding on limited working memory resources and requires effort.

Cloze exercises are very popular in many primary school classrooms because they help children develop prediction and contextual strategies. A cloze activity can be made from any reading passage by deleting every nth word. It derives its name from the ability to close the gaps by focusing on the whole. Typically, children are presented with a reading passage with a number of words deleted with the aim that they use the context to predict what the missing words should be. Cloze exercises can be commercially produced as sets of re-printable worksheets, or, alternatively, they can quite easily be developed from any printed material that children are currently working with (by using white-out to delete words). However, commercially developed cloze activities are not always helpful in many classroom situations, particularly when they are merely used for tests or for filling in time.

Obviously, cloze activities based on materials that children are using in the classroom are more relevant to the needs of the children. It is asserted that cloze exercises should be used in the context of classroom discussion so that the children can learn from each other and consider the various clues that are embedded in the text being studied.

Some suggestions for using cloze activities in the classroom are:

- Delete every 10th word.
- Do not delete a word from the first sentence in the paragraph.
- After the children have become accustomed to cloze activities, increase the frequency of deletions (keep in mind that the more words are deleted, the more difficult it will be).
- Initially, model the contextual strategies and thinking skills needed to perform the activity by using 'think-aloud talk'.

- To develop the children's ability to use the strategy, work with the class to jointly 'work out' the missing words.
- Be aware that without graphic cues, the missing word will be impossible to predict and so synonyms should be accepted as being a correct response.
- For an exact match, provide some graphic information as a clue (e.g. don't delete the first letter of all words, but alternatively draw the shape of the word to give a clue as to the correct word).
- Delete particular words to highlight the effect of syntax (e.g. delete every nth verb or noun), however keep in mind that content words such as verbs and nouns carry the most meaning and their omission can make prediction more difficult. Structure words such as 'and' and 'are' are much easier because they merely connect meaning and are more predictable.
- Remember that combinations of words such as phrases, clauses and even whole sentences or whole paragraphs can be deleted. When a whole paragraph is deleted, it enables the children to focus their attention on the more global structures and ideas embedded within the text.
- Ask the children to justify their inclusions, then to consider whether or not other words could have been used instead.
- When discussing substitutions, focus on grammar and semantics. When graphic cues are provided, the focus should also be on their graphic and phonic decoding ability.

Appropriate text selection is an essential issue in terms of encouraging students' reading and comprehension while using the cloze method. Worksheets may provide practice and diagnostic information but they should not be seen as a substitute for the discussion and feedback that is so essential in this learning activity (Hattie and Timperley, 2007). In contrast, teachers should encourage readers to use texts that are interesting, comprehensible and sufficiently varied so that the individual can relate to it in terms of interest and motivation; use text passages regularly so that readers can consolidate their learning of skills and strategies; and encourage the children to read more challenging texts (with support when necessary) in order to stretch their ability levels.

Sentence- and paragraph-level processing

The classroom practice of 'round robin reading' where students read aloud around the class using the same text should not be encouraged, unless the students have had considerable practice with some success before this activity. Reading aloud may be rewarding for skilled readers. However, the less skilled can be disheartened by this procedure because it highlights their reading inadequacy in front of their peers. It is important that students are exposed to listening to a variety of texts read aloud in the classroom. Teachers should model fluent and expressive oral reading on a regular basis. Experiences of this kind can be enhanced when parents or elders are invited to read, talk about and share highlights from their own childhood or current reading. In these situations, they can talk with the students about their impressions of the story, the exciting events in the story and the meaning of interesting words within the texts.

To be successful in text comprehension, the reader needs to be able to identify and process the information contained in connected text such as phrases, sentences and relationships between sentences. Joshi and Aaron (2000) proposed that adding speed of processing to the Simple View of Reading (see Chapter 3) significantly improved the prediction of reading comprehension. Unless a student is able to read words fluently, heavy demands are made on working memory during a slow and tedious decoding process that requires the reader to use focused attention to identify each succeeding word (Spencer and Hay, 1998). A number of other researchers have also shown that there is a strong association between speed of word reading and text comprehension (Hay et al., 2005; Jenkins et al., 2003). Fluent word recognition and decoding skills facilitate the good comprehension of texts because they free up students' working memory as the focus is on gaining meaning at the text level, rather than at the word or word segment (morpheme) level. When text is processed in larger chunks, the more meaningful the comprehension and the less taxing it is on working memory (Perfetti, 2007). In Table 7.2, grade-level reading rates can be used as a rough guide for developing fluency.

Table 7.2 Oral reading rates related to grade levels

Oral Reading Rate Table			
Grade	WCPM	Grade	WCPM
1	10–30	5	100–140
2	50–80	6	110–150
3	70–100	7	120–160
4	80–120	8	130–170

Notes: WCPM = words correct per minute; grade scores are based on mid-year levels; reading rate scores are based on data from http://www.nclack.k12.or.us/cms/lib6/OR01000992/Centricity/Domain/249/Fluency_Article_for_RTI_Website.pdf

Most people have a constant reading rate with which they comfortably read most reading material. However, it should be noted that reading rate may vary considerably according to the purpose of the reading and to the difficulty level of the text.

Fluency not only involves the efficient decoding of words, but in order for reading comprehension to progress efficiently, the reader must focus attention on making meaning while using automatic processes for word recognition. To a large degree, fluency will be affected by the quality of prior experiences and knowledge structures that children can apply to read text information (Reutzel et al., 2002). Moreover, faster rates of word recognition are directly related to comprehension because readers are more able to chunk information into larger meaningful units in working memory by enabling the expansion and elaboration of existing knowledge structures. Thus, the larger the chunk of information, the more meaningful it will be, requiring less cognitive resources in working memory. This is particularly important for older children, as there is evidence to suggest that comprehension contributes relatively more to fluency at higher levels of reading development (Jenkins et al., 2003; Pikulski and Chard, 2005).

A useful strategy for children who have adequate word recognition but need to develop reading pace is to select a reading passage of approximately 100 words and with 90–96% word accuracy (see Chapter 11) level for the child. Have the child read the passage, timing them and counting the number of words read correctly. This can be repeated three or four times with the same passage. Plot the child's progress on a chart and note their reading rate improvement. Use other passages from the same book to keep the passages at the same level. When the child's reading rate improves and he/she feels more confident, move on to a slightly harder book and follow the same procedure.

How readers engage with literacy to construct meaning

Activating background knowledge

Readers who possess a rich prior knowledge base related to a topic being covered will have a deeper understanding than peers with poorer prior knowledge and world experiences. This is because many less skilled readers lack knowledge about a topic that inhibits the generation of inferences and the construction of an interpretation. Some children may have adequate world and background knowledge but are unable to link their experiences to the particular topic or story (Catts, 2009). Normally, skilled readers fill in missing information from their background knowledge by making the closest match from their own life experience. Therefore, teachers should take every opportunity to discuss familiar and unfamiliar story elements and new vocabulary before the children undertake a reading activity. Rich talk can activate and develop the background knowledge that readers need to make appropriate inferences, ask questions and develop detailed situation models as they read.

The QAR (question–answer relationship) strategy (Raphael, 1984) is a particularly good method for demonstrating to students that not all the answers can be found in the text, whether they are literal or inferential. It requires students to connect text information to prior experience or knowledge. Students need to ask:

> Is the answer right there in the text? *Answers to literal questions can be answered there in the text.*
> Do you need to think and search the text? *The answer is in the text but the reader must tie it together from two or more sentences in the passage.*
> Is the answer found in my head? *The answer is not in the text. The reader needs to use his/her own background experiences to answer the question.*
> Is there a part of this text that reminds me of something else I have read? *or* Is there a part of the text that reminds me of something else?
> Is the answer a combination of the author and me? *The answer is not in the passage. It is found in the reader's own prior knowledge together with the text.*

Global inferences

The more global or macro-level inferences tie together meanings at the gist or theme level by connecting text ideas across sentences. Questions such as 'Why did the king banish the handsome prince?' will stimulate causal connections between actions and events in the story (Laing and Kamhi, 2002). Furthermore, Kintsch (2005) argued that the use of open-ended 'WH' questions (who, when, where, why and how) assists children in comprehending text by enabling them to elaborate and enhance their recall and processing of the words and themes in the text. 'Why' questions are particularly good at helping with the organisation and consolidation of relations at the discourse level (Trabasso, 1981). Children who have difficulty maintaining causal links across story propositions would be expected to have problems with generating explanatory inferences (Laing and Kamhi, 2002). However, Pressley (2002) maintained that this could be improved when children ask questions in order to generate explanatory answers.

The following are some suggestions that teachers can use with their students to enhance their students' ability to generate questions and make inferences from read texts:

- Set a goal for the reading.
- Ask, 'What do you think is the theme or the message in this story/text?'
- Make predictions about story content.
- Read the text for the big ideas. Ask, 'What is important about this story?'
- Generate some questions to get to those big ideas.
- Go from general to specific in talking and thinking about the story. Ask who, what, where, when and how questions.

- Is the story more about the place, the plot or the characters? Ask the children if they know of any characters like those in the story.
- What does the story tell us about how people behave and relate to each other?
- Work towards a unified understanding of the context, such as: What is the purpose of the writing of this text? How does it make you feel? What motivates or excites you in this story?

How readers use metacognition to regulate their own learning

Metacognition

Self-regulating learners are active readers who clarify, question and monitor their own comprehension strategies to gain meaning from read text (Duke and Pearson, 2002; Gersten et al., 2001; NRP, 2000; Pressley, 2002). It is asserted that poor readers not only need literacy interventions specifically aimed at the development of positive self-concepts, they also need specific training in self-regulation in order to develop independent learning and deep engagement in reading. A large body of research has demonstrated that self-regulatory processes lead to reading success at school (Cox and Guthrie, 2001; Paris and Winograd, 1990; Westwood, 2011). However, very few teachers are adequately trained to assist students in becoming independent learners. Many learning problems that students exhibit are related to the inability to use self-regulating strategies appropriately. Effective teaching of children with reading comprehension difficulties places emphasis on self-monitoring as well as on motivation and effort with increased independence. Teachers should encourage all students to self-generate positive goals, along with the thoughts and behaviours needed to attain their learning goals. Self-regulated readers are viewed as active constructors of meaning who integrate existing knowledge structures with new information. They also use reading comprehension skills strategically to foster, monitor and regulate their own comprehension before, during and after reading.

Prediction

Successful readers use predictive inference as a self-regulating strategy. A predictive inference focuses the reader's attention by speculating about events or actions that may occur in the text based on what the reader already knows about the story (Laing and Kamhi, 2002). Thus, when readers predict before reading, they activate past memories and experiences and test themselves as to whether they have sufficient knowledge about the topic in order to comprehend read text (Glazer, 1994). Predictive strategies help promote overall story understanding of and engagement with the text information during further reading. They also help the reader to verify their understanding of the read text by comparing and contrasting their predictions with text information (Block, 2004; Duke and Pearson, 2002). You may scaffold this prediction strategy by asking questions such as 'What clues helped you make this prediction?' After the story is finished, readers may be asked, 'What part of your predictions came true?' These types of questions can become a framework to demonstrate the questioning process so that readers eventually internalise self-questioning and self-testing strategies.

Visualisation instruction

Prediction and comprehension can be enhanced by visualising story content. As discussed earlier, reading comprehension is not just about remembering words and ideas, it also involves situation modelling using both verbal and imaginative visual information. As students read texts, they should be taught to picture in their minds the situation that is occurring in a story. You can facilitate this mental activity, for example, by asking the children to visualise the setting of the story, the activity, the people and how they look and react to the situations within the plot. Class discussions centred on the children's own imagined scenes would improve the linking of visual and verbal material in working memory (Van Meter et al., 2006). Furthermore, it has been widely demonstrated that encouraging children to develop visual imagery while they read or listen to a story improves comprehension because it helps to organise and build coherence within the mind of the reader (Woolley, 2011). This strategy enables the linking of the incoming text information to the reader's prior knowledge, which in turn increases the reader's involvement in and enjoyment of reading.

Vignette 7.2

The following is an excerpt from Emily Kissner's blog on 15 May 2011 (http://emilykissner.blogspot.com.au/2011_05_01_archive.html).

Help for word callers: using manipulatives

For me, some of the hardest readers to reach are those that seem to decode accurately and quickly, but have trouble with retelling or answering questions. Sometimes these readers are called 'word callers'. They have often done just fine with reading in the primary grades, when their ability to decode quickly and accurately puts them at the top of their class.

In fourth grade, however, things start to change. As text becomes more complex and readers need to make more inferences, these students start to feel a little lost. They might look around the room and see the other students quickly writing summaries, while they struggle to think of what to include. They might listen to a conversation about the theme of a story, but not understand how stories can show different themes. It's easy for these readers to become frustrated – reading used to be so easy, but now it's so hard.

[As I wrote about in January,] These readers may not be building elaborate mental models. A mental model is a reader's impression of a text and understanding of the main ideas. Dr Gary Woolley's [2010] article, 'Developing reading comprehension: Combining visual and verbal cognitive processes', is an excellent introduction to helping students build mental models.

One of the ideas mentioned in the article is the use of manipulatives for reading. While much of the research about this focuses on manipulatives for early readers, I've found this strategy to be useful in the intermediate classroom as well. When readers have to move around pictures and objects, they have to make more meaningful connections between ideas in the text. It's not enough to just read a sentence and blunder on to the next – the reader needs to stop, find the relevant pictures and show how they carry out the actions in the text.

Why is this strategy not used more often? I think it's a question of materials. Materials for retelling and acting out text with manipulatives are simply not widely available, especially at the intermediate level. (In some of the original research, they referred to using Playmobil toys, with texts written especially to fit the toys that they had. Playmobil did make some fairytale sets, but they're becoming hard to find.)

(Continued)

(Continued)

I've tried to create some items for my classroom, using simple illustrations for the manipulatives. Once students are familiar with the process, they are eager to create their own retelling figures. This is a great activity, because it harnesses both drawing and manipulative use to enhance comprehension. While I started using this activity to help the word callers, I found that all of the readers in my room enjoyed this.

If you haven't yet tried manipulatives with your readers, the end of the year is the perfect time to try it out. Kids find this strategy inherently motivating, while you can do some 'kid-watching' to see how all of your readers – and especially those who show word-calling tendencies – react to this kind of activity.

Questions

1   How do readers process text?
2   How do readers engage with literacy to construct meaning?
3   How do readers use metacognition to regulate their own learning?

Whole-of-text treatments

A number of researchers and teachers from around the world have noted a slump in students' reading and reading comprehension around year 4. It has been suggested that this slump in reading is partly related to the increase in text complexity and an increase in the level of difficulty of the vocabulary in that text. At this stage, words across all subject areas become increasingly phonologically and morphologically complex (Leach et al., 2003). Furthermore, readers are expected by their teachers to read more accurately and there is more of a need to process large texts at a rapid pace without assistance.

Duke and Pearson (2002) have demonstrated that when you instruct students about text structure it will have positive results for a wide population of students including those with reading difficulties. In general, their research implies that a wide variety of approaches to teaching text structure improves both comprehension and recall of important text information. Text structure devices such as graphic organisers and graphic post-organisers can be used as organisation strategies to assist with developing recall of the read text information (Duke and Pearson, 2002; Kintsch and Van Dijk, 1978). This approach may also include showing students how to identify the main ideas and the relevant supporting details.

The narrative structure is a more familiar text structure and one that is generally more widely used in lower primary classrooms. It normally has a three-part structure with a goal-action-outcome format. In more complex narratives, this structure will be repeated within the overall Goal – Action – Outcome (G-A-O) structure. In other words, each incident within a story will also echo this same structure. Usually, the structure is highly predictable. However, some genres, such as mysteries and detective stories, use a surprise ending to keep the reader guessing.

Most narratives involve events that take place in time and space. A graphic post-organiser (see Figure 7.2) can be used after reading a passage to help students organise the global structure of the story and guide their story recall and retelling. Retelling is an effective technique because it enables the reader to reflect on and reorganise important information. It can also be an indicator of reading comprehension.

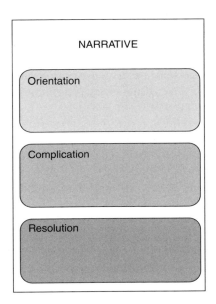

Figure 7.2   Graphic organiser for the narrative genre

Retelling

The following are some suggestions that teachers can consider using with their students to increase the effectiveness of graphic organisers and retellings:

- Use card or a large piece of paper to write the main ideas in large writing.
- List contributing paragraph ideas on the same card under the main idea.

- Draw or divide a poster board into story frame sections that reflect the structure of the read text, such as introduction, developments and conclusion.
- Use Post-it notes to write down ideas about the story and add these to the story frames.
- Imagine and describe sections of the story or passage to match each section of the story frame.
- As the teacher, model the construction of story frames in the graphic organiser by using think-aloud talk to reveal appropriate thinking processes.

Conclusion

Reading comprehension is a two-way constructive process. Readers use their own prior knowledge together with their understanding of the message conveyed in print to develop an interpretation. As such, reading instruction should engage learners as active constructors rather than passive receptors of information. Reading comprehension is not only influenced by the characteristics of the learner but also by the nature of the reading material and by the instructional and task requirements. All of this is influenced by the socio-cultural context that gives meaning and relevance to any literacy activity.

Children in primary school need to be taught to use a wide repertoire of vocabulary enhancement and comprehension strategies to increase their comprehension of text. Comprehension is more than testing; it is at the very core of the reading process. Educators should provide their students with a rich set of learning opportunities so they can develop both breadth and depth of vocabulary and acquire the necessary language skills, content knowledge and reasoning skills to develop their understanding.

Effective reading comprehension requires readers to use their own background knowledge to make inferences and to develop a situation model of a text. Automatic decoding skills and word recognition enable efficient readers to focus on meaning rather than on attention-demanding sounding-out strategies. Comprehension also relies on the reader's knowledge of the vocabulary and meaning of the words in that text and the ability to read fluently. This economises on effort, and the chunking of text into larger meaningful wholes enables more efficient use of limited working memory capacity.

Knowledge of how narrative texts are constructed will enhance readers' global understanding of a story. These reading attributes can be both taught and encouraged and this is particularly important for students who come into our classrooms from disadvantaged backgrounds.

Discussion questions and activities

 Points for discussion

1   What are the thinking processes that occur in reading comprehension?
2   What instructional approaches are needed to enhance reading comprehension?
3   How do you foster reading engagement and reading independence?

††††   Group activities

1   Discuss the importance of setting a purpose for a reading activity.
2   Go to www.readabilityformulas.com/fry-graph-readability-formula.php and assess the readability of a reading passage that children are likely to read. Discuss the pros and cons of using the formula to grade a book or article.
3   Place an unseen object in a black bag and describe it so that others have to guess what it is. Discuss, 'How does this develop language?' and 'How does this develop visualising skills?' and then discuss, 'How are language and visualising skills linked?'
4   Divide the children into pairs. Provide each pair with a picture so that one student cannot see the picture. (You may need to place a barrier between each pair so that one participant can see the picture while the other is blocked from seeing it.) Have the participant with the picture describe it as best they can so that the other person can imagine and draw the picture.

Whole-class activities

1   Read a descriptive passage from a children's novel and ask the students to close their eyes and imagine the scene.
2   Ask, 'What do you think about asking children to read a passage and then giving them ten questions at the end?' Make a chart of pros and cons.
3   In groups of two, make up a cloze activity using a photocopied page from a story and join with another group to fill in the gaps. As a whole group, discuss the pros and cons of this.
4   In groups, visit http://reading4meaning.blogspot.com.au or http://emily kissner.blogspot.com.au and discuss activities that enhance reading comprehension in terms of text processing, learner engagement and the fostering of metacognition.

References

Anderson, J. R. (2000). *Cognitive Psychology and its Implications*. New York: Worth Publishers.

Anderson, J. R. and Freebody, P. (1981). Vocabulary knowledge. In J. T. Guthrie (ed.), *Comprehension and Teaching: Research Reviews* (pp. 56–75). Chicago, IL: International Reading Association.

Bartlett, F. C. (1932). *Remembering: A Study in Experimental and Social Psychology*. New York: Cambridge University Press.

Block, C. C. (2004). *Teaching Comprehension: The Comprehension Process Approach*. Boston: Pearson.

Bryant, P. and Nunes, T. (2006). Morphemes and literacy. In T. Nunes and P. Bryant (eds), *Improving Literacy by Teaching Morphemes* (pp. 3–34). London: Routledge.

Carroll, L. (1866). *Alice's Adventures in Wonderland*. London: Macmillan.

Catts, H. W. (2009). The narrow view of reading promotes a broad view of comprehension. *Language, Speech and Hearing Services in Schools*, 40(2), 178–183.

Cox, K. and Guthrie, J. T. (2001). Motivational and cognitive contributions to students' amount of reading. *Contemporary Educational Psychology*, 26, 116–131.

Duke, N. K. and Pearson, P. D. (2002). Effective practices for developing reading comprehension. In A. E. Farstrup and S. J. Samuels (eds), *What Research has to Say about Reading Instruction* (3rd edn) (pp. 205–242). Newark, DE: International Reading Association.

Gambrell, L. B., Kapinus, B. A. and Wilson, R. M. (1987). Using mental imagery and summarization to achieve independence in comprehension. *Journal of Reading*, 30(7), 638–642.

Gersten, R., Fuchs, L. S., Williams, J. P. and Baker, S. (2001). Teaching reading comprehension strategies to students with learning disabilities: A review of research. *Review of Educational Research*, 71, 279–320.

Glazer, S. M. (1994). Can children assess their own work? *Teaching K-8*, January, 114–116.

Graesser, A. C., Singer, M. and Trabasso, T. (1994). Constructing inferences during narrative text comprehension. *Psychological Review*, 101, 371–395.

Greene, S. B., McKoon, G. and Ratcliff, R. (1992). Pronoun resolution and discourse models. *Journal of Experimental Psychology*, 18, 266–283.

Harris, K. R. and Pressley, M. (1991). The nature of cognitive strategy instruction: Interactive strategy instruction. *Exceptional Children*, 57, 392–404.

Hattie, J. A. (1992). *Self-concept*. Hillsdale, NJ: Erlbaum.

Hattie, J. and Timperley, H. (2007). The Power of Feedback. *Review of Educational Research*, 77(1), 81–112.

Hay, I., Elias, G., Fielding-Barnsley, R., Homel, R. and Frieberg, K. (2005). Language delays, reading delays and learning difficulties: Interactive elements requiring multidimensional programming. *Journal of Learning Disabilities*, 40, 400–409.

Horner, S. L. and Shwery, C. S. (2002). Becoming an engaged, self-regulated reader. *Theory into Practice*, 41, 102–109.

Jenkins, J. R., Fuchs, L. S., Van den Broek, P., Espin, C. and Deno, S. L. (2003). Sources of individual differences in reading comprehension and reading fluency. *Journal of Educational Psychology*, 95(4), 719–729.

Jenkins, J. R., Matlock, B. and Slocum, T. A. (1989). Two approaches to vocabulary instruction: The teaching of individual word meanings and practice in deriving word meaning from context. *Reading Research Quarterly*, 24, 215–251.

Joshi, M. and Aaron, P. G. (2000). The component model of reading: Simple view of reading made a little more complex. *Reading Psychology*, 21, 85–97.

Kintsch, W. (1998). *Comprehension: A Paradigm for Cognition*. New York: Cambridge University Press.

Kintsch, E. (2005). Comprehension theory as a guide for the design of thoughtful questions. *Topics in Language Disorders*, 25(1), 51–64.

Kintsch, W. and Van Dijk, T. A. (1978). Toward a model of text comprehension and production. *Psychological Review*, 85, 363–394.

Laing, S. P. and Kamhi, A. G. (2002). The use of think-aloud protocols to compare inferencing abilities in average and below-average readers. *Journal of Learning Disabilities*, 35(5), 436–447.

Leach, J. M., Scarborough, H. S. and Rescorla, L. (2003). Late-emerging reading disabilities. *Journal of Educational Psychology*, 95, 211–224.

Lewis, C. S. (1955). *The Magician's Nephew*. London: The Bodley Head.

Nation, K. and Norbury, F. (2005). Why reading comprehension fails; Insights from developmental disorders. *Topics in Language Disorders,* 25, 21–32.

National Reading Panel (NRP) (2000). *Teaching Children to Read: Report of the Comprehension Instruction Subgroup to the National Institute of Child Health and Development*. Washington, DC: NICD.

Neal, J. C. and Kelly, P. R. (2002). Delivering the promise of academic success through late intervention. *Reading and Writing Quarterly, 18,* 101–117.

Paris, S. G. (2005). Reinterpreting the development of reading skills. *Reading Research Quarterly*, 40, 184–202.

Paris, S. G. and Winograd, P. N. (1990). How metacognition can promote academic learning and instruction. In B. F. Jones and L. Idol (eds), *Dimensions of Thinking and Cognitive Instruction* (pp. 15–51). Hillsdale, NJ: Erlbaum.

Pearson, D. P. and Johnson D. D. (1978). *Teaching Reading Comprehension*. New York: Holt, Rinehart & Winston.

Pearson, D. P. and Raphael T. E. (1990). Reading comprehension as a dimension of thinking. In Jones, B. F. and Idol, L. (eds), *Dimensions of Thinking and Cognitive Instruction* (pp. 209–240). Hillsdale, NJ: Erlbaum.

Perfetti, C. (2007). Reading ability: Lexical quality to comprehension. *Scientific Studies of Reading*, 11(4), 357–383.

Pikulski, J. J. and Chard, D. J. (2005). Fluency: Bridge between decoding and reading comprehension. *The Reading Teacher*, 58(6), 510–519.

Pressley, M. (2002). *Comprehension Instruction: What Makes Sense Now, What Might Make Sense Soon*. Newark, DE: International Reading Association. Available at: www.readingonline.org/articles/handbook/pressley/index.html

Raphael, T. E. (1984). Teaching learners about sources of information for answering questions. *The Reading Teacher*, 28, 303–311.

Reutzel, D. R., Camberwell, K. and Smith, J. A. (2002). Hitting the wall: Helping struggling readers to comprehend. In C. Collins Block, L. B. Gambrell and M. Pressley (eds), *Improving Comprehension Instruction* (pp. 385–389). San Francisco: Jossey-Bass.

Ricketts, J., Nation, K. and Bishop, V. M. (2007). Vocabulary is important for some, but not all reading skills. *Scientific Study of Reading*, 11(3), 235–257.

Snow, C. E. (2002). *Reading for Understanding: Toward a Research and Development Program in Reading Comprehension*. Santa Monica, CA: Rand Corp. Available at: www.rand.org/publications/MR/MR1465/ (accessed 12 December 2002).

Snow, C. E. and Sweet, A. P. (2003). Reading for comprehension. In A. P. Sweet and C. E. Snow (eds), *Rethinking Reading Comprehension* (pp. 1–11). New York: The Guilford Press.

Spencer, R. and Hay, I. (1998). Initial reading schemes and their high frequency words. *Australian Journal of Language and Literacy*, 21, 222–233.

Stanovich, K. E. (1986). Matthew effects in reading: Some consequences of individual differences in the acquisition of literacy. *Reading Research Quarterly*, 21, 360–407.

Stull, A. and Mayer, R. E. (2007). Learning by doing versus learning by viewing: Three experimental comparisons of learner-generated versus author-provided graphic organisers. *Journal of Educational Psychology*, 99(4), 808–820.

Swanborn, M. S. L. and de Glopper, K. (2002). Impact of reading prose on incidental word learning from context. *Language Learning*, 52, 95–117.

Thorndike, E. L. (1917). Reading as reasoning: A study of mistakes in paragraph reading. *Educational Journal of Psychology*, June, 323–332.

Trabasso, T. (1981). On the making of inferences during reading and their recall. In J. T. Guthrie (ed.), *Comprehension and Teaching: Research Reviews* (pp. 56–75). Chicago, IL: International Reading Association.

Van Dijk, T. A. and Kintsch, W. (1983). *Strategies of Discourse Comprehension*. New York: Academic Press.

Van Meter, P., Aleksic, M., Schwartz, A. and Garner, J. (2006). Learner-generated drawing as a strategy for learning from content area text. *Contemporary Educational Psychology*, 31, 142–166.

Vygotsky, L. S. (1962). *Thought and Language*. Cambridge, MA: Harvard University Press.

Westwood, P. (2011). *Commonsense Methods for Children with Special Educational Needs: Strategies for the Regular Classroom* (6th edn). London: Routledge.

Wharton-McDonald, R. (2002). The need for increased comprehension instruction. In M. G. Pressley (ed.), *Reading Instruction that Works: The Case for Balanced Teaching* (pp. 236–288). New York: The Guilford Press.

Woolley, G. (2010). Developing Reading Comprehension: Combining Visual and Verbal Cognitive Processes, *Australian Journal of Language and Literacy*, 33, 109–125.

Woolley, G. (2011). *Reading Comprehension: Assisting Children with Learning Difficulties*. Dordrecht, The Netherlands: Springer International.

Worthy, J., Patterson, E., Salas, R., Prater, S. and Turner, M. (2002). More than just reading: The human factor in reaching resistant readers. *Reading Research and Instruction*, 41, 177–202.

Zhang, H. and Hoosain, R. (2001). The influence of narrative text characteristics on thematic inference during reading. *Journal of Research in Reading*, 24, 173–186.

CHAPTER 8

INFORMATION TEXTS, INQUIRY AND ICT

Chapter objectives

- To understand the nature of different text genres.
- To develop suitable teaching pedagogy.
- To develop a repertoire of strategies to locate, organise, synthesise and consider issues related to the use of information for other sources.

Key questions

1. What is the difference between traditional print media and new technologies?
2. What is the inquiry process?
3. How can learners benefit from the use of electronic literacies in your classroom?

Key words: comprehension, context, fluency, language, memory, questioning, reading, strategies, vocabulary.

Introduction

This chapter builds on the notion of comprehension as presented in the previous chapter. Often, students with reading comprehension difficulties have more exposure to the narrative as a text genre and less exposure to exposition or information texts. The notion of purpose is also pivotal to successful literacy learning because it not only determines the writer's use of genre and content but also affects reader engagement and responses. This chapter examines the variables that impact on literacy engagement within a socio-cultural context. First, it examines some variables within the learner that impact on learning outcomes, such as memory and motivation. Second, it examines text variables – exposition text genres, in particular, present unique challenges for all students and require them to use more complex cognitive processes to construct meaning during reading. Each genre has specialised features that need to become familiar and to be navigated regularly. For example, the vocabulary in exposition texts is usually subject- or domain-specific and often unfamiliar to young learners. Consequently, unskilled and novice readers will have more difficulty in using the context to construct the meaning of new words. Third, the chapter will discuss some instructional ideas related to information texts in the contemporary classroom and how you should facilitate children's ability to inquire about a topic of interest. This chapter will also discuss the various electronic information texts and the visual and verbal modes that they incorporate.

> It is no longer possible to think about literacy in isolation from a vast array of social, technological and economic factors. Two distinct yet related factors deserve to be particularly highlighted. These are, on the one hand, the broad move from the now centuries-long dominance of writing to the new dominance of the image and, on the other hand, the move from the dominance of the medium of the book to the dominance of the medium of the screen. (Kress, 2003: 1)

This quote represents a departure from a reliance on print only to a position of *ascendency* by the medium of the screen. The modes of print and image have different rationalities afforded to them. The organisation of writing is governed by speech with the logic of time sequence. On the other hand, the organisation of the image is governed by the logic of space and concrete objects represented by their position within that space. In the medium of print, the flow of communication is in one direction; in English-speaking and western cultures it is in the direction of left to right. In print-based texts, the author generally structures the sequence and flow of ideas.

Information texts are predominantly multimodal. They are composed of a combination of text and image, and the learner will need to rely on a number of resources or skills to navigate, synthesise and integrate new information. New electronic technologies have also changed the way in which the reader/viewer navigates pages and screens. The eyes do not necessarily move from left to right or from top to bottom but their movements are more likely to be determined by readers' interests and purposes. Thus, the reading of multimodal texts often requires added navigation skills combined with goal-directed and self-regulated behaviours.

The above quote by Kress (2003) assumes that there are a number of socio-cultural factors – technological, social and economic – that determine the function and modes of communication a particular culture will engage with. Figure 8.1 shows the factors that influence learning outcomes within the socio-cultural context of the classroom. Within this context, three things have a direct influence on learner outcomes: learner, text and activity-based factors. Learner factors relate to literacy skills, modes of learning, memory and engagement. Text-related factors include print, illustrations and technology. The third factor relates to the types of teaching, expectations and tasks that students are required to perform. Central to this model is the notion of purpose because it draws together text, activity and learner competence to give meaning to the product of any literacy endeavour (Figure 8.1).

In this chapter, you will understand how these important variables can be incorporated in engagement with factual print-based and multimedia texts. It is important for you to realise that the three factors – text, learner and activity – will vary according to the socio-cultural context and to the particular purpose that is desired. In this chapter, the overall aim will be to examine these variables as they relate to the comprehension of exposition texts.

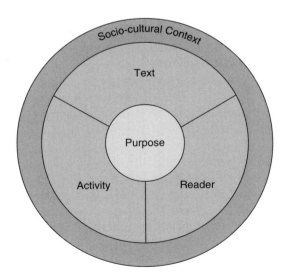

Figure 8.1 Variables that affect reading performance

Source: Snow, 2002; Woolley, 2011

Learners

In the previous chapter on reading, it was asserted that comprehension was enabled when readers construct a mental situation model as they read, by the incorporation of elaborated text-based information into the reader's own prior knowledge. Situation models are flexible mental representations that are constantly updated to reflect the most recent understandings of textual information. However, the ability to form an adequate situation model may largely depend on the efficiency of working memory in effectively allocating cognitive resources and efficiently storing information. The ability to coordinate and appropriately allocate these cognitive resources within a limited working memory is vitally important for effective reading and comprehension. In particular, this discussion focuses on using visual and verbal processes that will enhance students' ability to comprehend information texts. It also explores related aspects that deal with reading engagement, learning styles, motivation, metacognition, self-regulation, direct instruction and learning through inquiry.

Working memory

In the classroom, children use their working memory to remember instructions, learn language and perform thinking tasks. One theoretical working memory model that is useful for conceptualising and explaining how thinking processes function was originally put forward by Baddeley and Hitch (1994) and developed further by Baddeley (2000). In this model, working memory can be separated into a visual and verbal subsystem under the direction of a central executive (or central processing unit). The visual-spatial working memory is used to remember patterns, images and special relationships. The verbal subsystem operates in a sequential and linear mode but has a very limited storage capacity. For example, the average 7-year-old will normally only retain and remember about three separate verbal items at any one time for a short period without decay. Another limitation on the efficiency of verbal memory is how quickly information is presented (Alloway, 2011).

Dual Coding theory complements the Baddeley working memory model because it assumes that all thinking is composed of the activity of two mental codes: a verbal code that uses language and a non-verbal code that uses mental imagery (Sadoski et al., 2000). According to Dual Coding theory (Paivio, 1986, 1991), there are three levels of cognitive processing. The *representational level* involves the perception of a mental representation in either the verbal or visual code in working memory. The *associative level* involves the association of concepts within the code, while the *referential level* involves connections between the visual and verbal codes (Sadoski et al., 2000). The interconnectedness of the visual and verbal systems of working memory can overcome the capacity limitations in working memory and make learning more efficient (Woolley, 2011).

Images in texts are used to give visual representations of topic material, to classify, to depict events, to show part/whole relationships, topographical accuracy and timelines, and often use symbolic images to portray interaction of one kind or another. Thus, reading comprehension will be strengthened when visual and verbal information are linked in working memory. For example, when children are encouraged to visualise story content, the quality of their mental representations will be enhanced through discussion and elaboration. This process should enable the student to make links between verbal and visual memory content in a much more integrated way. Thus, the quality of a reader's situation model will be enhanced by the quality of the dialogue during learning activities. Moreover, images are often quite motivating because they inherently draw on the student's own world experience.

Motivation

A motive is any condition in a student that affects their readiness to initiate an activity or set of activities. Students differ in the quality of motivation and in their motivational orientation. However, all human behaviour can be considered to be goal-directed and success or failure in attaining goals will draw corresponding positive or negative motivational responses (Linnenbrink and Pintrich, 2002). Orientation of motivation involves the underlying attitudes and goals that give rise to engagement in literacy or other learning activities (Ryan and Deci, 2000). Furthermore, individuals may be motivated by a number of competing psychological needs. For example, a student may be motivated to read a chapter of a book in class but may then be motivated to switch their attention to a distraction beyond the classroom window.

Motivation is driven primarily by three psychological needs: (a) competence, (b) autonomy and (c) relatedness (Ryan and Deci, 2000). Learners who believe themselves to be competent are more likely to persist at a task when they are confronted by difficulties (Paris et al., 2001). Autonomy involves one's need to know and understand and relies on the learner's desire for significance and self-actualisation. This is usually determined by their sense of purpose and perceived control over their learning (Beach, 1994). Relatedness is influenced by the learning orientation or learning style orientation, together with the value that the individual places on the task (see Chapter 10). It is also strongly influenced by one's expectation of success or failure at a task (Gambrell et al., 1996). What influences a student's lack of motivation and progress will be discussed in Chapter 10.

Text

Images and diagrams

Images used in information and multimodal texts may vary quite considerably from simple photographs or drawings to quite complex diagrams and flow charts containing labels, boxes, circles and other devices. On-screen diagrams and illustrations may also have interactivity with hyperlinks built into them. Graphs and diagrams have their own unique visual conventions and children should be made aware of how the data should be analysed. Many of the visual codings will be similar to those presented in narrative picture books or graphic novels (see Chapter 6). The problem is that unless readers are provided with either an opportunity to engage in an inquiry-based science programme, for example, or are given additional information and support, they will often have difficulty making inferences from the text passage (Pearson et al., 2007). In the same way, post-modern picture books (as discussed in Chapter 6) use different semiotic systems that provide different codes and conventions through which meaning is conveyed. Multimodal information texts also use linguistic, visual, audio, gestural and spatial conventions.

Genre

A text is usually the product of social action, and literacy is always seen as a matter of social action and social forces. All aspects of literacy can be seen as deriving from these actions and forces as the author shapes language into text genre (Kress, 2003). Thus, the text-maker's purpose for writing, the targeted audience and the mode of delivery will determine the type of genre used.

Genre is not just about how content is arranged but also about form and the way in which it should be navigated. Information is presented differently according to whether the text content is dealing with cause and effect, problem/solution, compare/contrast, or is simply a list. Narratives and recounts can also convey information, as can newspaper articles, cooking recipes and timetables of various kinds. Top-level structuring is concerned with knowing the structural elements and vocabulary that are embedded in the different information text genres. Graphic organisers (see Table 8.1) can help children form appropriate situation models by explicitly teaching structural design elements.

Explicit instruction

The quality of the learning outcomes for children is ultimately related to the quality of instruction. For example, rather than merely introducing students

Table 8.1 Genre structures and signalling words

Design Features of the Genre

Compare/Contrast

	Signalling words	
Compare/Contrast	**Comparison**	**Contrast**
	Similar to, likewise	Different to
	Both, share	Compared with
	Compared to	In contrast to
	Just as … so…	One has…
	Resemble	The other has…
	Alike	In spite of, in contrast to
	Like	However
	Have in common	But
	In comparison	In opposition to
	Instead	Unlike
	Similarly	Not everyone
		On the other hand
		While, whereas

List

	Signalling words
List	Description
	Sequence
	Elaboration
	And
	Then
	Next
	Main idea is a list or sequence
	Main ideas have a time order
	Main idea is usually followed by details that elaborate on it

(Continued)

Table 8.1 (Continued)

Problem/Solution

	Signalling words	

Problem
Consequently
Whereas
Alternatively therefore
Question
Query
Predicament
Trouble
Dilemma
Puzzle
The challenge was
What had to be discovered was
Enigma

Solution
Answer
Reply
Resolution
Clarification
Response
Comeback
Rejoinder
To fix this problem
To set this issue at rest
So (we did this)

Problem/Solution

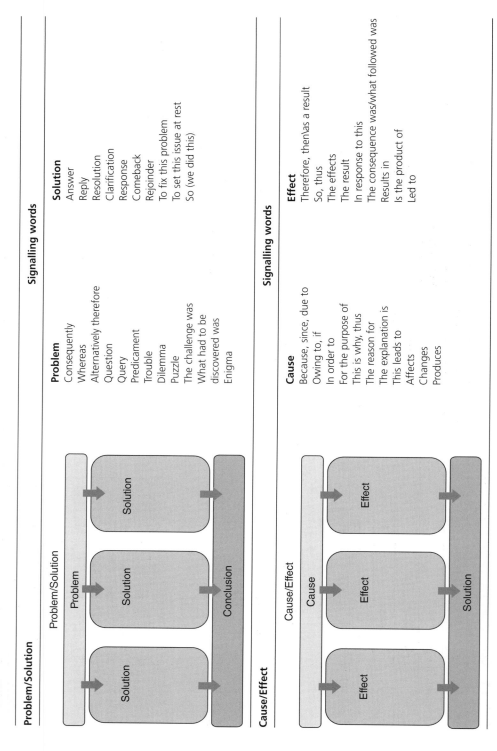

Cause/Effect

	Signalling words	

Cause
Because, since, due to
Owing to, if
In order to
For the purpose of
This is why, thus
The reason for
The explanation is
This leads to
Affects
Changes
Produces

Effect
Therefore, then\as a result
So, thus
The effects
The result
In response to this
The consequence was/what followed was
Results in
Is the product of
Led to

Cause/Effect

to a comprehension strategy and then testing them on it, they should be taught the strategy using explicit teaching techniques. Explicit instruction usually refers to a whole-class or focus group expository teaching technique. It involves the transfer of three types of knowledge: *declarative* knowledge refers to what it is; *procedural* knowledge to how it is; *conditional* knowledge to when and why to apply a strategy, and is needed for application strategies in different contexts.

It is asserted that the more explicit the comprehension instruction, the more likely children are to use such strategies in their everyday reading activities. However, unlike reading decoding skills, comprehension strategies take time and practice to develop. Furthermore, the teaching of reading comprehension should provide students with guidance on when and where to use these strategies, and they should be given ample practice with a wide range of texts and different genres.

There are a number of strategies that will need to be taught so that students can develop as independent learners and this is usually delivered through explicit instruction. However, the combination of explicit instruction and modelling of comprehension strategies such as inference-making and self-monitoring has been found to be more effective (NRP, 2000; Troegger, 2011). Think-aloud strategies can be used by the teacher during explicit instruction to model the kinds of thinking processes that students should use (Duke and Pearson, 2002; Zhang, 2002).

When children use strategic processing, they develop metacognitive and self-regulatory processes. They clarify, self-question and monitor their own comprehension-making strategies (Duke and Pearson, 2002; Gersten et al., 2001; NRP, 2000; Pressley, 2002). However, an emphasis should be placed on the gradual release of teacher responsibility so that children learn to take control of their own strategic processing. To further enable this transfer of responsibility, teachers should complement explicit teaching approaches with the provision of implicit learning opportunities so that readers can exercise self-regulation through activities designed to promote inquiry and self-discovery.

Your explicit teaching of reading comprehension strategies should involve the following steps:

1 Explain the strategy in terms of its importance for learning.
2 Use explicit teacher modelling.
3 Provide opportunities for scaffolded practice with the fading out of expert support.
4 Provide prompts where possible (fade out prompts as the students become more competent).
5 Monitor students' progress and give specific feedback.
6 Provide new task opportunities for transferring learnt skills to new situations.

7   Provide opportunities to reflect on students' meaning making and strategy usage with a view of bringing their reading performance closer to that of the 'expert' model. (Horner and Shwery, 2002; Schunk, 2003; Woolley, 2011)

It is important that you explain exactly what a strategy involves and why the strategy is important, together with when and how to use it in different genres and contexts (Duke and Pearson, 2002). You should model the strategy by using 'think-alouds' to demonstrate the types of self-talk and self-questions to use when performing the task (Gambrell et al., 1987; Horner and Shwery, 2002). You should also provide instruction to students on when and how to use these new strategies (Vaughn et al., 2000; Woolley, 2011). After you have modelled the reading strategies, students practise the skills while you guide them by giving corrective and specific feedback. You, as the teacher, can explicitly teach your students a range of reading strategies by explaining and modelling them, and encouraging your students to become independent users of these strategies. You can do this in a systematic way by gradually withdrawing support and providing ample opportunities for the students to practise taught strategies using a variety of texts and genres (Afflerbach et al., 2008).

Comprehension strategies

There are a few comprehension strategies that you should be well acquainted with and use frequently. In the USA, a seminal study entitled 'The National Reading Panel Report' (NRP, 2000) identified eight reading comprehension strategies that were deemed to be the most effective and these were: multiple strategies, question answering, question generating, comprehension monitoring, text structure, graphic organisers, cooperative learning, and summarising.

Multiple strategies (a blend of individual strategies used flexibly and in natural contexts): the teacher models an approach by showing how they would try to understand the text, using combinations of strategies. Evidence shows that actively involved, motivated readers read more text as a result of multiple strategy instruction. The panel found that in studies involving even a few hours of preparation, instructors taught students who were poor readers but adequate decoders to apply various strategies to expository texts in reading groups, with a teacher demonstrating, guiding, modelling and scaffolding the strategies. Even limited use of these strategies produced a noticeable improvement in students' level of comprehension, though with only modest improvement in standardised test scores. While it is held that teaching even one comprehension strategy can lead to improved comprehension, the teaching of multiple strategies can have an even greater impact

(Duke, 2004; NRP, 2000; Pressley, 2002). The National Reading Panel was concerned that, at present, teachers are not employing effective comprehension practices (NRP, 2000).

Question answering: teachers ask questions and steer students to correct answers, enabling them to learn more from the read text.

Children are more engaged in their learning when metacognitive skills such as asking appropriate questions are modelled and practised. This enables them to clarify understanding and develop deeper meaning by encouraging more elaborate discussion and monitoring their responses. The use of metacognitive strategies such as self-questioning and using prompt cue cards can enable students to 'think about their thinking'. According to Kamhi and Catts (2002), a key element of good questioning treatments is where learning is considered to be a dialogical activity that is modelled by an expert other and progressively internalised in the form of self-questioning by the learner. Such focused dialogue can also enhance students' comprehension of read text by developing a more proficient use of language (Snow, 2002).

Question generating: when readers are taught to use self-questioning before, during and after reading, there are significant gains in the ability to make inferences about text and in text comprehension (Palincsar and Brown, 1984; Snow, 2002). The types of questions used in comprehension instruction will elicit different inferences by the reader (Duke and Pearson, 2002; Palincsar and Brown, 1984).

Successful questioning treatments that enhance comprehension should involve coherence building at both the local and global levels. Local-level processes tie together meanings at the sentence level. For example, 'when', 'where' and 'what' questions elicit associative inferences. Who/what questions assist in the formation of concepts within sentences, usually at the word level (Trabasso, 1981). An associative inference also makes generalisations about characters, actions, objects or events in a story (Laing and Kamhi, 2002). Associative inferences can also build and elaborate on the mental imagery of story content (Gambrell et al., 1987).

Other research suggests that self-questioning benefits students' learning when it is interspersed throughout the text (Kintsch, 2005). Kintsch suggested that children should be taught to ask questions at logical break points in the text and that each question should be presented close to the item in the text that provides cues for appropriate inferences.

Cue cards can be used to provide suitable scaffolding for children to develop their discussion around words and to encourage independent reading. Thus, progression from teacher direction to student self-regulation is an essential component for the development of meaningful word learning. The following list developed from Bloom's taxonomy (1956) shows this progression from lower-order thinking to higher-order comprehension and problem solving:

- Knowledge: the reader simply recalls information from the text.
- Comprehension: the reader is involved in translating, interpreting or extrapolating.
- Application: this requires the reader to use principles or abstractions to solve novel or real-life situations.
- Analysis: this requires the reader to break down complex information or ideas into simple parts to see how the parts relate to each other.
- Synthesis: the reader creates or designs something that did not previously exist.
- Evaluation: this requires the reader to judge something against a standard. (Also see Bloom's revised taxonomy, Krathwohl and Anderson, 2010)

Comprehension monitoring: students need to be aware of their understanding of the text and to use appropriate strategies as required. Comprehension monitoring is 'thinking about thinking'.

Text structure: this involves making students aware of the text genre structure. Graphic organisers, map timelines, characters and story events (the narrative) can be used here (see the above discussion on text genre).

Graphic organisers: students write or draw meanings and relationships of read text ideas. Graphic organisers help the reader to concentrate on the main ideas or specific words found in the text. In terms of narrative text, a story frame can be used that highlights the setting, the characters, the plot, the problem and how it was resolved (Roser et al., 2007). This process can be a way to tie together story ideas at the sentence level and also at the whole text or global level. The main effect appears to be the improvement of readers' recall of read text content. Improvement is particularly found in social science and science content areas.

Cooperative learning: students work together to learn comprehension strategies. This enhances the learning of strategies and supports rational discussion and improved reading comprehension in test performance (see Chapter 10).

Summarising: instruction in summarising improves text recall and reorganisation of ideas. It involves incorporating ideas related to the main idea, generalising and removing redundancy. Students need to be shown how to identify the main idea in each paragraph and how to link ideas together. A summary involves two parts – one where the text is expanded and the technical words explained, followed by a more telegraphic and compact statement once the vocabulary is understood. Many readers are unable to get to this second stage without going via the expansion stage, and teachers need to teach both processes if they want students to effectively comprehend and summarise the content of the text (see Figure 8.2).

Clarifying: this skill involves identifying new vocabulary and text-related concepts that may be unclear. It requires the student to scan the

---

Use graphic organiser/write a summary/draw a diagram

Follow these steps when summarising read text:

- **Delete** duplication.
- **Combine** ideas with the same subject.
- **Restate** in fewer words.
- **Use** summary words.
- **Remove** details that are not about the main subject.

Figure 8.2   Summary cue card

text for words that are unfamiliar and to decode correctly. It also requires that the student use the context to elicit possible meaning and to monitor and check those perceived meanings from further reading, e.g. 'Does it make sense?'

Organising: students select important details and construct relationships among them. This involves identifying the main ideas, classifying them, and noting sequences or categories.

Comparing and contrasting: this requires students to make judgements by looking for similarities and differences in the subject matter. For example, if the subject of the text passage is lions, then the focus may be on comparing and contrasting the physical features and behaviours of cats and dogs. This can be enhanced by what, where and how questions. It may be further extended by the introduction of why questions.

Elaborating: this entails making connections between information from the text and prior knowledge, and includes making inferences and analogies and evaluating and judging.

Imagining: this requires students to make mental images of a subject by noting information in the text and pictures and combining it with elements from students' own background knowledge. It also requires some comparing and contrasting as well as guided elaboration to develop and intensify mental imagery that becomes more memorable.

Monitoring: this means being aware of the cognitive processes used by a reader during a reading activity. It involves knowing whether a text element or reading strategy makes sense and what steps need to be taken to repair comprehension.

Learning through inquiry

The inquiry-learning model is associated with the cross-disciplinary mode of learning because it provides opportunities for students to do research and make links between learning processes across different genres. It requires a number of thinking and learning processes such as asking relevant questions, planning and locating suitable sources of information. These processes can provide an opportunity for group discussions about the text. When students share ideas around this type of activity, they are more able to compare and contrast their own thinking with that of their peers. Moreover, you will find that an important way to induce students to focus on an important issue is to have them develop their own research questions.

Inquiry requires a number of skills that are linked to progressive stages:

- Exploring: initiating the inquiry, predicting, developing questions, planning
- Investigating: locating sources, narrowing the focus
- Monitoring: analysing and synthesising information and organising findings
- Reflecting: filtering, organising, analysing, evaluating the information
- Presenting: sharing an answer to the research question by reporting, presenting and displaying
- Reviewing: further inquiry.
  (Ansty and Bull, 2012; Killen, 2007; Zimmerman, 2002)

Ultimately, inquiry is about reading engagement and the establishment of a specific purpose to enable children to set their own reading goals and obtain answers to self-generated questions (Guthrie et al., 2004; Hay and Woolley, 2011). While engaging in inquiry, students need to know how to navigate and use the appropriate study or investigation skills. Many of these skills are needed no matter whether the sources are books, letters, diaries, plays, presentations, websites, films or social media such as Facebook. For example, in some paper-based texts we need to know how to use an index, table of contents, chapter headings, captions and illustrations. In contrast, some of the types of navigation skills that are required to use digital electronic technologies include knowing how to use: the URL, homepage, menus, tool bars, drop-down menus, breadcrumbs and footers.

ICT

The ability to find, analyse and evaluate information sources has always been a critical component of information literacy and this landscape is constantly in a state of flux. The terminology that is used to describe these new forms of literacy is also diverse and includes such terms as: digital literacy, e-literacy, multimedia literacy, computer literacy, Internet literacy, ICT literacy or just plain literacy. Both the media and the context in education are evolving and so too are the types of environments that young people populate. It will be important for you as a teacher to find ways for students to become highly engaged, by critically reflecting on the content of texts that they view and read. Students do, however, need to feel excited about their learning. This will often be an outcome of their creative endeavours and their growing confidence in using the new literacies (Beavis, 2007).

Durrant and Green's (2000) 3D model is useful as a framework for conceptualising how technology can be used in the classroom. They propose that we think about literacy and technology in terms of three dimensions simultaneously: cultural, critical and operational. The model identifies a contextually situated set of social practices and builds in prospects for young people to be actively engaged in inquiring and evaluating ICT-mediated skills, knowledge and literacies. The model prioritises and balances learning experiences with an activity-oriented curriculum of teaching for learning rather than learning from direct teaching.

The rapid expansion of the World Wide Web and other multimedia technologies demands a complex skill set for children to function appropriately in the age of the Internet. However, many teachers posit that web-based texts are more complex than traditional print media and students must now acquire added literacy skills to critically and effectively evaluate the quality of materials and consider any potential bias of that material. Students should be formally introduced to the concepts of copyright theft, intellectual property and plagiarism in an age-appropriate manner as early as possible.

Some important questions that students may need to ask themselves as they engage with new literacies are:

- Who is the audience?
- What is the message?
- Who is sending the message?
- Why are they sending this message?

Enthusiastic teachers sometimes embrace the new technologies, claiming they offer a panacea for educational problems. The challenge for you, however, will be to learn how to utilise these new technologies appropriately, ethically and responsibly, with a view to tapping the educational potential of all students. You will need to include in your understanding and teaching of literacy the unique literacy skills that children have developed outside school: text messaging, Facebook, blogs, video, wikis and emails using the new technologies: mobile phones, tablets and other devices (The New London Group, 2000).

The classroom as a learning community

It has been demonstrated that when reading and thinking processes are taught to students through dialogic interactions, they increase students' engagement and control of the reading comprehension process (Cole, 2002;

Guthrie and Davis, 2003; Hareli and Weiner, 2002). Higher student achieve-ment and more positive social, motivational and attitudinal outcomes have also been found to occur in collaborative learning contexts (Gambrell et al., 2007; Woolley, 2007). The involvement of students in group discussions during and after listening to a story has been shown to lead to improved comprehension, particularly when the teacher asks questions or prompts students to describe what they have read (Gambrell et al., 2000). Directed questions may also contribute to reading comprehension by focusing atten-tion on text segments containing the information being sought (Taboada and Guthrie, 2006). Explanatory answers to those questions can further improve students' comprehension of read text and enable a more efficient use of language through focused dialogue (Snow, 2002). Thus, requiring students to self-explain during re-reading will promote active learning that has been shown to lead to a significant improvement in self-monitoring for all readers (Woolley, 2011).

Vignette 8.1

Interview with Ms Brennan

Interviewer: Ms Brennan, would you tell me about your regular inquiry lessons?

Ms Brennan: I implemented the inquiry lesson as part of the reading hour in my classroom. The reading hour is comprised of a whole/part/whole approach. For example, our last theme centred on an animal unit entitled 'All Creatures Great and Small'. We were studying the characteristics and habitats of different animals. At the beginning of our reading hour, I introduced the big book *Please Don't Feed the Bears* (Fowler, 1991) and encouraged the students to activate prior knowledge by posing the question 'What do I already know about bears?' I then modelled making a concept map on the whiteboard of the students' known words and information about bears.

Interviewer: How do you organise these groups?

Ms Brennan: I conduct cooperative literacy lessons several times a week. I make these times a priority and organise a number of parent helpers and the learning support teacher to work with group activities around the theme. Each group works on a literacy-learning task such as developing a graphic organiser by using specialised software, such as 'Inspiration', on classroom laptops, building models, writing reports, etc.

Interviewer: I understand that you work more intensively with one of your groups in each session?

Ms Brennan: That is correct. I work with the literacy circles group where children read and research together. However, I tend to facilitate their activity rather than direct their learning. I tend to use a lot of cue cards (or prompt cards) to prompt the students. For example, I use 'Clunk Expert Cue Card' (Figure 8.3) to enable the children to provide prompts during the reading phase. The student holding the card will assume the role of reading 'expert' and prompt students, using the suggestions on the card where necessary, to use compensatory reading strategies to self-correct while reading.

Clunk expert: Reminds members to use clunk strategies for difficult concepts.

Clicks: When we understand what we read, everything 'clicks' along smoothly.

Clunks: When we don't understand, 'clunk', we stop.

When we get to clunk, we use fix-up strategies to try to figure out what the clunk means:

1. Reread the sentence with the clunk and the sentences before or after the clunk, looking for clues.
2. Reread the sentence without the word. Think about what would make sense.
3. Look for a prefix or suffix in the word.
4. Break the word up and look for smaller words.
5. Use a picture.
6. Use a glossary or dictionary.
7. If something is still not clear after trying all of these fix-up strategies, ask for help.

Figure 8.3 An example of a cue card to help children develop peer support

Interviewer: How do you promote an inquiry approach to learning?

Ms Brennan: The children are encouraged to generate their own questions before, during and after the reading of the text. They use question cue cards to assist them in generating questions (see Figure 8.4). This started as an oral lesson by activating prior knowledge, making predictions, identifying details, determining the main idea, identifying clunks, sharing information and generating questions to locate new information. Eventually, the students reached the stage where they were recording questions before, during and after reading texts in their learning journals and posing questions for their peers to answer. It was also successful in stimulating inferential questions, with students posing questions commencing with 'I wonder why...'.

(Continued)

(Continued)

Knowledge Question Cue Card
Stage 1

Sample question stems:
How many…?
Who was it that…?
Can you name the…?
Describe what happened at…?
What does … do?
Can you tell me why…?
Find the meaning of…
What is…?
Which is true or false…?
What happened after…?

Figure 8.4 Question stem cue card

Interviewer:	I noticed that the children were using a journal to reflect on their learning.
Ms Brennan:	One student wrote: 'Thinking about questions when you are reading helps you learn new words and helps you think better about the book. You can stop and think about it. Asking questions helps you find out what tricky words mean like frankfurter – it means a type of spicy smoked sausage that was made in Frankfurt (Germany) – and like pomegranate – it means a fruit with a tough skin, reddish flesh and many seeds. It helps me understand words.'
Interviewer:	How do the children reflect on their learning?
Ms Brennan:	The children celebrated the culmination of their project with a wide audience of parents and friends during a special evening session by sharing what they had created and learned. It was evident that they were genuinely proud of their achievements and were eager to begin a new phase.
Interviewer:	What has particularly worked well in these group activities?
Ms Brennan:	The graphic organiser group worked collaboratively to construct a concept map using coloured paper circles that they Blu-Tacked onto a large sheet of cardboard. The students used a familiar text and negotiated to re-read it again independently, in pairs, all together or in small groups. They worked together to determine the main idea and identify details in the text. The students worked with a teacher aide and generated a lot of discussion while constructing their concept maps. The movable paper circles and Blu-Tack allowed the students to move information around and group it in a particular way. It also provided

the opportunity to negotiate what information should be included, taken out or expanded on. The concept maps were displayed in the classroom and provided a visual aid to assist the students when they wrote their information reports on a particular animal.

Questions

1   In what ways did Ms Brennan encourage learner independence?
2   What are the benefits of children working in groups?
3   What other activities could be incorporated into an inquiry lesson?

Independent users

Children use and apply their ICT knowledge, skills and understanding confidently and competently in their learning and in everyday contexts. They become independent and discerning users of technology, recognising opportunities and risks and using strategies to stay safe. Children should be able to:

- know how and where to find relevant information and to judge its reliability
- explore, capture, manipulate and create new forms and combinations of information that use a variety of media to investigate their environment
- share, collaborate and connect to others to reach a variety of audiences within and beyond the school environment
- take advantage of the flexible nature of the technology to explore new ways of doing things.

The following are some suggestions to encourage an inquiry-focused classroom:

- Provide frequent opportunities for children to read silently for enjoyment.
- Give choice by providing a range of books in different genres from the library and supplement these with donated books.
- Regularly rotate borrowed books and encourage independent library borrowing.
- Have book-sharing opportunities for children to tell others about their favourite books.
- Create displays, dioramas, infographics, posters, models and collections of associated objects mentioned in a story or information text.
- Have the 'book of the week' displayed and read sections from the book to 'sell the book'.

- Provide awards and rewards of various kinds.
- Have regular interviews so that each child has an opportunity to share their reading experiences with the teacher.
- Read interesting books as a serial or read interesting and descriptive passages on a regular basis to model fluent and expressive reading and to create interest for particular books.

Vignette 8.2

Ms Beard has a year 3 class and they have been studying animals and their habitats in the second term. Ms Beard wanted the children to use the Internet to locate information that they needed to develop their PowerPoint presentation, which was to be presented in front of parents during education week.

Ms Beard had prepared the children well by teaching them some basic keyboard and navigation skills that they would be required to apply when using their computers to find the relevant information. For most of the first term, the children had devoted two lessons per week in the computer lab to developing the necessary computer skills. Ms Beard showed them how to find information on the Internet using key words to do a search and to decide whether or not their Internet site gave them the answers they needed. Ms Beard used a 'think aloud' strategy to explicitly show the children what sort of thinking processes she would use in deciding if a particular Internet site was appropriate or not. She also talked about layout, position of pictures, how the information was structured, whether it was easy to navigate and whether or not she should access the hyperlinks. She also showed them how to identify key words and how to make notes from a number of websites. She also showed them how to group the key words and how to write a short paragraph using the ideas gathered from the sites. Ms Beard also discussed the notion of author authority, purpose, objectivity and durability of the information.

The children were divided into groups of three and were required to produce an interesting slide as part of a whole-class slide presentation. Each group was expected to consider the overall layout of the slide including fonts, pictures and animations. At first, the children were asked in a whole-group session to decide on the style of fonts, pictures and background so that the presentation would have some consistency across groups. A number of different styles and formats were considered until the group decided on an overall theme and style of presentation.

The children decided that they would study life forms in the local pond, which was situated in the school grounds. They collected samples, took pictures and video-recorded the sounds with some iPads (one for each group – some parents were available to help with this activity). Ms Beard helped students identify the organisms using information texts that had been supplied by the school librarian. Once the organism had been identified, further information was found on the Internet.

One advanced group of students was assigned the role of making an introduction while another group was given the summary to do. After each group had finished, the slides were put together and the children decided on the best way to sequence the slides. Many of the slides also had an interactive button that would activate an audio file of group members speaking.

Questions

1 What prerequisite skills would be needed for this type of lesson?
2 Why did Ms Beard use the 'think aloud' strategy?
3 How could you use other technology in a similar series of lessons?

Walsh (2011) has offered you, as a teacher, a note of caution when using new technologies in the classroom: 'However, it is not the technology itself that will create a vibrant, engaging learning environment but the way teachers plan and structure the learning experiences with rich language, literature and literacy practices.' Teachers can have the mistaken idea that just by using technology children will be more motivated and engaged.

The technology of print utilised the tools of pencil and paper and later the photocopier, keyboard and word processor. Often, these tools require extra learning to enable efficient operation. However, once an electronic tool has been mastered it will save time and effort and enable the literacy user to become more productive. For example, students may become curators of information as part of the inquiry process. Curation enables the learner to identify, categorise and store information in the form of an electronic memory in the 'cloud' (or Internet space). Curating can also be viewed, for example, as an expansion of the notebook tool in the medium of print. There are many Web 2.0 resources that enable curation such as ScoopIt, Drop Box, Pinterest, Tumblr and Evernote. By using these tools, children can store information and ideas or even work on collaborative texts stored in Google Docs or Drop Box. The advantage over notepaper is that projects can be accessed by anyone (with permission) at any time and in any place, thereby giving an expanded meaning to the notion of collaboration and producers of new juxtapositions of information.

Most children in school will have had significant engagement with video games online and using consoles and laptops outside school. As a consequence, there has been an increased interest in exploring ways to incorporate video games into the classroom environment (Beavis, 2012). For example, narrative-based games such as quest-based role-play games can extend certain classroom topics by simulating processes and ideas around a topical theme. They can also link with other forms of literature such as the narrative by entering into the world of a fictional character. Some games have split screens that enable the viewer to view a map, for example, to help navigate the scene. There are also many other skills that are developed incidentally while children play games: keyboard skills, hand–eye coordination, memory and perception, reading and problem solving. Many games develop social skills where children have to negotiate and make joint decisions.

Conclusion

Reading comprehension is a two-way constructive process. Readers use their own prior knowledge and skills together with their understanding of the message conveyed by the medium to develop an interpretation or situation model of the message. As such, reading instruction should engage learners as users, curators, researchers and producers of information. Reading comprehension is not only influenced by the characteristics of the learner but also by the nature of the reading material and by the instructional and task requirements. All of this is influenced by the socio-cultural context that gives meaning and relevance to any literacy activity. There are a number of variables that can impact on learner outcomes such as task, learner and activity. However, children will be more intrinsically motivated to achieve if there is an authentic purpose for the activity, learning or teaching. When literacy learning is purposeful, it enables the learner to relate to the activity and learning. However, it should also enable the learner to become competent and autonomous. Electronic modes are extensions of traditional technologies but can be more complex or more enabling.

 Discussion questions and activities

 Points for discussion

1 How do literacy teachers use new technologies in their practice?
2 What sorts of principles can guide teachers in deciding what to incorporate into their classroom practice?
3 Can technology hinder rather than help children with their literacy development?
4 In Vignette 8.1, how could Ms Brennan have incorporated new technologies into her inquiry lessons?

†††† **Group activities**

1 Discuss the importance of setting a purpose for a reading activity.
2 What variables affect student learning outcomes? What are other examples not mentioned in this chapter? Brainstorm and make a chart showing these elements.
3 Form several groups with each group pairing with another group. One group in each pair will do a group activity while the other group observes the group

behaviours while performing the task. This is what is often referred to as a fishbowl activity, designed to give feedback to the group performing the task. The task for each activity group is to build a tower using paper, paper clips and tape with a 5-minute time limit. The group with the tallest tower will be the winning group. After the first 5-minute activity, the fishbowl groups and the activity groups will swap places.

4   At the end of the activities, each group is to present its observations about the functioning of each group.

5   Following activity 3, each group is to compile a list of skills that children will need to operate successfully in a discussion group.

6   Determine the types of roles that could be assigned to group members and develop cue cards as prompts for these roles.

7   In groups, design an inquiry lesson around a particular theme and show how the iPad (supplied) could be used.

 ### Whole-class activities

1   What technologies and software do you use at home?
2   Why should we try and incorporate new technology into classroom activities?
3   How could tablets or smartphones be used in the classroom?

References

Afflerbach, P., Pearson, D. and Paris, S. G. (2008). Clarifying differences between reading skills and reading strategies. *The Reading Teacher,* 61(5), 364–373.

Alloway, T. (2011). *Improving Working Memory: Supporting Students' Learning.* London: Sage.

Ansty, M. and Bull, G. (2012). *Using Multimodal and Factual Texts during the Inquiry Process.* PETAA paper 184. Newtown, NSW: Primary English Teaching Association Australia.

Baddeley, A. (2000). The episodic buffer: a new component of working memory? *Trends in Cognitive Sciences,* 4(1), 417–423.

Baddeley, A. D. and Hitch, G. (1994). Developments in the concept of working memory. *Neuropsychology,* 8, 485–493.

Beach, S. A. (1994). Engagement with print: Motivation to read and to learn. *Reading Psychology,* 15, 69–74.

Beavis, C. (2007). Critical engagement: ICTs, literacy and curriculum. In *Australian Literacy Educators Association: The Best of Practically Primary* (pp. 17–21). Norwood, SA: ALEA.

Beavis, C. (2012). Video games in the classroom: Developing digital literacies. *Practically Primary,* 17(1), 17–20.

Bloom, B. S. (1956). *Taxonomy of Educational Objectives, Handbook 1: The Cognitive Domain.* New York: David McKay.

Cole, J. E. (2002). What motivates students to read? Four literacy personalities. *The Reading Teacher*, 56, 326–336.

Duke, N. (2004). The case for informational text. *Educational Leadership*, 61(6): 40–44.

Duke, N. K. and Pearson, P. D. (2002). Effective practices for developing reading comprehension. In A. E. Farstrup and S. J. Samuels (eds), *What Research has to Say about Reading Instruction* (3rd edn) (pp. 205–242). Newark, DE: International Reading Association.

Durrant, C. and Green, B. (2000). Literacy and the new technologies in school education: Meeting the l(IT)eracy challenge? *The Australian Journal of Language and Literacy*, 23, 89–108.

Fowler, A. (1991) *Please Don't Feed the Bears* (Rookie Read-About Science series 11). Chicago: Children's Press.

Gambrell, L. B., Kapinus, B. A. and Wilson, R. M. (1987). Using mental imagery and summarization to achieve independence in comprehension. *Journal of Reading*, 30(7), 638–642.

Gambrell, L. B., Palmer, B. M., Codling, R. M. and Mazzioni, S. A. (1996). Assessing motivation to read. *The Reading Teacher*, 49, 518–533.

Gambrell, L. B., Malloy, J. A. and Mazzoni, S. A. (2007). Evidence-based best practice for comprehensive literacy instruction. In L. B. Gambrell, L. M. Morrow and M. Pressley (eds), *Best Practices in Literacy Instruction* (3rd edn) (pp. 11–29). New York: The Guilford Press.

Gambrell, B., Mazzoni, S. A. and Almasi, J. F. (2000). Promoting collaboration, social interaction, and engagement. In L. Baker, M. J. Dreher and J. T. Guthrie (eds), *Engaging Young Readers: Promoting Achievement and Motivation* (pp. 119–139). New York: The Guilford Press.

Gersten, R., Fuchs, L. S., Williams, J. P. and Baker, S. (2001). Teaching reading comprehension strategies to students with learning disabilities: A review of research. *Review of Educational Research*, 71, 279–320.

Guthrie, J. T. and Davis, M. H. (2003). Motivating the struggling readers in middle school through an engagement model of classroom practice. *Reading and Writing Quarterly*, 19, 59–85.

Guthrie, J. T., Wigfield, A., Barbosa, P., Perencevich, K. C., Taboada, A., Davis, M. H., et al. (2004). Increasing reading comprehension and engagement through concept oriented reading instruction. *Journal of Educational Psychology*, 96(3), 403–423.

Hareli, S. and Weiner, B. (2002). Social emotions and personality inferences: A scaffold for a new direction in the study of achievement motivation. *Educational Psychologist*, 37, 183–193.

Hay, I. and Woolley, G. (2011). The challenge of reading comprehension. In T. Le, Q. Le and M. Short (eds), *Language and Literacy in a Challenging World* (pp. 197–210). New York: Nova Science Publishers.

Horner, S. L. and Shwery, C. S. (2002). Becoming an engaged, self-regulated reader. *Theory into Practice*, 41, 102–109.

Kamhi, A. and Catts, H. (2002). The language basis of reading: Implications for classification and treatment of children with reading disabilities. In K. G. Butler & E. Silliman (Eds.), *Speaking, reading, and writing in children with language learning disabilities: New paradigms in research and practice* (pp. 45–72). Mahwah, NJ: Lawrence Erlbaum Pub.

Killen, R. (2007). *Effective Teaching Strategies: Lessons from Research and Practice*. Melbourne: Thomson Science Press.

Kintsch, E. (2005). Comprehension theory as a guide for the design of thoughtful questions. *Topics in Language Disorders*, 25(1), 51–64.

Krathwohl, D. R. and Anderson, L. W. (2010). Merlin C. Wittrock and the Revision of Bloom's Taxonomy. *Educational Psychologist*, 45(1), 64–65.

Kress, G. (2003). *Literacy in the New Media Age*. London: Routledge.

Laing, S. P. and Kamhi, A. G. (2002). The use of think-aloud protocols to compare inferencing abilities in average and below-average readers. *Journal of Learning Disabilities*, 35(5), 436–447.

Linnenbrink, E. A. and Pintrich, P. R. (2002). Achievement goal theory and affect: An asymmetrical bi-directional model. *Educational Psychologist*, 37, 69–78.

National Reading Panel (NRP) (2000). *Teaching Children to Read: Report of the Comprehension Instruction Subgroup to the National Institute of Child Health and Development*. Washington, DC: NICD.

Paivio, A. (1986). *Mental Representations: A Dual-Coding Approach*. New York: Holt, Rinehart & Winston.

Paivio, A. (1991). Static versus dynamic imagery. In C. Cornoldi and M. A. Daniel (eds), *Imagery and Cognition* (pp. 221–246). New York: Springer-Verlag.

Palincsar, A. S. and Brown, A. L. (1984). Reciprocal teaching of comprehension-fostering and comprehension-monitoring activities. *Cognition and Instruction*, 1(2), 117–175.

Paris, S. G., Byrnes, J. P. and Paris, A. H. (2001). Constructing theories, identities, and actions of self-regulated learners. In B. J. Zimmerman and D. H. Schunk (eds), *Self-regulated learning and academic achievement* (pp. 253–287). New Jersey: Lawrence Erlbaum Associates.

Pearson, P. D., Hiebert, E. H. and Kamil, M. L. (2007). Vocabulary assessment: What we know and what we need to learn. *Reading Research Quarterly*, 42(2), 282–296.

Pressley, M. (2002). *Comprehension Instruction: What Makes Sense Now, What Might Make Sense Soon*. Newark, DE: International Reading Association. Available at: www.readingonline.org/articles/handbook/pressley/index.html

Roser, N., Martinez, M., Fuhrken, C. and McDonnold, K. (2007). Characters as guides to meaning. *The Reading Teacher*, 60(6), 548–559.

Ryan, R. M. and Deci, E. L. (2000). Intrinsic and extrinsic motivations: Classic definitions and new directions. *Contemporary Educational Psychology*, 25, 54–67.

Sadoski, M., Goetz, E. T. and Rodriguez, M. (2000). Engaging texts: Effects of concreteness on comprehensibility, interest, and recall in four text types. *Journal of Educational Psychology*, 92(1), 85–95.

Schunk, D. (2003). Self-efficacy for reading and writing: Influence of modelling, goal setting, and self-evaluation. *Reading and Writing Quarterly*, 19, 159–172.

Snow, C. E. (2002). *Reading for Understanding: Toward a Research and Development Program in Reading Comprehension*. Santa Monica, CA: Rand

Corp. Available at: www.rand.org/publications/MR/MR1465/ (accessed 12 December 2002).

Taboada, A. and Guthrie, J. T. (2006). Contributions of student questioning and prior knowledge to construction of knowledge from reading information text. *Journal of Literacy Research*, 38(1), 1–35.

The New London Group (2000) A pedagogy of multiliteracies: Designing social futures. In B. Cope and M. Kalanatzis (eds), *Multiliteracies: Literacy Learning and the Design of Social Futures* (pp. 9–42). Melbourne: Macmillan.

Trabasso, T. (1981). On the making of inferences during reading and their recall. In J. T. Guthrie (ed.), *Comprehension and Teaching: Research Reviews* (pp. 56–75). Chicago, IL: International Reading Association.

Troegger, D. (2011). Teaching reading strategies by using a comprehension framework. *Practically Primary*, 16(1), 10–13.

Vaughn, S., Gersten, R. and Engle, D. (2000). The underlying message in LD intervention research: Findings from research synthesis. *Exceptional Children*, 67, 99–114.

Walsh, M. (2011). *Multimodal Literacy: Researching Classroom Practice*. Newtown, NSW: Primary English Teaching Association Australia.

Woolley, G. (2007). *The COR Reading Framework*. Brisbane: Desktop Publishing.

Woolley, G. (2011). *Reading Comprehension: Assisting Children with Learning Difficulties*. Dordrecht, The Netherlands: Springer International.

Zhang, L. (2002). Thinking styles: Their relationships with node of thinking and academic performance. *Educational Psychology*, 22(3), 331–348.

Zimmerman, B. J. (2002). Becoming a self-regulated learner: An overview. *Theory into Practice*, 41, 64–70.

CHAPTER 9

DIVERSE LEARNERS AND LITERACY

Chapter objectives

- To understand the scope and nature of diversity within the modern classroom.
- To develop appropriate instructional approaches to accommodate and adjust to individual needs within the literacy learning classroom.
- To develop a repertoire of strategies to foster literacy engagement and reading independence.

 ## Key questions

1. How are literacy learners different to one another?
2. How do diverse readers engage with literacy to construct meaning?
3. How do teachers develop self-regulating strategies to promote independent learning for all students?

 Key words: accommodations, adaptations, difference, diversity, inclusion, language, literacy.

Introduction

In Chapter 5, it was shown that children's literature has the capacity to explore some of the deeper issues and attitudes in society. Many issues such as social justice, discrimination, prejudice, caring for one another and tolerance can be discussed openly in the classroom by introducing children to good quality literature. These same issues and attitudes can also be dealt with in practical ways within the classroom. Every classroom will have a diverse population of students with different backgrounds in terms of class, socio-economic circumstances, ethnic differences and (dis)abilities and gifts. In other words, the classroom is a natural platform for the ideas presented in children's literacy to be put into practice. For example, the book *Let the Balloon Go* (Southall, 1972) could be a useful starting point for creating a more tolerant and accepting classroom environment while providing a forum for developing strength of character and responsible citizenship.

There is an increasing awareness that the classroom is a diverse community of learners. You, as a classroom teacher, will be required to have the necessary skills to adjust your teaching environment to support children with individual differences. This chapter examines the learner, the learning tasks and the teaching and learning environment, and discusses the kinds of adjustments that will need to be made in terms of literacy learning. Literacy is inherently a social enterprise and as such many of the practices will have a cooperative aspect. In addressing classroom diversity, teachers of literacy will need to make some accommodations so that all children can be treated fairly within the context of the classroom. The issue of fairness should be seen in terms of giving all students equal access to the curriculum. However, many teachers have the mistaken impression that fairness means treating all students exactly the same no matter what their circumstances are. It often requires teachers to make some accommodations and adaptations within the classroom for some children so that they are able to have the opportunity to function as normally as possible.

In this chapter, there will be a discussion about how to make appropriate accommodations and adaptations within the classroom and about ways in which children can work individually and collaboratively. We will discuss the efficacy of a team approach by working with others, such as peers, helpers, teacher aides, support teachers, reading specialists, parents and school administrators.

In any classroom, there will be a diversity of learner characteristics and capabilities but learning tasks and texts are not always conducive to effective learning for every student. Good teaching requires that you are able to provide challenging materials that are age-appropriate and developmentally considerate.

> Regular schools with an inclusive curriculum are the most effective means of combating discriminatory attitudes, creating welcoming communities, building an inclusive society and achieving education for all; moreover, they provide an

effective education to the majority of children and improve the efficiency and ultimately the cost-effectiveness of the entire education system. (UNESCO, 1994: ix)

The above quote emphasises the importance of accommodating the diverse needs of children. It also highlights the benefits for the personal development of all children and society in general. For you as a teacher, it is of the utmost importance that you realise that the way in which you treat the most needy affects the overall moral and character development of all children in your care.

Diversity and inclusion

In England, as many as one fifth of all primary-aged children have been identified as having special education needs (Alexander, 2010; Rose, 2009); these figures are similar in Australia (Louden et al., 2000; Rohl and Rivalland, 2002). In most classrooms, there is a broad spectrum of learning needs and learning styles that do not necessarily fit into neat categories. You should also keep in mind that learning problems are not always entirely located within the child but may be influenced by external factors such as family experiences, school, friendships, the effectiveness of teaching methods and the wider social context that individuals are placed in. The term inclusion, however, implies that the education needs of all children should be met within the mainstream classroom.

In recent years, there has been a greater acceptance of difference in society. In the past, it was assumed that children would have to meet certain rigid expectations in the classroom. Children were often required to conform to the classroom norm or standard, whether or not they had the capability to perform to the level expected. Differences were often not tolerated and some groups, particularly those with a disability, were often excluded from having the same educational opportunities as others. As a consequence, many underachieving students dropped out early and this added to the cycle of poverty and juvenile delinquency in society. Today, in many western countries, difference is acknowledged and children with diverse needs are expected to be included in mainstream schooling. However, the inclusion of all children in literacy practices within mainstream classrooms can pose considerable challenges to most education practitioners.

One of the main theoretical frameworks driving this move towards inclusion is social constructivism, which proposes that knowledge and meaning are constructed through interactions between people and society. This guides ideas about human gender, sexuality, race, class and even what is regarded as being normal. In society, these views have changed over time and from place to place and various groups of people negotiate these meanings differently, resulting in particular actions (Carrington et al., 2012).

Changing attitudes and views of inclusion have been largely influenced by the widespread social justice movement, which has led to important changes in society, such as an acceptance of the right to vote for indigenous people and women. These changing ideas have led to anti-discrimination legislation in many countries seeking to enforce standards of behaviour in society and within school (Foreman, 2011). In most western countries, the law now expects that schools will not discriminate on the basis of gender, ethnicity and disability. This means that the social and educational needs of all children must be catered for in regular classroom settings regardless of their particular circumstances.

As human beings, we are distinguished from other animals because we use complex language to communicate with one another. It is through language that people communicate their ideas and reflect their perceptions, beliefs and understandings such as tolerance or even prejudice. Language, however, is a powerful tool that can be used to categorise and stigmatise groups of people. For example, the word 'retarded' is a label that can refer to an entire group of people, however this label can mask the unique qualities of individuals and lead to prejudice and human devaluation in many cases. Thus, it is important to view disability or even gender or socio-cultural circumstances as one aspect of a person's personality. A general principle for you to apply when using language is that the person's name should be used first and their condition second. For example, rather than saying the 'ADHD kid', it would be much more appropriate to say, 'George, who has ADHD...'. You should model this approach with your colleagues, parents and other children by avoiding using labels and by the way you speak to or address individuals within the classroom and wider school community.

Most children with a learning difficulty will experience issues with literacy. This is because reading is a cognitively demanding activity requiring a large amount of information to be processed quickly. For example, a child with dyslexia or a speech/language difficulty may need more time to process the language content. Normally, skilled readers develop automatic reading decoding and comprehension. However, this progression increasingly draws on a wide range of different language skills, presenting poorer readers with greater challenges (Droop and Verhoeven, 2003; Perfetti, 2007; Snowling et al., 2001; Van Gelderen et al., 2004). Thus, students will encounter new, unfamiliar content, more complex grammatical structures and the increasing need to use higher-level text processing skills such as inference generation and comprehension monitoring (Cain and Oakhill, 2006, 2007; Ehri and McCormick, 1998).

Learning differently

The major dilemma in regard to inclusion is reflected in the problem of conceptualising and categorising pupil differences (Alexander, 2010). In the remainder of the chapter, learner diversity will not only consider learning difficulties but will also include gifted and talented learners and learners with English as a second language. The chapter develops the notion of intervention as 'response to intervention' (RTI). This is a whole-school three-tier approach that is gaining acceptance as a process to assist those that struggle with literacy. It promotes the notion of the teacher being part of a team that includes other professionals, parents and caregivers.

It is important that children with disabilities are recognised for their strengths. A learning difficulty or disability should be seen merely as a part of the whole learner rather than as a reflection of the total person (Reid, 2013). Often, when children are assessed, the emphasis is on looking for their weaknesses, which can contribute to a negative, deficit view of the child (Alexander, 2010), where the child's problems are seen solely as being within the child. For example, sometimes children with dyslexic difficulties can be misunderstood and labelled as lazy or lacking interest. This view can lead to the victim being blamed and to professionals ignoring the fact that behaviour can be changed, for example, by adjusting the learning environment.

The categorisation of students can often cause frustration and confusion because children can exist on a broad continuum of needs that do not fit into neat classifications (Alexander, 2010). Furthermore, there is now considerable evidence, from recent research studies, that reading difficulties in most beginning readers may not be directly caused by biologically based cognitive deficits intrinsic to the child, but may in fact be related to the learning experiences provided for children learning to read (Vellutino, 2010). Thus, by providing all children with evidence-based reading instruction, the number of children who struggle with learning to read should be dramatically reduced.

However, some children do not respond adequately to the normal evidence-based pedagogy. What is required to meet each child's unique academic needs is a responsive approach that considers individual differences. Response to intervention (RTI) has gained in popularity as a general education framework in which multi-tiered evidence-based interventions are provided early to support struggling learners in general education settings (Allington, 2012; Bryant and Barrera, 2009; Reeves et al., 2010). The RTI framework ensures the provision of increasingly intensive interventions that are informed by assessment and frequent monitoring of student progress (Barge, 2012; Bryant and Barrera, 2009). Tier 1 is considered to be accessible to regular classroom education and received by all students (Barge, 2012; Bryant and Barrera, 2009). Tier 2 interventions increase in duration and intensity with progress more frequently monitored than for tier 1 interventions, and will often involve differentiated group work. Tier 3 would involve referral to a specialist learning support teacher and access to withdrawal intervention programmes.

Approximately 1.4% of children in England have educational needs severe enough to warrant an official statement of those needs and how they should be met (Alexander, 2010; Rose, 2009). Once again, these figures and the process of identification are similar in the Australian context. Normally, the learning needs of children with learning disabilities are severe enough to warrant an Independent Education Plan (IEP) or Individual Support Plan (ISP), which draws together a team of stakeholders such as education practitioners, paraprofessionals, other professionals, parents and administrators under the guidance of an assigned team manager. This process aims to identify, individualise, prioritise and simplify the teaching of the agreed essential elements of the curriculum (needed for the individual) so that all stakeholders can work in harmony.

Multi-disciplinary teams

Schools will also enhance the overall assessment and intervention process for all students with a learning difficulty by developing a team method by utilising wider sources of expertise to provide a systematic and whole-school approach. As a consequence, this should minimise the classroom teacher's over-reliance on special educators (Ortiz et al., 2006). For example, a classroom teacher may seek the assistance of the multi-disciplinary team when he/she realises that classroom-based literacy interventions are not working for a particular student. Teams should collaboratively develop solutions with the teacher to provide suitable classroom strategies to meet the needs of the student and develop a follow-up plan to monitor progress.

Cycle of failure

Falling behind can lead to a cycle of failure in literacy (see Figure 9.1). As a consequence, the student will begin to lack confidence, especially after comparing their performance to that of their more successful peers. The student may then develop anxiety and a reluctance to participate in future reading activities. They will have less motivation to try because they expect to fail and seek to avoid embarrassment, particularly if they are expected to read in front of others. Often, this leads to avoidance or other behavioural problems, and to learned helplessness. Learned-helpless students tend to think that it is better to avoid doing a learning task than to attempt the task and experience failure once again. Sometimes the 'reward' for misbehaviour is exclusion from an unwanted activity. This reinforces the behaviour and ensures the behaviour will be repeated in the future. A typical example is Emily's failure at spelling meant writing out spelling words and missing out on sport. Since she hated sport, she would deliberately fail at spelling.

These behaviours often contribute to the teacher having lower expectations of the child and lower performance goals. This becomes a self-fulfilling

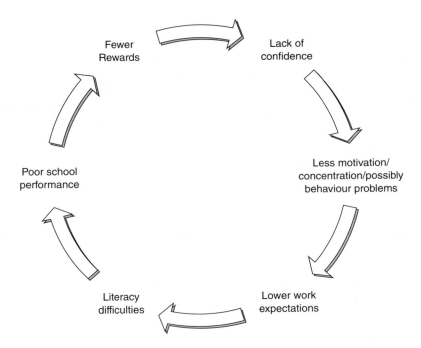

Figure 9.1 Cycle of failure

prophecy: when significant others expect less of you, you tend to meet those low expectations. This leads to further literacy difficulties: the lower reading rate leads to less exposure to new words and less reading practice (Stanovich, 1986). Thus, the gap begins to widen between those who read more and those who don't. As literacy impacts on other domains of the curriculum, the child begins to experience failure in other areas. Poor school performance leads to fewer rewards and contributes to lack of confidence and performance anxiety. And so the cycle continues, but each time round the negative cycle becomes stronger (see Figure 9.1).

Self-management

What often contributes to this cycle of failure is the notion that the student has little control over their learning. However, you as a teacher can reverse this downward trend by implementing strategies that focus more on the student's own thinking processes and knowledge of what is involved in performing a set task (Johns et al., 1994). Self-regulation refers to the learner monitoring his/her thinking actions, often through language mediation and self-monitoring of the learning process (Schunk, 2005; Zimmerman, 2002). The verbalising of thinking strategies is a self-monitoring and self-regulation strategy that enables the reader to build metacognitive understanding (Palincsar and Brown, 1984).

Students can be taught metacognitive and self-regulatory processes to promote self-management and self-determination. Instructional strategies that support self-monitoring and self-regulation are important in promoting independent and efficient learning (Schunk, 2004; Vaughn et al., 2000; Zimmerman and Schunk, 2001). Strategies that support self-management include clarifying, self-questioning and self-monitoring of comprehension, and reflection on learning (Duke and Pearson, 2002; Gersten et al., 2001; NRP, 2000; Pressley, 2002). The development of effective self-management skills by a child with a learning difficulty is one of the most important factors contributing to the successful social integration of that child into a regular classroom (Westwood, 2011). Teaching students to use metacognitive strategies encourages them to become more efficient and independent in their learning (Bos, 1999; Ernsbarger, 2002; Vaughn et al., 2000; Whitney and Bud, 1996). You as a teacher can support these metacognitive strategies by giving prompts and specific feedback and by encouraging students to reflect on the efficacy of the strategies employed.

Instruction

The indications are that children with ADHD and other less able readers have more difficulty preventing unimportant information from entering their working memory. In contrast, skilled readers are more able to inhibit or resist potential interference from irrelevant information (Bayliss et al., 2005; Kendeou and Van den Broek, 2005; Swanson et al., 1996). To reduce this cognitive overload, you as a teacher will need to focus readers' attention on the relevant text information and help them clarify the purpose of the reading task in which they are engaged (Alfassi, 2004).

Effective reading instruction also requires different kinds and amounts of learning experiences for different learners (Duke and Pearson, 2002). Think-aloud strategies can help to provide a balance of practice and explicit instruction and teachers can model thinking processes during instruction (Duke and Pearson, 2002; Zhang, 2002).

Vignette 9.1

Oliver is a year 5 student attending a co-educational public metropolitan school. Throughout his relatively short school career, Oliver has been regarded as a difficult student. In the first couple of years of formal schooling, Oliver's teachers had noticed that he was falling behind in reading and spelling and was somewhat reluctant to engage in classroom discussions. However, when questioned about social studies, science or general knowledge, he often astounded his teachers by his level of understanding and his ability to apply this knowledge to new or novel situations. He was good at mathematics, science and physical education but he particularly excelled in art. However, his poor reading and spelling skills affected some of the subjects that he normally did well in.

Most of his teachers assumed that he was a bright child but that his reading and literacy skills were retarding his academic development. By the time he had finished year 4, his teachers had tried to give him extra help in one form or another. Most of these interventions targeted his poor phonic skills and so a number of times he was included in withdrawal classes to boost his knowledge of phonics. However, Oliver did not make very good progress with these extra sessions. Some of his teachers even made remarks on his report cards such as, 'Oliver is lazy' or 'Oliver is a bright student but he does not try hard enough'. He repeated year 3 because it was felt that the extra year would help him catch up to his peers. By the end of the extra year, he had made very little progress.

By year 5, Oliver was resigned to the fact that he was behind in these vital areas of the curriculum but had gained the impression that he was just dumb and that for some unknown reason he was not able to learn. His constant failure had dampened his enthusiasm to try in literacy tasks that he knew he could not do well in. In some areas of the curriculum, he had developed learned helplessness and preferred to avoid doing tasks that would reinforce this perception of being dumb. Sometimes he would even misbehave to avoid doing these onerous tasks.

In the middle of year 5, however, Oliver's academic performance was showing signs of improvement, particularly in English, reading and spelling. Along with this, his attitude to work had changed in that he was now willing to give most activities a try. He appeared to be much more motivated and expressed a particular connection to his teacher who had given Oliver some targeted help.

At the beginning of the year, Oliver's teacher, Mr Thomson, had noticed that Oliver was very bright and could not understand why he was so far behind in his literacy and spelling skills. After Mr Thomson had interviewed some of his former teachers and his parents, he decided to use a different approach to accommodate Oliver's learning style. As an experienced year 5 teacher, Mr Thomson could see that Oliver was a predominantly visual learner and had difficulty hearing sounds correctly and following aural instructions. Consequently, he decided to introduce Oliver to some visual techniques that he could use to help him focus his attention, listen to instructions and guide his reading and study skills.

In class, Oliver was seated near the front so that he could hear the instructions and explanations more clearly while being delivered in simpler sentences. Where possible, Mr Thomson would reinforce what was said in class by writing the instructions on the board in short sentences as sequential numbered points. These instructions were often supplemented by diagrams or by highlighting key points with coloured markers on the whiteboard. The other children also

(Continued)

(Continued)

seemed to appreciate the accommodations because the ideas were presented to them more clearly. The teacher also introduced the 'look, cover, write, check' method of learning spelling words to the class. Sometimes Mr Thomson would supplement this spelling method by having Oliver write in shaving foam on the table or write the word in the air or close his eyes and imagine what the word looked like.

He also taught Oliver some study skills that would help him visualise ideas and concepts. For example, he taught him about top-level structuring – a technique in which graphic organisers are used to show how different genres are structured and organised. Main idea sentences were also identified and highlighted along with key words. Mr Thomson showed Oliver how these ideas could be used in his own made-up diagrams and sketches. He also showed him how to organise his notes in the form of an anagram as an aide to remembering key points.

In spelling, he showed him how to break a word up into syllables and to decide which graphic representation would be the best one for the particular word. For example, Oliver was asked to write the word several times by writing the difficult syllable or syllables in different ways. He was then asked to highlight the word form that looked closest to the targeted word. These techniques were taught to the whole class because Mr Thomson felt that it would benefit all of the students.

By the end of the year, Oliver's academic report had acknowledged a big improvement as reflected in class and across grade assessments. His parents were very pleased with his progress and had higher expectations than before for Oliver's future academic progress (as did Oliver).

Questions

1   Why had Oliver been lagging behind for so long?
2   Why did Mr Thomson's teaching methods work for Oliver?
3   Can you think of examples from your own experience that seem to echo this vignette which you can relate to the rest of the group?

Gender, digital divide and literacy

In the past few decades, there has been an emphasis on eliminating gender inequality in schools. This has had some very positive gains, particularly for girls. There are now more girls moving into tertiary education with increasing numbers of girls opting for further study in mathematics and science, previously dominated by boys. There has also been an emphasis on eliminating stereotypical gender role models in books and on the elimination of language that supports this stereotyping.

While there have been gains for girls, boys are now consistently showing poorer attainment than girls in English, reading and literacy in general. Boys, as mentioned earlier, have long been disproportionately represented in most forms of special education but have dominated the higher levels of classroom performance. Recently, the number of boys performing at high levels has been steadily declining. It would appear that this decline might be explained by social and environmental factors rather than by differences in cognitive reasoning abilities (Alexander, 2010). It is thought that the model of masculinity most often presented to boys in the media and on the sporting field is one that often dismisses books and reading as being inherently feminine: boys develop a poor attitude to books, reading and possibly schooling altogether. Furthermore, masculinity is often judged by what a boy can do rather than by what he knows. His prowess on the sporting field or in computer games seems to be all-important. The biggest challenge, then, is to show boys that reading does not threaten their masculinity and in fact can develop strength of character, a sense of personal and collective responsibility, a compassionate outlook, a tolerance to difference, etc. Hawkes (2001) has suggested that schools are not boy-friendly: schools can fail to cater for the different learning style of many boys. Alarming numbers of boys are becoming distant from reading, being diagnosed with learning and emotional problems and dropping out of school (Zambo, 2007). In fact, three times as many boys as girls are placed into learning disability programmes in schools, and 70–80% of these students are found to be lacking in motivation (Gurian and Henley, 2001; Kush and Watkins, 1996).

Because reading and writing are often perceived as activities for girls, men who read can be valuable role models for both boys and girls. This is highlighted by the fact that most primary school teachers are female. To circumvent this situation, teachers can invite men and boys who enjoy reading and writing to share their literacy experiences with the class (Senn, 2012).

Boys tend to enjoy non-fiction and are attracted to books that have high visual appeal. The school librarian should be able to provide a wide variety of non-fiction books that focus on areas of particular interest and/or classroom themes. Fiction books by male authors featuring male characters that appeal to the interest areas of boys can also be included. Wherever possible, boys should be provided with access to technology and with opportunities to be more actively engaged in activities that involve reading. Boys generally enjoy humorous books, magazines, newspapers, comics and graphic novels, and should be given the opportunity to choose their own topics, to collaborate and share their ideas with others.

ESL/EFL learners

The proportion of children who have a first language other than English has been steadily increasing in British schools (Alexander, 2010; Rose, 2009) over the last few decades and this has given teachers added challenges. In

Australia, there has always been a high proportion of English-as-a-second-language (ESL) or English-as-a-foreign-language (EFL) learners. Normally, it takes several years for such students to gain English-language proficiency.

Some facets of English print, such as phonemic awareness, can be quite challenging for these students. Phonological awareness has a strong relationship to word-level reading skills and this is more evident in the first few years of formal reading instruction (Lindsey et al., 2003; Verhoeven, 2000; Wade-Woolley and Geva, 2000). However, second-language (L2) learners are generally less capable of discriminating between sounds in the second language than first-language (L1) learners, particularly when phonological elements that are specific to the second language are met with (Verhoeven, 2000; Wade-Woolley and Geva, 2000). Consequently, L2 learners would not be expected to achieve the same level of automaticity as L1 learners, particularly since English is a non-transparent language and one of the hardest languages to master (Verhoeven, 2000). Normally, this disadvantage dissipates after two to three years of reading instruction (Lindsey et al., 2003; Lipka and Siegel, 2007; Verhoeven, 2000).

You need to be aware that even though ESLs may have enough L2 language skills to function reasonably well in the playground, they may lack the depth of language expected in the classroom. Thus, teacher observations and thorough assessments that draw on multiple sources of evidence should provide you with the appropriate information to adjust the curriculum to suit their unique educational needs (Deponio et al., 2000; Lindsey et al., 2003; Spinelli, 2008).

Gifted and talented students

In recent years, it has been recognised that gifted and talented children may need special arrangements (Alexander, 2010). Children exist on a broad continuum of needs and learning styles that do not fit into neat categories. An inclusive approach in your classroom would cater for all children irrespective of their level of ability or disability. For this reason, schools should individualise the curriculum for a whole range of students, including those who are gifted and talented. Many of these students, out of the fear of being different, often try to hide the fact that they are gifted or have talents that normally make them stand out amongst their peers. Some are teased or bullied while others become bored and uninterested in the curriculum (Foreman, 2011). The challenge will be to extend these children within the classroom without creating an entirely separate curriculum.

Multiple intelligences

In your classroom, you will have children who learn differently: normally, children have strengths in different areas. Howard Gardner challenged the notion of intelligence when he developed the multiple intelligences model

(1993). Gardner maintained that you, as a teacher, should be able to strategically use activities that require one or more intelligences to develop and enhance children's cognitive strengths and develop their creativity.

The following list gives examples of teaching ideas for Gardner's multiple intelligences:

- *linguistic:* respond to a text you are reading by writing a poem
- *musical:* compose and perform a song about a character from a book
- *logical-mathematical:* at the end of the year, survey your classmates about the top ten books; kelly, graph and present your results
- *spatial:* draw a map of the characters' journey throughout the book
- *bodily/kinesthetic:* play charades with book titles and favourite characters
- *interpersonal:* co-work in a small group to present a readers' theatre performance
- *intrapersonal:* read silently and independently and respond to your book in a personal way
- *naturalistic:* after reading books about animals, make a chart to classify the different types of animals.

By offering all your students opportunities to engage in a range of literacy learning experiences across the intelligences, you will begin to see which students have particular talents (Farris et al., 2004).

Pedagogical practices that can provide a challenge within the classroom include: questioning based on Bloom's taxonomy, using open-ended questions, debating, philosophy discussions, project extension activities, the Gardiner–Bloom matrix (see Chapter 10), computer simulation games, programming, etc.

Texts

When selecting suitable texts, you should take into consideration the complexity of the texts and their semantic density. Obviously, gifted students will need engaging texts where they can learn new vocabulary and be challenged by new ideas. The ability to read with ease is determined by factors related to the text and also by what the reader brings to the reading task. For example, interests, background knowledge and reading goals facilitate the integration of propositions and text information into readers' understanding. When choosing a particular text, a teacher needs to consider a number of text features, such as the complexity of the language, vocabulary, sentence structure, causal relationships, illustrations and genre structure. Since the reading process involves readers bringing meaning to print, other factors within the reader also need to be considered: interest, topic familiarity and reading ability. These principles apply to all readers regardless of their ability level. A discussion about the promotion of children's literature and the importance of choosing texts that are rich in language and imagination will give balance to what would seem to be a very technical discussion about readability issues (see Chapter 11).

Modes of learning

Traditional teaching methods have tended to favour analytical thinkers while penalising holistic thinkers. Often, traditional teaching methods are suited to those students who have thinking styles similar to their teachers (Zhang, 2002). The three modes of thinking are: the holistic (originally referred to as right-brained dominance); the analytic (originally left-brained dominance); and the integrative (originally whole-brained). Kozhevnikov et al. (2002) also identified three groups of learners based on their learning style preferences. The first group, the geometric type, are those who prefer to use imagery. The second group, the analytic type, consists of people who prefer verbal-logical modes when attempting to solve problems. The third group, the harmonic type, consists of individuals who have no tendency one way or the other and use both images and verbal codes equally. Both studies demonstrate that matching individual student learning style preferences with complementary instruction improves academic achievement and attitudes towards learning for all students (Cano-Garcia and Hughes, 2000; Lovelace, 2005; Zhang, 2002).

A student's academic achievement can also be influenced by personal preferences such as environmental, emotional, social, perceptual, physiological and psychological conditions and their ability to master new and difficult academic tasks (Lovelace, 2005). The first level of preferences is biological, such as a penchant for noisy or quiet environments. The second level includes emotional elements like the desire to persist rather than take a break. The third preference is sociological and reflects the individual's predisposition to work alone, in pairs, in a group or with an adult. The fourth and fifth levels correspond more closely to personality modes and thinking styles (Dunn and Dunn, 1981). For example, a student with ADHD may have a visual learning style and a learning preference for a quiet environment, so elimination of visual distractions and extraneous noise would be a priority. To complement this, for example, you as the teacher could use clear and simple explanations that are accompanied by visual prompts or diagrams.

Vignette 9.2

Sarah, a year 3 student, excelled in reading, English, music and public speaking; in class she would often finish her work well before the other children. Her teacher would give her extra work to keep her occupied. This seemed to partly solve the problem of her behaviour because while she was occupied she would not distract the other children. However, her parents made an appointment with her teacher, Ms Blainey, earlier in the year because even though she was doing well in class her parents reported that she was often bored and needed extending. The learning support teacher was also at the meeting and together they discussed the possibility of accelerating her into the next grade. However, her parents were not keen on this option because they felt that she wasn't as mature as the children in the grade above and her social development was a priority. It was decided that she would stay in year 3 and be given the same work as the other children but that she would also be given extended open-ended activities that would be challenging but not overlap with the next year level.

The school had other programmes to supplement the activities within the class. For example, Sarah was asked to join the year 5 debating team and was encouraged to attend the after-school viola class and to join the school orchestra. After the meeting with the teachers, her father decided to attend the local public speaking group, called Toast-masters, with her to encourage her oral skills. This was supplemented in the classroom by having her research the topics in the library with the teacher aide and some gifted students from other classes.

In the classroom, she was given a contract or an agreed independent project to complete. This was extended to all students in the class, and, to facilitate this, a Bloom–Gardiner matrix was used to give the students some guidelines as to what sort of activities to put in their contract (see Chapter 10). Some of the less capable students were encouraged to select activities that were challenging but within their ability to do well. Sarah and some other students were encouraged to select higher-order thinking activities and to work towards a more intense project. So that the teacher could manage this, she asked a mentor with particular expertise to help Sarah work towards displaying her project and present a 5-minute speech about the project at a special awards night for students who had excelled in some area of study. Sarah made a study of the history of the viola and wrote a musical score to be presented with her talk.

When asking questions in the classroom, the teacher made sure that many of the questions were open-ended so that Sarah and other students could more easily contribute their own ideas. This approach was used in literacy circles when studying children's literature and seemed to benefit the rest of the class as evidenced by their keenness to add their own ideas and thoughts. It also seemed to lift the overall tone of the classroom: some students commented that the teacher was always interested in their ideas. As a result, many of the classroom projects were generated in this way. Not only did Sarah's motivation improve, but other children in the class also showed improvement in many aspects of the curriculum.

Questions

1   When might it be appropriate for a child experiencing difficulties in the classroom to repeat a year?
2   Why was the social aspect of Sarah's education so important?
3   Why do you think that the other children responded well to Ms Blainey's classroom accommodations?

Classroom accommodations and adaptations

There are many ways for you to adapt the classroom curriculum to accommodate individual differences (see Table 9.1). These adjustments will not only support the learning needs of the relevant individuals but may also be beneficial to the other children in the class. For example, a student with speech language difficulties may need to have instructions stated in shorter sentences, accompanied by having the instructions written on the board. Obviously, this teaching strategy will help all children because it gives clarity and makes instruction more explicit.

Table 9.1 Making adaptations in the classroom

Variables affecting performance	Accommodations	Examples of adaptations
Content	How	Establish a daily routine, make a contract and reinforce with rewards, use choice where possible.
	Where	Provide specific places to hand in work or to find materials, keep the layout and format of work consistent.
	What	Before students encounter new material, discuss the new vocabulary, use a feature analysis chart, use concept maps, show how to use an online dictionary, show how to use the context to work out meaning.
		Discuss the content with students before reading, provide top-level structuring, use diagrams and coloured markers to highlight important information, use supplementary material dealing with the same topic, use repeated readings, provide audio tapes or CDs of the text.
Process	Attention focus	Break the instructions into short sentences, follow a routine, write instructions on the whiteboard, ask the child to articulate the instructions, prioritise steps in completing assignments, provide a checklist, assign a teacher aide as a guide.
	Procedural processes	Use cooperative group activities/note-taking skills, have students submit a draft before handing in assignments, give extra time on learning tasks, reduce the amount of content, assign a peer helper or work in a small group, use worksheets that require minimal writing, use alternative ways to present new knowledge.
	Comprehension	Discuss pictures, use graphic organisers, use reading guides, teach skimming and scanning skills, use reciprocal teaching techniques, use self-monitoring (see below).
	Self-monitoring procedures	Set goals, ensure that students are familiar with the procedures, provide advanced notes, teach self-monitoring techniques, self-monitor progress, use checklists, give specific and targeted feedback, reflect on outcomes and apply insights.

Variables affecting performance	Accommodations	Examples of adaptations
Product	Content development	Allow alternative formats for products of work, use a voice-to-text-conversion computer program, use the cloze procedure by placing only the important information in the gaps.
Purpose	Differentiation and quality	Use real-world tasks, allow for spelling errors, use peer helper or teacher aide as a scribe, use a word processor with a spell checker.

Source: Polloway et al., 2013; Shaddock et al., 2007; Woolley, 2011

Motivation

'He doesn't seem to be motivated.' This is a comment frequently found on report cards for children who struggle with literacy. Many teachers and parents maintain the mistaken belief that student motivation is a global personality trait and hence students are either motivated or unmotivated across all domains of learning (Bong, 2004). What is certain is that motivation is strongly influenced by the kinds of experiences children have at school. Furthermore, we know that young children's competency beliefs and intrinsic motivation are differentiated across subject areas (Wigfield et al., 2004). They often form motivational beliefs and attitudes that are subject-specific and some beliefs generalise more than others across different learning situations (Bong, 2004). To some extent, this may be related to their preferred thinking styles.

Often, what is not understood is that motivation is dependent on the student's level of competency. Motivation is also influenced by autonomy and relatedness (See Chapter 8). Autonomy is enhanced when teachers provide children with meaningful choices of learning activities based on their individual learning styles or preferences within a lesson. Thus, when children exercise choice they are more likely to perceive that they have control over their learning. As a result, they will be more intrinsically motivated and engage more deeply with the reading activity (Guthrie and Davis, 2003; Wigfield et al., 2004). Engaged readers tend to be more deeply involved in their learning and apply more effort which is likely to persist over time (Ryan and Deci, 2000; Wigfield et al., 2004). Improved literacy outcomes are observed when teachers provide choices that capitalise on children's thinking styles: children tend to be more creative and persist at higher levels of complexity (Zhang and Sternberg, 2005).

When most children read informational text, they do so for an authentic purpose – to obtain information that they want or need to know. Some aspects of reading motivation may be unique to reading, such as the social aspects of sharing books with others or the experience of getting totally involved in a captivating book (Wigfield et al., 2004). Instruction that emphasises reading to learn and the sharing of information with others has proven effective in increasing students' engagement, application of strategies and comprehension (Duke, 2004; Guthrie and Davis, 2003). The depth of children's understanding and motivation to read can be enhanced when the goal of reading is to share information from expository text in some meaningful way. For example, children can choose to present information using a multimedia presentation. Activities that focus on tasks that appeal to their preferred learning style can enhance students' motivation to achieve because they are intrinsically interesting (Hattie, 1992; Zhang, 2002).

Conclusion

Within most classrooms in western countries, there are diverse populations. Many of the factors that lead to a student's underachievement at school are found within them as individuals but there are some factors – such as the type of teaching, and social or ethnic circumstances – that are located outside of the learner. This situation often requires adaptations and accommodations to the curriculum to enable all students to attain academic outcomes consistent with their potential.

 Discussion questions and activities

 Points for discussion

1 Why should students with disabilities be included in the regular classroom?
2 What is meant by a team approach and how should it be applied in the regular classroom? Give examples from your experience.
3 Give an example of a child learning differently and how the curriculum was/ was not adjusted/differentiated to accommodate their needs.

†††† Group activities

1 In groups, ask students to think of a child in a class they have visited and to give an outline of their strengths and educational needs. Brainstorm ideas by noting key words in three columns: strengths, weaknesses and classroom adaptations.
2 Alternatively, present the group with a scenario and do the same as above.
3 Use Gardner's multiple intelligences to differentiate instruction in the classroom. In groups, plan and develop suitable literacy activities for a particular theme at an assigned grade level. Come together as a whole class with each group presenting their unit of work.
4 After completing activity 3, show how you would adapt the activities for a child with fine motor difficulties, with ADHD, with dyslexia, that is gifted and

talented or with ESL. Each group could choose one of these conditions and report back to the whole group with their adaptations.

⊞ **Whole-class activity**

1 Obtain the book *Let the Balloon Go* (Southall, 1972) (or some other book with a disability or learning difficulty theme), divide into groups of about eight and simulate a literacy circle in the primary classroom.

Ask:

(a) How is the topic sensitively presented in the book?
(b) If you had a student with a disability in the class, would you discuss their situation with the class? If so, how would you do this?
(c) Do you think that books, films and interviews are good ways to promote social justice?
(d) Can you give examples of how literacy has influenced your own views?
(e) How would you assist a child with vision impairment when working with a novel in class?
(f) What is intrinsic motivation and how can this support children who have become learned-helpless?

References

Alexander, R. (ed.) (2010). *Children, their World, their Education: Final Report and Recommendations of the Alexander 2010 Primary Review*. Oxon: Routledge.

Alfassi, M. (2004). Reading to learn: Effects of combined strategy instruction on high school students. *Journal of Educational Research*, 97, 171–184.

Allington, R. (2012). Struggling does not mean learning disabled. *Reading Today*, 29(5), 35.

Barge, E. T. (2012). Teacher empowerment in the implementation of response to intervention: A case study. A dissertation presented in partial fulfilment of the requirements for the degree of Doctor of Education, Liberty University, Lynchburg, VA.

Bayliss, D. M., Jarrold, C., Baddeley, A. D. and Leigh, E. (2005). Differential constraints on the working memory and reading abilities of individuals with learning difficulties and typically developing children. *Journal of Experimental Child Psychology*, 92, 76–99.

Bong, M. (2004). Academic motivation in self-efficacy, task value, achievement goal orientations, and attributional beliefs. *Journal of Educational Research*, 97(6), 287–297.

Bos, C. S. (1999). Informed flexible teaching: Promoting student advocacy and action. In P. Westwood and W. Scott (eds), *Learning Disabilities: Advocacy and Action* (pp. 9–20). Melbourne: Australian Resource Educators' Association.

Bryant, D. P. and Barrera, M. (2009). Changing roles for educators within the framework of Response-to-Intervention. *Intervention in School and Clinic*, 45(1), 72–79.

Cain, K. and Oakhill, J. (2006). Assessment matters: Issues in the measurement of reading comprehension. *British Journal of Educational Psychology*, 76, 683–696.

Cain, K. and Oakhill, J. (2007). Reading comprehension difficulties: Correlates, causes, and consequences. In K. Cain and J. Oakhill (eds), *Students' Comprehension Problems in Oral and Written Language: A Cognitive Perspective* (pp. 41–75). London: The Guilford Press.

Cano-Garcia, F. and Hughes, E. H. (2000). Learning and thinking styles: An analysis of their interrelationship and influence on academic achievement. *Educational Psychology*, 20(4), 413–428.

Carrington, S., McArthur, J., Kearney, A., Kimber, M., Mercer, L., Morton, M., et al. (2012). Towards an inclusive education for all. In S. Carrington and J. McArthur (eds), *Teaching in Inclusive School Communities* (pp. 3–38). Milton, Australia: John Wiley & Sons.

Deponio, P., Landon, J., Mullin, K. and Reid, G. (2000). An audit of the processes involved in identifying and assessing bilingual learners suspected of being dyslexic: A Scottish study. *Dyslexia*, 6, 29–41.

Droop, M. and Verhoeven, L. (2003). Language proficiency and reading ability in first- and second-language learners. *Reading Research Quarterly*, 38(1), 78–103.

Duke, N. K. (2004). The case for informational text. *Educational Leadership*, 61(6), 40–4.

Duke, N. K. and Pearson, P. D. (2002). Effective practices for developing reading comprehension. In A. E. Farstrup and S. J. Samuels (eds), *What Research has to Say about Reading Instruction* (3rd edn) (pp. 205–242). Newark, DE: International Reading Association.

Dunn, L. M. and Dunn, L. M. (1981). *Peabody Picture Vocabulary Test – Revised*. Circle Pines, MN: American Guidance Service.

Ehri, L. C. and McCormick, S. (1998). Phases of word learning: Implications for instruction with delayed and disabled readers. *Reading and Writing Quarterly*, 4(2), 135–163.

Ernsbarger, S. C. (2002). Simple, affordable, and effective strategies for prompting reading behaviour. *Reading and Writing Quarterly*, 18, 279–284.

Farris, P. J., Fuhler, C. J. and Walther, M. P. (2004). *Teaching Reading: A Balanced Approach for Today's Classrooms*. Boston: McGraw-Hill.

Foreman, P. (ed.) (2011). *Inclusion in Action* (3rd edn.) Melbourne: Cengage.

Gardner, H. (1993). *Multiple Intelligences: The Theory into Practice*. New York: Basic Books.

Gersten, R., Fuchs, L. S., Williams, J. P. and Baker, S. (2001). Teaching reading comprehension strategies to students with learning disabilities: A review of research. *Review of Educational Research*, 71, 279–320.

Gurian, M. and Henley, P. (2001). *Boys and Girls Learn Differently: A Guide for Teachers and Parents*. San Francisco: Jossey-Bass.

Guthrie, J. T. and Davis, M. H. (2003). Motivating the struggling readers in middle school through an engagement model of classroom practice. *Reading and Writing Quarterly*, 19, 59–85.

Hattie, J. A. (1992). *Self-concept*. Hillsdale, NJ: Erlbaum.

Hawkes, T. (2001). *Boy oh Boy: How to Raise and Educate Boys*. Frenchs Forest, NSW: Prentice Hall.

Johns, J. L., Van Leirsburg, P. and Davis, S. L. (1994). *Improving Reading: A Handbook of Strategies*. Dubuque, IA: Kendall/Hunt.

Kendeou, P. and Van den Broek, P. (2005). The effects of readers' misconceptions on comprehension of scientific text. *Journal of Educational Psychology*, 97, 235–245.

Kozhevnikov, M., Hegarty, M. and Mayer, R. (2002). Revising the visualizer-verbalizer dimension: Evidence for two types of visualizers. *Cognition and Instruction*, 20(1), 47–77.

Kush, J. C. and Watkins, M. W. (1996). Long-term stability of children's attitudes towards reading. *Journal of Educational Research*, 89(5), 315–319.

Lindsey, K. A., Manis, F. R. and Bailey, C. E. (2003). Prediction of first-grade reading in Spanish-speaking English-language learners. *Journal of Educational Psychology*, 95(3), 482–494.

Lipka, O. and Siegel, L. S. (2007). The development of reading skills in children with English as a second language. *Scientific Studies of Reading*, 11(2), 105–131.

Louden, W., Chan, L. K. S., Elkins, J., Greaves, D., House, H., Milton, M., et al. (2000). *Mapping the Territory: Primary Students with Learning Difficulties – Literacy and Numeracy* (vols 1, 2 and 3). Canberra, ACT: Department of Education, Training and Youth Affairs.

Lovelace, M. K. (2005). Meta-analysis of experimental research based on the Dunn and Dunn model. *Journal of Educational Research*, 98(3), 176–183.

National Reading Panel (NRP) (2000). *Teaching Children to Read: Report of the Comprehension Instruction Subgroup to the National Institute of Child Health and Development*. Washington, DC: NICD.

Ortiz, A. A., Wilkinson, C. Y., Robinson-Courtney, P. and Kushner, M. (2006). Considerations in implementing intervention assistance teams to support English language learners. *Remedial and Special Education*, 27(1), 53–63.

Palincsar, A. S. and Brown, A. L. (1984). Reciprocal teaching of comprehension-fostering and comprehension-monitoring activities. *Cognition and Instruction*, 1, 117–175.

Perfetti, C. (2007). Reading ability: Lexical quality to comprehension. *Scientific Studies of Reading*, 11(4), 357–383.

Pressley, M. (2002). Metacognition and self-regulated comprehension. In A. E. Farstrup and S. J. Samuels (eds), *What Research has to say about Reading Instruction* (3rd ed, pp 291–309). Network, D1: International Reading Association.

Reeves, S., Bishop, J. and Filce, H.G. (2010). Response to intervention (RtI) and tier systems: Questions remain as educators make challenging decisions. *Delta Kappa Gamma Bulletin*, 76(4), 30–35.

Reid, G. (2013). *Dyslexia and Inclusion* (2nd edn). London: Routledge.

Rohl, M. and Rivalland, J. (2002). Literacy learning difficulties in Australian primary schools: Who are the children identified and how do their schools and teachers support them? *Australian Journal of Language and Literacy*, 25, 19–40.

Rose, J. (2009). *Independent Review of the Primary Curriculum: Final Report.* Nottingham: DCSF Publications.

Ryan, R. M. and Deci, E. L. (2000). Intrinsic and extrinsic motivations: Classic definitions and new directions. *Contemporary Educational Psychology*, 25, 54–67.

Schunk, D. H. (2004). Learning theories: An educational perspective (4th edn). Saddle River, NJ: Pearson.

Schunk, D. H. (2005). Commentary on self-regulation in school contexts. *Learning and Instruction*, 15, 173–177.

Senn, N. (2012). Effective approaches to motivate and engage reluctant boys in literacy. *The Reading Teacher*, 66(3), 211–220.

Shaddock, A., Giorcelli, L. and Smith, S. (2007). *Students with Disabilities in the Mainstream Classrooms: A Resource for Teachers.* Canberra: Department of Education Employment and Workplace Relations, Australian Government.

Snowling, M. J., Adams, J. W., Bishop, D. V. M. and Stothard, S. E. (2001). Educational attainments of school leavers with a preschool history of speech-language impairments. *International Journal of Language and Communication Disorders*, 36, 173–183.

Southall, I. (1972) *Let the Balloon Go.* Harmondsworth: Penguin.

Spinelli, C. G. (2008). Addressing the issue of cultural and linguistic diversity and assessment: Informal evaluation measures for English language learners. *Reading and Writing Quarterly*, 24, 101–118.

Stanovich, K. E. (1986). Matthew effects in reading: Some consequences of individual differences in the acquisition of literacy. *Reading Research Quarterly*, 21, 360–407.

Swanson, H. L., Ashbaker, M. H. and Lee, C. (1996). Learning-disabled readers' working memory as a function of processing demands. *Journal of Experimental Child Psychology*, 61, 242–275.

United Nations Educational, Scientific and Cultural Organisation (UNESCO) (1994). *Salamanca Statement and Framework for Action on Special Needs Education.* Paris: United Nations.

Van Gelderen, A., Schoonen, R., de Glopper, K., Hulstijn, J., Simis, A., Snellings, P., et al. (2004). Linguistic knowledge, processing speed, and metacognitive knowledge in first- and second-language reading comprehension: A componential analysis. *Journal of Educational Psychology*, 96(1), 19–30.

Vaughn, S., Gersten, R. and Engle, D. (2000). The underlying message in LD intervention research: Findings from research synthesis. *Exceptional Children*, 67, 99–114.

Vellutino, F. R. (2010). Learning to be learning disabled: Marie Clay's seminal contribution to the response to intervention approach to identifying specific reading disability. *Journal of Reading Recovery* (fall), 5–23.

Verhoeven, L. (2000). Components in early second language reading and spelling. *Scientific Studies of Reading*, 4(4), 313–330.

Wade-Woolley, L. and Geva, E. (2000). Processing phonemic contrasts in the acquisition of L2 word reading. *Scientific Studies of Reading*, 4(4), 295–311.

Westwood, P. (2011). *Commonsense Methods for Children with Special Educational Needs: Strategies for the Regular Classroom* (6th edn). London: Routledge.

Whitney, P. and Budd, D. (1996). Think-aloud protocols and the study of comprehension. *Discourse Processes*, 21, 341–351.

Wigfield, A., Guthrie, J. T., Tonks, S. and Perencevich, K. C. (2004). Children's motivation for reading: Domain specificity and instructional influences. *Journal of Educational Research*, 97(6), 299–309.

Woolley, G. (2011). *Reading Comprehension: Assisting Children with Learning Difficulties*. Dordrecht, The Netherlands: Springer International.

Zambo, D. (2007). Using picture books to provide archetypes to young boys: Extending the ideas of William Brozo. *The Reading Teacher*, 61(2), 124–131.

Zhang, L. (2002). Thinking styles: Their relationships with node of thinking and academic performance. *Educational Psychology*, 22(3), 331–348.

Zhang, L. and Sternberg, R. J. (2005). A threefold model of intellectual styles. *Educational Psychology Review*, 17(1), 1–53.

Zimmerman, B. J. (2002). Becoming a self-regulated learner: An overview. *Theory into Practice*, 41, 64–70.

Zimmerman, B. J. and Schunk, D. H. (2001). Reflections on theories of self-regulated learning and academic achievement. In B. J. Zimmerman and D. H. Schunk (eds), *Self-regulated Learning and Academic Achievement* (pp. 289–307). Hillsdale, NJ: Erlbaum.

CHAPTER 10

PLANNING, ORGANISATION AND LITERACY ENGAGEMENT

Chapter objectives

- To understand how the organisation of the classroom environment impacts on learning.
- To understand how connectedness is an important element within the social environment of the classroom.
- To develop knowledge about the ways in which pedagogical methods can be structured and employed to develop intellectual quality.
- To develop a repertoire of strategies to foster literacy engagement using students' individual learning styles.

Key questions

1. How can you become proactive as a teacher?
2. How can you organise your classroom and resources to support the diverse needs of your students?
3. How do literacy learners engage with a unit of work to develop levels of intellectual quality?

Key words: goals, group work, learning environment, organisation, planning, strategies.

Introduction

There are two aspects to planning and organising classroom lessons: the learning intention and the success criterion. The first aspect relates to clear and transparent learning aims. The second aspect relates to having a way of knowing that the desired learning has been achieved. In other words, teachers need to know what the learning goals should be and they need to know how to evaluate these goals (Hattie, 2012). This chapter will focus on how you can establish appropriate learning and teaching goals, while Chapter 11 ('Assessment') will focus on the second aspect of evaluation.

> A 'learning-friendly' environment is 'child-friendly' and 'teacher-friendly'. It stresses the importance of students and teachers learning together as a learning community. It places children at the centre of learning and encourages their active participation in learning. It also fulfils the needs and interests of teachers, so that they want to and are capable of giving children the best education possible. (UNESCO, 2004: 4)

This quote from UNESCO makes it clear that you should be proactive in making your classroom an interesting place where your students are at the centre of learning activities. Furthermore, student enthusiasm is more likely to be generated within a collaborative learning community where the participants support one another. As a result, students will be more likely to be on-task and well behaved (Churchill et al., 2011).

To become a proactive teacher, you will need to develop productive pedagogies of practice to engage your students. Pedagogy comes from the Greek word, *paidagogas*, which means 'to lead the child'. It incorporates the ways in which you interact with your students and foster their interests by asking appropriate questions. Good organisation considers complex social relationships and the complex processes by which students create new knowledge. For you to use pedagogy productively in the classroom, you need to develop four elements: a supportive classroom environment; a connected community of learners; the promotion of intellectual quality; and a recognition of the diverse learning styles of your students.

Supportive classroom environments

You will be more likely to provide a motivating and engaging instructional classroom environment when it is characterised by a clear and explicit organisational arrangement that allocates space efficiently, along with well-defined boundaries, rules, directions, schedules and familiar routines. Such a learning environment will develop coherent knowledge, skills and structures that encourage social interaction, collaboration and joint construction of new meanings, while supporting individual literacy learners and their progress towards self-regulation (Zimmerman, 2002). In this, you will need to provide the essentials for the development of different forms of literacy practices and instructional techniques by scheduling time and resources appropriately.

A crucial issue is that the students need to know what the learning goals are and the criteria on which they will be assessed. As a new teacher, thorough planning will enable you to teach well and ensure you experience success. This means that you have to design a series of organisational steps and record the necessary information to allow you to implement your teaching programme. With experience, you will develop effective techniques that will streamline your planning. However, it must be emphasised that there is never a point at which planning is not necessary (Killen, 2007). Moreover, good learning intentions are those that explicitly make clear to the students the type or level of performance that they need to attain. Once this is understood, they will know where and when to invest energy, use appropriate learning strategies and apply thinking skills that will position them for successful learning (Hattie, 2012).

Organisation of resources

Environments in which we all function well usually have a powerful effect on one's behaviour and readiness to learn. For example, a supermarket and an executive boardroom have different layouts because there are different expectations, rules and routines embedded in those spaces (Dempsey and Arthur-Kelly, 2007). Thus, you should be mindful of the layout and ecology of your classroom and consider whether or not the physical arrangement encourages the type of learning that should take place.

Most primary school teachers place a lot of importance on the physical arrangement and layout of their classrooms. This is because it is important to provide students with learning spaces to promote their social as well as their intellectual development. In more traditional teaching environments, where teachers have viewed themselves as instructors who impart knowledge, the tables and chairs are more likely to be arranged only in rows. However, the ecology of the classroom may have many variations – in the end, it boils down to three types of seating arrangements: in rows, in groups or at activity centres, depending on the style of teaching and the quality of the learning expected (see Figure 10.1).

Learning spaces

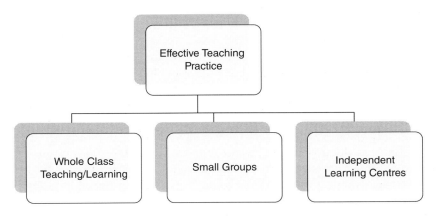

Figure 10.1   Organisation

A connected community of learners

There are strengths and weaknesses with each type of arrangement. Seating in rows (in some cases) helps to promote direct teaching and allows the teacher to monitor student behaviours. Seating in groups promotes group activity and cooperative learning methods. Activity centres will allow activities that individuals or groups can work at but are often harder to set up and usually require a semi-permanent corner of the room where activities and displays can be showcased over time. You may like to include all three types of grouping in flexible sub-environments located in different parts of your room. For example, learning centres can be set up in corners or other out-of-the-way areas while rows or semi-circle arrangements could function for direct or explicit teaching in another area of the classroom (Dempsey and Arthur-Kelly, 2007).

Whatever type of group arrangements you intend to operate in the classroom, you will need to train the children to function according to the nature of the group and the type of learning to take place (Woolley, 2011). Thus, successful and meaningful interactions within classroom spaces often mean spending some time developing the necessary expectations, routines, behaviours and skills. Group participants will need some measure of training, practice and scaffolding. Thus, critical aspects of cooperative learning will involve systematic and structured instruction with adequate opportunities for students to experience frequent success. When you promote dialogic group interaction, the difficulty is in stepping back and allowing discussions to take place between the children while still providing frequent monitoring and adequate feedback. Discussion skills need to be taught such as: restating what another person has said; inviting someone else to participate in the conversation; agreeing; disagreeing; focusing or refocusing the conversation; elaborating on a point that someone else has brought up; and giving an example of a point that someone has made. If you want to promote, for example, elaboration, you might model the question: 'Does anyone want to add a little bit to what Juan had to say about that point?' These are just a few of the prompts you can use to promote this kind of student-centred dialogue.

When children are working in groups, there should be a progression from teacher direction to student self-regulation. This is an essential component for the development of meaningful learning but it will not happen automatically (Gambrell et al., 1987; Woolley, 2006). Cue cards are one way to provide scaffolded prompts for children to guide their discussions around key issues. In such a situation, you should gradually hand over the responsibility of learning to the students as they become more skilled (Pressley, 2002; Snow, 2002).

Peer tutoring is another arrangement that enables cooperative learning on a one-to-one basis (Rhodes, 1993). Student relationships with peers are often critical in influencing student motivation and academic progress (Rohrbeck et al., 2003). The fostering of self-management, individualised evaluation and immediate rewards are common outcomes of the peer intervention, particularly if the arrangement requires one of the pair to have more ability than the other (Rhodes, 1993). Research suggests that this is not always necessary. Same-aged students who are of similar reading ability have also been shown to make improvements in reading (Pagett, 1994).

In peer tutoring, students are normally matched using tutors from their age group or class, while cross-age tutoring arrangements utilise tutors from higher grades. It is possible to use tutors and tutees with reading difficulties across years 1 to 6 in a cross-age tutoring programme, resulting in good reading outcomes (Scruggs and Osguthorpe, 1986). One of the other benefits of cross-age tutoring is that the participants learn to help each other (Cohen et al., 1982). At-risk primary school children have been shown to have gained much from being read to regularly by older students who were at-risk readers themselves (Juel, 1996). Thus, a wide range of cooperative situations can be used effectively in literacy programmes.

If you want to employ small groups to develop particular skills using direct or explicit teaching, you will need to engage the rest of the class in suitable activities. One way to do this is to create literacy centres. Designate areas of the classroom where small groups can engage in independent activities. For example, a reading centre may be set up in a quiet corner of the classroom where children can either sit at desks or on pillows, lie on mats or sink into a beanbag. A large selection of books borrowed from the library, class sets or books donated by parents can be arranged attractively and colour-coded according to level of difficulty, so that children can choose books according to their interests. It is important to display books on rotational racks or on bookstands so that covers can be viewed easily. Listening centres can be set up using an iPad or other tablet with headphones for children to listen and read. Children's book-based projects and book reviews can also be displayed to encourage reading. This print-rich environment could also be supplemented by activities to dramatise the stories being read, by a puppet theatre and puppet or readers' theatre scripts.

In another corner of the room, a computer centre could be set up so that children can look for information on the Internet, type reports, captions, design illustrations, etc. Mobile technology such as tablets or mobile phones could also be used. Children could write posts to blogs or Facebook, or design mind maps with hyperlinks to link information that they are collating for particular projects they are working on.

Elsewhere in the room, a poetry centre could be established where children can read poems together or individually. They could practise reciting a poem as a group or using a template or pattern to produce a poem on a particular topic. They could use magnetic word labels to move words around on a magnetic board and use a cue card with hints to help them design the poem. Alternatively, they could use a tablet to orally record their own poems and use a drawing app to illustrate them.

There are many other types of learning centres that could be set up in the classroom – for example, students could practise particular skill sets such as identifying morphemes, syllables and phonemes or making summaries and notes or sequencing activities using commercial or teacher-constructed games. Another possibility is that the children themselves could design games to practise specific skills and use those games in the learning centre. Computer games are readily accessible on the Internet to practise particular skill sets and students are often quite keen to use those.

There are many ways to use learning centres in the classroom – for example, some learning centres could be used for students who finish their work early as a reward. At other times, students could be given free choice as to which learning centre they go to for a period of time. Learning centres could be used on a rotational basis whereby the teacher rotates from one group to the next so that all students have an opportunity to use each centre, and the teacher has the opportunity to work intensively with a small group (Farris et al., 2004).

Literacy blocks and using technology in the classroom

One way to organise the literacy programme is to have blocks of time devoted to literacy activities each day. This can be organised as formal lessons – for example, 20 minutes can be allocated to spelling each day. Process writing sessions might be allocated 30-minute sessions each day. Other skills-based or open-ended activities can also be timetabled in regularly as well. In the morning, desks could be arranged for a block of more directed teaching of skills. In the afternoon, the desks could be rearranged to promote group or individual work activities or a block could be programmed to organise rotational group activities two or three times a week.

Rules, routines and transitions

Rules and routines are essential components of any classroom arrangement and are particularly important for children when they are transitioning from one activity to the next or from one sub-environment to another. The important thing is that children know what is important and what is expected in different spaces and at different times. For example, some spaces could be quiet spaces while others could be more conducive to discussion. In transitioning from one space to another, children may need a mental break from the previous activity and to re-energise. This is often a good opportunity to sing a song, recite a learned poem, view an example of a student's work, tell a joke and ask a riddle or do some physical or mental exercises such as creating mental imagery or performing a mime.

The role of resources

Suitable resources should be collected over time and can be sourced from myriad places, however you usually need to think ahead and be constantly on the look-out for resources. Many good resources are free or cheap and some can be found on the Internet. One of the most useful resources will be your local newspaper (Killen, 2007). You should consider viewing yourself as a curator of ideas and set up a 'Pinterest' or 'Scoop-it' account, for example, to collect and share teaching ideas and resources. It is important that you don't use a lack of resources as an excuse for not teaching well. You simply have to make the most of whatever resources you have available to you.

Promotion of intellectual quality

Teaching approaches

A teacher-centred approach, such as a lecture or an explicit teaching lesson (see Chapter 8) devoted to teaching a particular skill or strategy, may be preferred from time to time. This method gives the teacher more direct control over what is taught and how learners are presented with information.

At other times, learner-centred approaches, sometimes referred to as discovery learning, inductive learning or inquiry learning, are more desirable. These approaches place a much stronger emphasis on the learner's role in the learning process. When you are using learner-centred approaches for teaching, you can facilitate the learning agenda but you have much less direct control over what and how learners learn (Killen, 2007). Constructionist approaches to learning are based on the notion that children construct meaning from their background knowledge, experiences and previous understandings together with new conceptualisations. In the classroom, a constructionist approach usually requires students to use active methods such as experiments, real-world problem solving and their own research-based inquiry projects. Often, the best place for this to take place is in a social or collaborative context where children can share ideas and opinions and learn from one another. In this context, the teacher becomes a facilitator and a guide, helping children to find information by providing resources and prompts. In this collaborative situation, you are more able to assist children to clarify ideas, ambiguities and misconceptions. This is a much more open style of learning and it usually requires careful monitoring and assessment at each stage.

In the literacy classroom this approach works well, particularly for students with diverse needs, by providing choices and learning at different levels; students with English as a second language and students who are gifted or talented can be included (Cohen and Cowen, 2008).

Learner choice

Each learner has unique needs and abilities, so providing choice and giving responsibility to the student is a vital aspect of the overall learning process. Through negotiation and guidance, learners should be given as much choice and control as is feasible over what and how they learn, how much time they will spend on particular activities and the criteria by which they will be assessed. To achieve high levels of student self-direction, teachers need to engage students in specific activities that offer them opportunities to make decisions and solve problems on their own, as far as possible, with minimal supervision. Teaching strategies such as cooperative learning and research projects can help to foster students' self-direction. As a consequence, your students are more likely to develop self-confidence, particularly when they are encouraged to become more reflective about their own learning processes. However, student self-direction should not be at the expense of the teacher taking an active role in the classroom. Learning engagement will necessitate you guiding and focusing their learning endeavours (Killen, 2007). Above all, learning activities should be purposeful and meaningful by resembling, as far as possible, real-life situations.

Purposeful and meaningful classroom activities

The essential element of education is student learning, in other words you teach so that students can learn. Whatever you teach, the main principle is that you help your students acquire the cognitive strategies they will need to make sense of their learning (Killen, 2007). In doing so, you will need to develop outcomes for student learning. Outcomes are demonstrations of learning and are the substance of what is done as a result of learning. Thus, an outcomes-based education means that the focus of the curriculum will be on the essential learning assigned for your cohort of students.

Planning a unit of work

Thematic units provide students with an opportunity to delve into topics across curriculum boundaries and to use discovery learning. Units can be constructed in a variety of ways and may even arise from the student's own interests and inquiry. This enables students to collaborate in selecting, planning and implementing thematic units. Meaningful learning can take place when children learn to accept one another's opinions and create joint projects on purposeful activities. Thematic units offer students real choices and ways to investigate problems and provide avenues to disseminate their findings. The school curriculum may dictate a particular focus but there are usually subtopics where children can exercise some real choice. You should be guided by their interests but in such a way that the theme will also provide a challenge.

Some considerations for designing a unit of work:

1. Establish appropriate learning goals.
2. Involve students in the planning process wherever possible.
3. Look for ways in which the theme can integrate with other elements of the curriculum.
4. Gather appropriate resources.
5. Look for suitable sources of information on the Internet that the children may be able to access.
6. Structure the learning environment so that each student is working to their capacity.
7. Make sure that the activities are authentic and meaningful.
8. Differentiate the activities so that all children can participate.
9. Look for ways in which teacher aides or parent helpers can be involved.
10. Develop suitable assessment tools and think of ways to give students feedback on their performance.

Recognition of diverse learning styles

Most students have a unique learning style and tend to gravitate towards particular types of learning activities. This is because not all children are the same; they have different talents, abilities and interests. Gardner has identified eight intelligences that can be useful in designing activities to support the curriculum (see Chapter 9). The idea is that children can be given a choice of activities according to their particular learning style.

Bloom (1956) proposed that outcomes in the cognitive domain could be classified into a hierarchy of six levels. This was developed further by Anderson and Krathwohl (2001, see also Krathwohl and Anderson, 2010); a later version uses key words to help with planning suitable activities that are pitched at the six levels of thinking (see below).

Key words

- Knowledge: define, identify, label, list, match, name, pronounce, quote, recite, reproduce, state. Answer, who? What? Where?
- Comprehension: change, depict, describe, discover, give examples, illustrate, interpret, relate, rephrase, represent, restate, reword, summarise, translate, vary.
- Application: apply, compute, demonstrate, direct, discover, manage, predict, prepare, present, relate, show, solve, use. Answer, how many? What? Give an example.
- Analysis: analyse, determine, diagnose, diagram, difference, divide, examine, find, outline, reduce, separate. Answer, why?
- Synthesis: combine, create, design, develop, devise, expand, generalise, integrate, modify, plan, propose, revise, rewrite, Answer, what would happen…? How can we solve…?
- Evaluation: appraise, assess, compare, conclude, contrast, criticise, critique, deduce, evaluate, judge, weigh.

By combining Bloom's (1956) taxonomy with Gardner's (1993) eight intelligences, a matrix could be developed to provide students with real choices for their literacy projects. For example, students may be required to choose five activities from the matrix and to make a contract with the teacher. A contract can be made up with spaces for the children to fill in their particular choices. After agreeing on a completion date, the filled-in contract is then signed by the students and the teacher. This device can also be used effectively to differentiate literacy learning activities so that children can be challenged at their own particular developmental level.

Levels of cognitive engagement

Whatever the activity, students will need to process information at three different levels if effective learning is to take place (see Table 10.1). At the surface level, children will need to attend to the task and this often requires

Table 10.1   Three COR framework meaning levels

COR levels	Activity
Factual (decode)	Highlight the new word in a read-aloud story.
	Examine the phonic, orthographic and morphological structure of the new word (e.g. use word feature analysis – see Table 7.1).
Conceptual (encode)	Use the context to work out the meaning.
	Put the word in a new sentence.
	Make up a new word using the different morphological units.
Metacognitive (recode)	Ask questions such as:
	Do I like this word?
	Does it make sense in this sentence?
	How will I remember this word?
	Can I use another word instead?
	How can I use this word in the future?

Source: Woolley, 2007

them to attend to the factual content. At a deeper or conceptual level, students will need to comprehend, problem solve or form opinions about the content. This often requires students to create new understandings and meanings. At an even deeper level, students will need to step back and consider their own learning by considering their goals, monitoring performance, making decisions about learning strategies and reflecting on their achievements.

Prompts

You will be able to support learning at these particular levels by using suitable questions and prompts. Prompts enable students to identify learning difficulties more quickly and invite students to invest more effort by planning and implementing fix-up strategies in order to enhance their learning (Hattie, 2012).

Prompts should target learning at the three levels:

1. Factual

   • What is this passage saying?
   • Does it sound right?
   • Does it make sense?

2. Conceptual

   • What strategies will I use?
   • What questions can I ask about the task?
   • What are the relationships with other parts of the task?

3. Metacognitive

- What is the goal of the activity?
- Are the strategies that I am using helping me achieve my goals?
- What have I learned about:
  - the topic?
  - myself as a learner?

The key to using prompts is to use them appropriately for each phase of the learning task.

Vignette 10.1

Mr Johnson developed a science unit of work on the re-introduction of wolves into Yellowstone National Park with his year 6 class. At the beginning of the unit, he used a KWoL chart on the interactive whiteboard to list all the things that the children already knew about wolves. After this initial brainstorming activity, the children were asked to think about what they wanted to learn about wolves. The 'o' (organisation) and the 'L' ('What have I learned?') would be filled in during the middle and end of the unit. Often, the KWL strategy is used in individual lessons but Mr Johnson decided to use a variation called 'KWoL' (Woolley, 2011) to organise the unit.

Questions

1 Why do you think that Mr Johnson chose to use the KWoL strategy to launch this unit of work?
2 Why would it be better to start the unit with the KWoL strategy rather than, say, watch a video on wolves?
3 Why is it important to activate the children's background knowledge before beginning a unit?

The *decoding level* requires children to process the surface features of words and to be aware of the word parts and forms as well as their semantic or morphological features (see Table 10.2). A feature analysis chart may be useful as a visual representation of a targeted word by displaying its morphological constituents so that they can be more easily decoded and compared with other word elements. The *conceptual level* requires students to encode words with meaning by using their own background knowledge and story context. Children also need to construct new words and create new sentences using their new and existing vocabulary. The *metacognitive level* requires that children plan, monitor and reflect on their own word learning. It requires

Table 10.2   Pedagogical treatments

Pedagogical treatments	Activity
Text enhancements	Text highlighting, illustrations, skills training, reinforcement, using context, questioning
Cognitive strategies	Activating background knowledge, inferencing
Behavioural treatments	Goal-setting, self-monitoring (self-questioning), self-reflection

the student to self-question – for example, 'If I place this word in a sentence, will it still make sense?'

Scaffolding, explicit teaching and the gradual release of responsibility

The notion of scaffolding comes from Vygotsky's (1962) zone of proximal development whereby the learner is given a learning task that is pitched at just about the level of learning that can be independently achieved. This space usually requires some support by the teacher so that it can take the student beyond their normal level of comfort and into the zone where optimal learning can take place. Teachers often use what they call scaffolding techniques to achieve this. The notion of scaffolding implies that these supports are put in place temporarily and gradually dismantled as the student becomes more competent and confident.

Duke and Pearson (2002) have emphasised that literacy activities in instructional classroom environments need to reflect this notion of the gradual release of responsibility. This principle requires you as a teacher to progressively transfer the responsibility of the learning process to the learner. In essence, it is the transferral of the locus of control from the teacher to the learner.

Learning centres

A learning centre is the type of workstation that can be set up in a corner of the room to enable students to work in groups or individually on various types of activities across a range of domains. Children can focus on a particular theme or activity with displays, posters, picture prompts or equipment such as laptops or tablets to support independent learning or small group work. The activities should be structured to enable children to practise skills that they have developed in the classroom and to complete tasks in the time allocated. For example, a reading centre could be designed so that students are able to practise their fluency by reading a book and listening to a recording of the story or article (Cohen and Cowen, 2008).

Scheduling for learning centre activities is easy to plan and implement. For example, the entire learning session could be broken up into 15–20-minute time segments with rotational activities. For example, if there are 4 x 15-minute segments, allow 60 minutes for group work or alternatively allow one hour and 20 minutes for a rotation of six groups. One of the 15-minute sessions could be organised as a large group with the teacher giving explicit instruction. Other small-group activities could be organised to operate in other areas of the classroom and be facilitated by a teacher aide or parent volunteer. Other groups could work independently on activities that involve skill practice using self-correcting games.

Other learning centre activities could include:

- sustained silent reading
- engaging in research
- engaging in inquiry projects while collaborating with others
- engaging in writing workshops
- using practice games, e.g. a phonics memory game via the Internet
- using a computer centre with set tasks
- working on a puppet play centre project.

Teachers who use learning centres have found that a sizeable amount of time will have been devoted to designing appropriate activities and training children to work interdependently. However, the time invested by the teacher usually pays off throughout the school year because students learn how to work cooperatively on tasks that are meaningful to them (King-Sears, 2005).

Vignette 10.2

After the initial KWoL activity, Mr Johnson used a class set (one copy between two children) of *National Geographic* magazines (Chadwick, 2010) entitled 'Wolf wars' to introduce the problem of the re-introduction of the wolves into the national park. He used the chart above (Table 10.1) to help analyse the unfamiliar vocabulary. After questioning the children and having a thorough discussion with them about the article, he decided to organise class group work using this format and rotate the groups around each workstation every 20 minutes during their block literacy schedule (Figure 10.2).

(Continued)

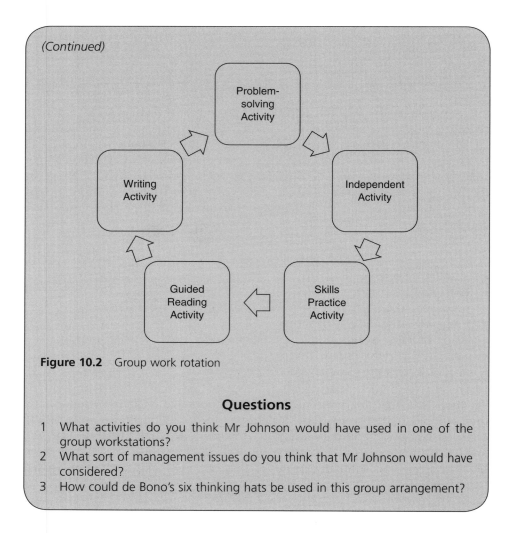

Figure 10.2 Group work rotation

Questions

1 What activities do you think Mr Johnson would have used in one of the group workstations?
2 What sort of management issues do you think that Mr Johnson would have considered?
3 How could de Bono's six thinking hats be used in this group arrangement?

Largely as a result of the work of Benjamin Bloom and his colleagues (Bloom, 1956), it is common practice for curriculum designers and teachers to group learning outcomes into three domains: the cognitive (concerned with mental processes); the psycho-motor (concerned with the control of bodily movements and physical actions); and the affective (concerned with feelings, attitudes and values).

Classroom libraries

It is important to provide suitable resources for independent classroom reading, so you should ensure you have a well-stocked classroom library with plenty of choices for children to choose from. It should be well organised and appealing with a variety of magazines, comics and books from various genres. It should be organised so that the students have a couple of books that they can go on with rather than using their free reading time to browse the bookshelf.

Conclusion

Learning intentions and the success criterion are two aspects of planning and organising classroom lessons. Being a proactive teacher and providing a classroom environment that is conducive to learning and good behaviour require some thought and organisation. A supportive classroom environment should provide a connected community of learners, the promotion of intellectual quality and recognition of the diverse learning styles of your students.

 ## Discussion questions and activities

 ### Points for discussion

1   What are the advantages and disadvantages of using whole-class, group work or peer tutoring? Make up a pros and cons chart to use for this brainstorming activity.
2   What should you consider in the first week of class to make sure that routines and expectations are organised? How should you implement these?
3   Why is it important to plan for transitioning from one activity to another?

✝✝✝✝ Group activities

1   With your mobile device, look up 'Bloom–Gardner matrix' and discuss how this could be used as an alternative way to organise a unit of work.
2   How could you create a contract system to organise open-ended or independent activities within a unit of work?
3   What are the advantages of having open-ended activities in the classroom as compared to direct teaching methods?

 ### Whole-class activities

1   Read the article 'Wolf wars' (Chadwick, 2010) or a similar article about the re-introduction of wolves into national parks in Scotland or Portugal, and design a mini unit of work for a particular grade level of your choosing.
2   De Bono (1996) emphasised the importance of teaching students appropriate thinking skills or ways of moving from one level of knowledge to a higher one. He argued that students needed to be taught how to think

(Continued)

(Continued)

constructively. Using a mobile device (e.g. a smartphone, tablet or laptop), conduct an Internet search to find out about de Bono's six thinking hats and answer the questions below:

(a) How can the six thinking hats be used in group-work activities?
(b) Why do you think that children need to use this type of thinking structure?
(c) Often, this technique is used for gifted students. Why do you think this is appropriate?
(d) Do you think that this could help students with learning difficulties? Why/why not?

References

Anderson, L. W. and Krathwohl, D. R. (2001) *A Taxonomy for Learning, Teaching, and Assessing: A Revision of Bloom's Taxonomy of Educational Objectives.* New York: Longman.

Bloom, B. S. (1956). *Taxonomy of Educational Objectives, Handbook 1: The Cognitive Domain.* New York: David McKay.

Chadwick, D. H. (2010). Wolf wars. *National Geographic*, March.

Churchill, R., Fergusson, P., Godinho, S., Johnson, N. F., Keddie, A., Letts, W., et al. (2011). *Teaching: Making a Difference.* Milton, QLD: John Wiley & Sons.

Cohen, V. L. and Cowen, J. E. (2008). *Literacy for Children in an Information Age: Teaching Reading, Writing, and Thinking.* Belmont, CA: Thomson.

Cohen, P., Kulik, J. A. and Kulik, C. L. (1982). Educational outcomes of tutoring: A meta-analysis of findings. *American Educational Research Journal, 19,* 237–248.

De Bono, E. (1996). Critical thinking is totally inadequate. *Across the Board,* 33(3), 25–26.

Dempsey, I. and Arthur-Kelly, M. (2007). *Maximising Learning Outcomes in Diverse Classrooms.* Melbourne: Cengage Learning Australia.

Duke, N. K. and Pearson, P. D (2002). Effective practices for developing reading comprehension. In A. E. Farstrup and S. J. Samuels (eds), *What Research has to Say about Reading Instruction* (3rd edn) (pp. 205–242). Newark, DE: International Reading Association.

Farris, P. J., Fuhler, C. J. and Walther, M. P. (2004). *Teaching Reading: A Balanced Approach for Today's Classrooms.* Boston: McGraw-Hill.

Gambrell, L. B., Kapinus, B. A. and Wilson, R. M. (1987). Using mental imagery and summarization to achieve independence in comprehension. *Journal of Reading*, 30(7), 638–642.

Gardner, H. (1993). *Multiple Intelligences: The Theory into Practice.* New York: Basic Books.

Hattie, J. (2012). *Visible Learning for Teachers: Maximising Impact on Learning.* London: Routledge.

Juel, C. (1996). What makes literacy tutoring effective? *Reading Research Quarterly*, 31, 268–289.

Killen, R. (2007). *Effective Teaching Strategies: Lessons from Research and Practice*. Melbourne: Thomson Science Press.

King-Sears, M. E. (2005). Scheduling for reading and writing small-group instruction using learning centre designs. *Reading and Writing Quarterly*, 21, 401–405.

Krathwohl, D. R. and Anderson, L. W. (2010). Merlin C. Wittrock and the revision of Bloom's taxonomy. *Educational Psychologist*, 45(1), 64–65.

Pagett, L. (1994). 'No fears with peers': A personal reflection on peer group tutoring in the context of reading development. *Reading*, 28, 31–35.

Pressley, M. (2002). At-risk students: Learning to break through comprehension barriers. In C. Collins Block, L. B. Gambrell and M. Pressley (eds), *Improving Comprehension Instruction* (pp. 354–369). San Francisco: Jossey-Bass.

Rhodes, J. (1993). How pupils and staff experienced a peer tutoring project involving paired reading. *Reading*, 27, 14–19.

Rohrbeck, C. A., Ginsburg-Block, M. D., Fantuzzo, J. W. and Miller, T. R. (2003). Peer assisted learning with elementary school students: A meta-analytic review. *Journal of Educational Psychology*, 95, 240–257.

Scruggs, T. E. and Osguthorpe, R. T. (1986). Tutoring interventions within special education settings: A comparison of cross-age and peer tutoring. *Psychology in the Schools*, 23, 187–193.

Snow, C. E. (2002). Reading for understanding: Toward a research and development program in reading comprehension. Santa Monica, CA: Rand Corp. Available at: www.rand.org/publications/MR/MR1465/ (accessed 12 December 2002).

Vygotsky, L. S. (1962). *Thought and Language*. Cambridge, MA: Harvard University Press.

UNESCO (2004). Understanding and Responding to Children's Needs in Inclusive Classrooms: A Guide for Teachers. Available at: www.unescobkk.org (accessed 30 November 2009).

Woolley, G. E. (2006). Comprehension difficulties after year 4: Actioning appropriately. *Australian Journal of Learning Difficulties*, 11(3), 125–130.

Woolley, G. (2007). A comprehension intervention for children with reading comprehension difficulties. *Australian Journal of Learning Difficulties*, 12(1), 43–50.

Woolley, G. (2011). *Reading Comprehension: Assisting Children with Learning Difficulties*. Dordrecht, The Netherlands: Springer International.

Zimmerman, B. J. (2002). Becoming a self-regulated learner: An overview. *Theory into Practice*, 41, 64–70.

ASSESSMENT

Chapter objectives

- To understand the purposes of assessment for teaching and learning.
- To develop a repertoire of assessment strategies to foster a dynamic and flexible approach to assessment.
- To develop appropriate instructional approaches.

Key questions

1. What should teachers assess?
2. How is assessment linked to learning and instruction?
3. Why is it important to involve children in the assessment process?

Key words: assessment, dynamic assessment, formative assessment, process, product, self-assessment, summative assessment, testing.

Introduction

Chapter 11 considers assessment as an integrated and essential aspect of all teaching. Assessment should not be considered as a separate activity but you should think about it as part of the whole learning process. This chapter discusses the dynamic application of informal assessment along with other more formal assessment procedures. It will look at the learner within the learning context rather than assuming that all of the problems are situated within the learner. A balanced approach to assessment can be the means by which you will be enabled to develop high-quality evidence-based teaching and effective literacy programmes to enhance students' learning. To achieve this, you need a range of assessment activities or methods that are capable of measuring and describing student growth and that will foster appropriate literacy skills and strategies. This growth in learning should also include other affective aspects such as: positive motivation, perseverance in the face of difficulties, appropriate attributions made for literacy success or failure, and an increased literacy self-concept (Afflerbach, 2007).

> Over the course of a school year, carefully teaching to students' individual needs can obviate the need to teach to the test. We must know where students are in terms of their skill and strategy development, motivation and engagement, prior knowledge for the texts they read, and self-esteem as readers. When reading assessment provides us with this balance of information, we can identify the next steps for student learning and for our teaching. (Afflerbach et al., 2011: 323)

The above quote conveys the notion that assessment is about catering for a whole range of students' needs. The word assessment is often used in two senses: as a process carried out to provide data about something or someone, and as a product, as in referring to teachers' assessments. Assessment in education involves making judgements about children's attainments. It involves deciding what information is relevant, how to collect it, how to make informed evaluations and how to communicate those evaluations to those who want to know what your children are achieving.

All of these assessments depend on the reason for conducting your assessment. Many people and organisations have their own reasons for using assessment results: to assist students with their learning: for parents to know how their children are progressing; for teachers to regulate their teaching and to diagnose problems; for school administrators and governors to know where to allocate resources more effectively; for local authorities and central governments to ascertain the effectiveness of their schools. There are different types of assessment. Assessments that are initiated externally are often mandated by federal or state authorities in order to assess students' achievements on standardised or norm-referenced achievement tests, with the assumption that these tests will reflect student achievement on identified essential learning. The content of these tests may or may not resemble the types of learning tasks that are normally conducted in the classroom. The results of these high-stakes tests usually provide a measure of accountability of the educational system: of teachers, schools or districts generally, and are rated on the basis of how well the students perform. Taken by themselves, these tests have the potential to narrow the scope of the curriculum as teachers endeavour to train students to perform on the actual test items.

Similarly, system-based assessments generally stem from the particular educational system where all schools desire to examine the effectiveness of a range of instructional practices or curricula within schools and districts. This form of assessment may involve classroom observations, students' self-evaluation, peer review, teacher-made tests or standardised test instruments. On the basis of these tests, immediate curricula or instructional modifications will be made to enhance students' learning outcomes. Such assessments usually provide important information related to instructional practices and on individual students' learning performance in the classroom.

Classroom assessment, on the other hand, is a process that occurs over an extended period of time. Usually, ongoing classroom assessments mirror or stem from what actually occurs in day-to-day learning activities within the classroom. Assessments that are most effective here include everyday tasks such as real-life, hands-on problem solving, computer simulations, and students' evaluation and profiling of their own work over an extended period of time. Collectively, this form of assessment is called authentic assessment because it evaluates the actual learning tasks and products that appear in the classroom.

Assessment is not a simple task – effective teachers make use of a wide range of assessment information to differentiate and contextualise their instruction and to support the practices they choose after considering the range of data provided. They are then enabled through research and collaborative discussions with colleagues in their schools to inform curriculum development in order to make the necessary changes and modifications (Gambrell et al., 2007).

Assessment: is it a process or a product?

Is educational assessment a process or a product? It can be used as a process to measure student progress and attainment of certain standards or it can be used as a product of that process, e.g. a teacher's assessment of a child's abilities and a set of judgements about students' progress. In general, assessments of processes focus on students' skills, strategies and work as they unfold. In contrast, product assessments focus on what students produce as a result of a literacy activity. Often, most attention is given to product assessments, especially with answers to test items, and this creates an imbalance that favours product assessment at the expense of information about actual learning processes (Afflerbach, 2007). In contrast, a process-oriented literacy assessment focuses on the thinking skills and strategies that students use to construct meaning in real-world literacy activities. For example, when you observe a student re-reading a sentence to clarify meaning, you are observing a metacognitive process, often understanding how a student deals with the learning process itself. This will help you determine the skills and strategies that work or do not work as the student attempts to construct meaning. Examples of this type of assessment, focusing on readers' cognitive processing, are reading inventories and miscue analyses, while writing conferences can also focus on the writing process (Afflerbach, 2007; Clay, 1993; Goodman and Goodman, 1977).

The use of think-aloud protocols as a measure of comprehension and learning has become a respectable assessment tool popularised by Ericsson and Simon (1984). The think-aloud protocol encourages students to articulate their thought processes at any point in time during a learning activity.

You should be aware that assessment, whether formal or informal, is never completely error-free because there are a number of factors that impact on validity. Assessment involves deciding what information is important, how it should be collected and what educational decisions are most appropriate. Different reading tests, for example, may give different age-equivalent scores for reading. Test scores can be expected to fluctuate when administered to the same child on different occasions. It is likely that the same test administered a second time will give a higher score or that a test administered while the child is tired, unwell or not feeling comfortable will quite likely give a depressed score. Thus, tests should be conducted in a professional manner and balanced against other sources of information such as observations, checklists and anecdotal notes, etc. (Witt et al., 1994).

In the past, assessment was reliant on tools that were designed around simple literacy models that often focused on a narrow set of skills. However, in more recent times, literacy has been viewed as complex and multifaceted – no single instrument will be able to provide the necessary information to guide the design of appropriate individualised teaching interventions for struggling students. The problem is that most standardised instruments tend to be limited in focus and don't give adequate direction to inform suitable teaching practices. Assessment strategies and instruments should robustly reflect the dynamic, developmental nature of learning to include other external dimensions such as activity, text and context. Thus, you will need to have a broader understanding of literacy that goes beyond viewing learning problems as being situated solely within the learner.

Educators generally agree that assessment is fundamental to the effective teaching of literacy and to curriculum design (Coccamise and Snyder, 2005). In reading, for example, Joshi and Aaron (2000) claim that most assessment procedures currently being used in schools are based on limited theoretical models of reading and tend to give the impression that all difficulties are found within the learner. Generally speaking, these assessment procedures have sprung from specific theories that are either concerned with a single aspect of reading such as word decoding or are focused on global aspects such as overall cognitive ability (Freebody and Freiberg, 2001; Joshi and Aaron, 2000). The reality is that successful reading, for example, requires a complex interaction of language, sensory perception, memory and motivation (Pikulski and Chard, 2005). Thus, some researchers have called for better assessment tools and more appropriate intervention programmes to reflect this complex process (Pressley, 2002; Schunk, 2004).

From the 1960s until the late 1980s, criterion-referenced tests (CTR) became popular in classroom assessment and structured reading programmes. Mastery learning was the driving force behind CTR with its emphasis on precision learning. The idea behind mastery learning was that if the essential elements within the domain of learning could be identified and mastered, students would be able to achieve high levels of confidence as they learned the prerequisite lower-level skills (Paris and Stahl, 2005).

During the 1970s and 1980s, two different perspectives emerged. The first perspective focused on schema theory, which provided a framework to account for how knowledge is understood in terms of what is already known by the learner. This highlighted the notion that learners can have differing understandings due to different background experiences and prior knowledge. This notion encouraged educators to examine texts from the perspective of students' knowledge and cultural backgrounds. Schema theory supported a constructivist view of learning whereby learners construct the most coherent model of meaning according to what they understand and know. In other words, they build a model of meaning which is unique to their experience of the world (Paris and Stahl, 2005). A group of psychologists focused on the second perspective here: the role of story grammar or structure (Kintsch, 1974; Rumelhart, 1977; Stein and Glenn, 1977). From this perspective, educationalists were interested in how story structures impede or enhance narrative or expository text and guide the learner's understanding and memory.

By the late 1980s, constructivist approaches to literacy assessment had emerged which emphasised the need for assessment to reflect resources such as prior knowledge, environmental clues, the text itself and the key players involved in the reading process. They emphasised metacognition as a reflective element in literacy processes.

Each trend has added to our collective understanding of assessment and educational practice. It is obvious that any one approach has its limitations according to its particular theoretical base. To overcome the limitations of any one approach, educators may need a range of assessment strategies and instruments that robustly reflect the dynamic, developmental nature of literacy learning and their interaction with activity, text and the context of the classroom (Duke and Pearson, 2002; NRP, 2000; Snow, 2003).

Formal assessment

Formal assessment usually samples students' behaviour using uniform or standardised procedures for administering and scoring tests. Formal testing, on the other hand, usually involves real-life, hands-on and sometimes incidental learning activities and experiences. Formal tests can be either norm-referenced or criterion-referenced. Norm-referenced tests compare the performance of an individual student with large samplings of a wide population of individuals. Comparisons are made between individual students and standardised measures of the larger group, usually in the form of percentile score rankings. For example, a student attaining a percentile score of 72 would be regarded as performing better than 71% of the same-aged population at a particular grade level. Criterion-referenced tests, on the other hand, are a measure of attainment in relation to certain learning outcomes.

Formative and summative evaluation

Formative evaluation is the process of assessing learning as it occurs and is reflective of student performance, pedagogy and teaching in the regular classroom. Usually, this involves the day-to-day assessment of learning outcomes of particular activities that students may be engaged in. Formal evaluations may also involve students doing self-assessment activities (Lipson and Wixson, 2009). This form of assessment can provide valuable information on the usefulness of instructional approaches or curricular materials and provide an indication of individual students' learning over a fixed period of time. It can also provide teachers with feedback on the effect of classroom settings and instructional approaches.

As a teacher, you will need regular classroom-based assessment that will enable you to identify teachable moments for each student. Routine and frequent assessment will provide you with the information you need for effective literacy instruction. You must know where students are placed in terms of their literacy skills and strategy development, motivation and engagement, prior knowledge of the texts as they read and their self-perception as readers. You can then use the results of your assessment in a formative manner, to immediately shape your understanding of the individual and related instruction (Afflerbach, 2007).

Dynamic assessment is based on Vygotsky's view of learning, which sees children's learning as being mediated by interactions with adults and peers (Vygotsky, 1978). Thus, assessment should not only state how a child is operating on their own at any particular point in time, but should also identify what an individual can do with the assistance of a peer or adult. In essence, dynamic assessment provides information about an individual child's potential learning ability (Gunning, 2010).

Some key questions that you should ask to promote this type of dynamic assessment are:

1. For this subject area, what can the child already do unaided?
2. What can the child do if given a little guidance or prompting?
3. Are there any important gaps in the child's prior learning?
4. What does the child need to be taught next in order to make progress?
   (Westwood, 2001)

Assessment can also be used in a summative manner, as it provides evidence that students have (or have not) met key learning goals. Summative assessment usually takes the form of a formal teacher-made assessment at the end of a unit or school term. This type of assessment is important as it will help you understand whether students have reached grade-level benchmarks, unit and lesson goals, and standards in classrooms, systems and states (Afflerbach, 2007).

Knowing your students

Often, what is required is for the student to appraise their own learning by establishing goals for their instructional activity and to self-evaluate their progress toward those goals (Lipson and Wixson, 2009). Time spent getting to know students at the beginning of the year will be time well spent. School records and interviews with parents and previous teachers can also be very informative.

Almost any teaching technique or method can be used to inform you about students' performance. How they perform on any given task will reveal much about their competency. What is important is that you are methodical and that you use a number of ways to gather data. Data gathering can utilise direct observations and anecdotal notes, work samples, portfolios, inventories, conferences, rubrics, regular formal or informal tests and quizzes (Lipson and Wixson, 2009). Informal gathering of student performance data, such as inventories, will supplement information from standardised tests, broaden the focus and provide more relevant and specific evaluative data. Teacher-designed instruments will often be more informative but vary with the content, test conditions and assessor variables. Teacher ratings have also been shown to be more reliable when judged against specific criteria (August and Shanahan, 2006). This does require good teacher judgement but there is a danger that reliability may suffer without consistent assessment planning and implementation.

Assessment: a multi-layered approach

Israel, Bauserman and Block (2005) maintained that assessment procedures should incorporate the use of a metacognitive perspective by focusing on readers' thinking processes. Where possible, ongoing or formative assessment should be dynamic, and should ideally involve the reader in making choices and allow for metacognitive decisions to be articulated while reading. Feedback from think-aloud protocols should inform teachers as to the motivational and self-regulatory reading behaviours of the children they are attempting to assist. Feedback from the student is habitually a neglected source of information – often they are the best ones to know how they are thinking and are often surprisingly insightful. Student interviews are especially important as they signal to the student that self-evaluation is important and that they have some responsibility over the learning process. There is strong evidence to suggest that most students identified early as having literacy difficulties can be remediated successfully by a combination of good quality assessment procedures followed by more intense and focused intervention (Vellutino et al., 2004).

A metacognitive assessment should determine how learners could use declarative and procedural knowledge, such as knowing the what and how about a literacy learning process (Manset-Williamson and Nelson, 2005). They should also have conditional knowledge that will inform them as to when to utilise the learning process appropriately. Reflective knowledge is another form of learning self-awareness that relates to knowing when a learning strategy is working effectively, or not. Finally, adaptive knowledge is essential knowledge about how to combine or adapt practices or techniques to meet one's needs (Gambrell et al., 2007). Using a think-aloud protocol is a useful metacognitive assessment tool – for example, having readers verbalise their own thinking when applying self-correction and self-regulation strategies during reading will give insight into their actual thought processes (Gersten et al., 2001; Israel et al., 2005; Schunk, 2003).

Self-assessment

While our classroom-based assessment should contribute to the collection of valuable information that can inform our understanding of students and our instruction, it must also provide students with the means to eventually assume responsibility for assessing their own literacy development. A teacher- or teacher/student-designed rubric can provide the means for students to check their progress towards a particular performance level and to practise self-assessment. When you require children to self-assess, you do not give up your responsibility to conduct valuable classroom-based literacy assessments, rather you look for opportunities when using your assessments to help students become self-supporting learners (Afflerbach, 2007).

A rubric using the questions below, for example, can be used so that children have a tangible guide as to how they can self-assess while doing a reading activity:

- Have I checked to see if what I am reading makes sense?
- Did I remind myself why I was reading?
- Did I focus on the goal of my reading while I read?
- Did I check to see if I could summarise sentences and paragraphs?
- Did I ask myself if there were any problems if the reading got hard?
- Did I try to identify the problem?
- Did I try to fix the problem?
- When the problem was fixed, did I get back to my reading and make sure I understood what I read?

Vignette 11.1

Ms Black, a year 4 teacher, had introduced her class to the process approach to writing (see Chapter 5). The children had been working on individual stories that had been generated after the children had visited the zoo. Most of the children were almost at the stage where they had finished their first draft. In one particular lesson, Ms Black talked to the children about designing a rubric to help them with their editing. She provided a table on the interactive whiteboard and the children made suggestions about what to include in the rubric.

Questions

1 Why would it be a good idea to have the children take part in this activity?
2 Is this an assessment activity?
3 How could the children use the rubric in class?
4 What could Ms Black discover about the children by doing this with her class?

Feedback

Teachers can support readers' learning more effectively by providing timely and effective feedback. Hattie and Timperley (2007) maintain that effective reading performance feedback contributes to the student's sense of security, self-efficacy and confidence, which then encourages the reader to take more risks and to attempt unfamiliar tasks. Overall, the aim of reading performance feedback is to guide the student's learning, thereby reducing dependence on external feedback as they become more capable, confident and self-regulating. When providing performance feedback, it is important to focus on students' strengths rather than on their weaknesses. Poor use of feedback together with low expectations can be harmful to students' academic and social development. Conversely, expectations that are too high or unattainable can be frustrating and can stifle reading independence.

Feedback in the form of praise should not be vague. For example, 'Good boy!' or 'Well done!' does not provide adequate feedback on the actual performance of a specific learning task (Woolley, 2011), but may actually be counter-productive because the student may see such comments as being condescending or manipulative. The message that is given to the child may be perceived as, 'Oh, she says that to everyone' or 'She just expects me to do what she wants'. Rather, feedback should be related to the student's own performance in relation to a specific learning goal and teachers should avoid comparing an individual's performance to that of their peers. Feedback should be immediate and quite specific so that the student knows exactly why the feedback was given and how the information can be useful for future improvement. It is especially helpful when students are also provided with error-detection skills and when the belief is conveyed that their self-monitoring and self-correction will most likely lead to success.

The ultimate aim of giving feedback should be to develop students as thoughtful, self-regulating and reflective learners that are able to self-reward (tangible rewards are extrinsic rewards that often undermine intrinsic motivation). Hattie and Timperley (2007) have identified three levels of effective feedback: task level, process level and self-regulation level (see Figure 11.1). First, feedback can be directed at the task or product and can be directed at acquiring more, different or correct information. Process feedback is aimed at the actual processing of information or the understanding and skills needed to learn from the task. The third level of feedback is directed at the self-regulatory process. This latter level relates to metacognitive (see above) and behavioural treatment. In summary then, feedback should aim to move students from task to processing and then to self-regulation.

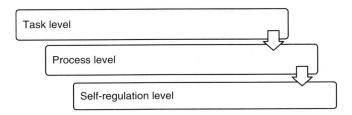

Figure 11.1   Levels of feedback

Assessment of resources

Readability

As discussed earlier, unfamiliar vocabulary can be very demanding on limited short-term memory capacity and comprehension may begin to suffer if the demand is too great. However, more complex sentences normally add to the meaning and can make comprehension easier because low-frequency words have a much more specific meaning. For example, some high-interest books with low-readability texts make reading comprehension more difficult for the struggling reader because meaning is lost due to oversimplification of the sentence structure incorporating simpler vocabulary. For example, the word 'stallion' conveys a specific meaning, whereas the word 'horse' is a much more general term. When texts are arranged in unfamiliar formats, they can also make it more difficult for the reader by slowing down the reading. This is because unfamiliar text organisation and syntactic complexity make higher demands on cognitive processing. For example, the more clauses that sentences contain, the harder it will be for children to read and understand them.

In understanding a narrative, for example, readers usually search for causal relationships between actions and events to make appropriate inferences (Pearson and Johnson, 1978). For this to happen, readers must be able to relate their background knowledge to the context or to a set of circumstances in the story sequence (Trabasso and Sperry, 1985). There are two things they can do to make a causal inference: they can either (1) find semantic and/or logical relations between events or propositions, which are stated or implied within the narrative structure, or (2) provide bridging inferences where information is not explicitly stated (Trabasso, 1981). The latter places a high cognitive load on working memory because readers must use extra memory resources to access background knowledge to imply causal relationships that are not explicitly stated in the text.

Furthermore, when readers are presented with very complex plots or storylines that are outside their existing world experience, then an extra cognitive load is placed on the reader. Similarly, if the reader has to deal with too many unfamiliar concepts, it will make it harder for the reader to adequately process meaning. Thus, comprehension involves relating the new information to what is already known and if there are too many unknowns then assimilation of the new material will become quite difficult.

Those who work with children may develop the ability to match text to student ability levels with some degree of success. Others have called for objective methods for judging readability (Elley, 1989). There are a number of methods to guide the assessment of readability of texts, although some factors such as interest and background knowledge are often beyond objective analysis. Because reading is a complex process, there is no simple and reliable formula for successfully matching all children to suitable books. However, readability formulas and checklists can give a rough indication of reader compatibility to reading material. Readability formulas use a limited range of factors as indicators, such as number of syllables, number of words and number of sentences for a given number of words (as in the case of the

Fry readability graph – a common readability formula). Table 11.1 summarises many other factors that also influence text readability.

Table 11.1 Factors that influence text readability

No.	Feature	Descriptor
1	Graphophonic complexity	Are the graphic and phonic word elements complex or simple?
2	Vocabulary	Are most of the words familiar to the children or are there some unknown words?
3	Print density	Are there a lot of words per page or only a couple of sentences?
4	Font size and familiarity	Are the words in large print or small print?
5	Punctuation	How much punctuation is there on the page?
6	Syntactic complexity	Are the sentences simple or complex?
7	Semantic density	Are the children familiar with the setting and cultural factors or are there a lot of unknowns?
8	Subject matter and interest	Are the children interested in the topic or plot?
9	Text organisation (genre)	Are the children familiar with this type of genre?
10	Plot	Is the plot simple or complex?

Measuring the percentage of known words in a text

When deciding what text to use with children, Vygotsky's (1962) concept, referred to as the 'zone of proximal development' (ZPG), can be used as a guide. The ZPG is the area between what the child can achieve without assistance and what can be accomplished with expert adult assistance. This is often referred to as the instructional level because it is the cognitive region in which learning can best take place. The instructional level is where teacher 'scaffolding' most effectively provides support and where guidance can be diminished as reading competence increases.

There are three levels of difficulty to consider when identifying the suitability of written materials. These levels of difficulty are based on the ratio of known words to unknown words in a given passage and are scored as a percentage of correct words.

To match students' reading level with a suitable text, you should:

- select a 100-word section of a reading passage
- have the reader start reading aloud while the observer checks the reading errors (if the reader self-corrects, do not count it as an error)
- after the child completes the 100-word segment, count the total errors (use Table 11.2 to assess suitable reading levels).

Table 11.2 Ease of reading chart

Level	Word accuracy	Word errors (per 100 words)
Independent level	96% accuracy and above	If there are 0 to 4 errors, the text is at an easy or *independent* reading level, and good for consolidation and reading for pleasure.
Instructional level	90% to 95% word accuracy	If there are between 6 and 10 errors, the text is at the *instructional* level (the level at which the student is able to function with assistance) and reading and comprehension support is required.
Frustration level	up to 89% word accuracy	If there are more than 10 errors, the text is at a *frustration* level (the level at which the student experiences frustration) and comprehension and meaning will be lost.

Source: Farris et al., 2004; Gunning, 2003; Hay and Woolley, 2011

While some commercially available texts are designed to allow students to apply specific word decoding and comprehension skills, there is little evidence to support their use (Reutzel, 2007). What is required are texts that appeal to interests and are relevant to what the children are doing in the classroom.

Repeated reading

One well-known strategy for enabling reading fluency and ease of reading is the repeated reading method. This method begins with the learner listening to a short text passage until text familiarity and fluency are sufficiently developed. The children are then required to re-read the text by focusing on reading fluently with expression. Another re-reading strategy, referred to as the 'neurological impress method' (NIM), can be used to supplement this activity. It requires children to read in concert with a more expert reader. However, the expert reader is usually expected to read at a slightly faster pace than the novice reader would normally be accustomed to. During this process, the novice reader is directed to concentrate on the flow of the text while trying to keep up with the expert reader as they read orally together. One of the advantages of re-reading text is that it increases the familiarity of the material and reduces the demands made on memory by the decoding process, thereby allowing students to attend less to the decoding of the text because it is more predictable. The overriding principle is that when the text becomes predictable, decoding is much easier. Choral reading, group oral reading activities, reading and performing plays, radio reading and poetry reciting are other activities where children can practise fluency in group or whole-class situations.

In the 1950s, Taylor (1953) developed the cloze procedure as an alternative to multiple-choice tests. Since then, the cloze technique has undergone a great deal of adaptation using a whole host of variations such as:

1. Allow synonyms as correct answers.
2. Delete every fifth content word (leaving function words intact).
3. Use an alternative to every fifth word deleted.
4. Provide a list of word choices from which examinees are to pick the best answer.

Assessment of teaching and pedagogical practices

What is increasingly clear from research is that the teacher is the most crucial factor in the classroom. The teacher who is knowledgeable and able to combine and adjust various methods, practices and strategies to meet the needs of a particular group of students is most likely to lead those students to higher levels of literacy engagement and achievement. You, as a future professional teacher, should regularly assess your own teaching routinely and systematically (Lipson and Wixson, 2009). However, for assessment of teaching to be effective, evidence-based best teaching practices should be strategically implemented and evaluated (Gambrell et al., 2007). Moreover, effective teachers are empowered when they identify and select evidence-based literacy practices to create integrated instructional approaches that adapt to the differentiated needs of their students.

Table 11.3 is a practitioner-designed rubric to be used as an instrument to evaluate teaching. A rubric such as this can easily be made into a checklist to be used by you or a colleague. It is often a good idea to ask a colleague to use the rubric while you observe each other's lessons from time to time.

Table 11.3 Teacher self-assessment rubric

Participation	Attention	Are all children focused on the literacy activities?
	Engagement	Are the children deeply absorbed in the literacy lesson/task?
	Stimulation	Do I motivate interest in literacy tasks, concepts and learning?
	Pleasure	Do I create an enthusiastic and energetic literacy classroom?
	Consistency	Do I use strong literacy routines that are recognised and understood by the children?
Knowledge	Environment	Do I use a literate physical environment as a teaching resource?
	Purpose	Do the children's responses indicate tacit or explicit understanding of the purpose of the literacy task?
	Substance	Does the lesson/task lead to substantial literacy engagement, not literacy work?
	Explanations	Are explanations of literacy concepts and skills clear and at an appropriate level?
	Modelling	Do the demonstrations of literacy tasks include metacognitive explanations?
	Meta-language	Are children provided with language for talking about and exemplifying literacy concepts?

(Continued)

Table 11.3 (Continued)

Orchestration	Awareness	Do I show a high level of awareness of literacy activities and participation by children?
	Structure	Have I made the environment predictable and orderly?
	Flexibility	Do I respond to learning opportunities that arise in the flow of the literacy lesson?
	Pace	Do I provide strong forward momentum in literacy lessons?
	Transition	Is a minimum amount of time spent in transitions or is there productive use of transitions?
Support	Assessment	Do I show the use of fine-grained knowledge of the children's performance in planning and teaching?
	Scaffolding	Do I extend children's literacy learning through modelling, modifying, correcting?
	Feedback	Do I give timely, focused and explicit literacy feedback to children?
	Responsiveness	Do I share and build on children's literacy contributions?
	Explicitness (word level)	Do I direct children's attention to explicit word and sound strategies?
	Explicitness (text level)	Do I make explicit specific attributes of a text?
	Persistence	Do I provide many opportunities to practise and master new literacy learning?
Differentiation	Challenge	Do I extend and promote higher levels of thinking in literacy learning?
	Individualisation	Do I differentiate literacy instruction and show recognition of individual differences?
	Inclusion	Do I facilitate the inclusion of all children in literacy lessons?
	Variation	Is my literacy teaching often structured around groups or individuals?
	Connection	Are connections often made between class and community literacy-related knowledge?
	Warmth	Am I welcoming and positive and is my classroom inviting and focused on literacy learning?
	Rapport	Does my relationship with the children support tactful literacy interventions?
	Credibility	Do I elicit respect that enables me to overcome any challenges to order and lesson flow?
	Citizenship	Do I encourage equality, tolerance, inclusivity and awareness of the needs of others?
	Independence	Do I make sure that the children take some responsibility for their own literacy learning?

Vignette 11.2

Ms Ryder was a keen teacher who wanted the very best for her students so she used the above rubric (Table 11.3) to self-assess her teaching.

> ## Questions
>
> 1 Why is it a good idea to use something like this rubric?
> 2 What are the pros and cons of having another teacher use the rubric to observe your teaching?
> 3 How else could you reflect on your teaching?

Informing and involving parents

Assessment information should be communicated regularly to students to inform them about what they are achieving at school to help them improve their learning. Parents also need to know how their children are progressing and how they can best be helped. It is also important for teachers to monitor their own teaching content and methods in order to diagnose problems so that they can make any necessary changes to the curriculum. School authorities and educational decision makers also need to make informed decisions on policy and implementation based on assessment. However, it should be emphasised that all of these decisions will depend on the particular reasons for conducting assessments (Alexander, 2010).

Conclusion

Assessment is a multi-faceted and multi-layered process that is ongoing. It is vital for good teaching as it informs and drives instruction. It is multi-faceted as it not only focuses on the learner but also involves assessment of the learning context, pedagogy and instructional processes. It is multi-layered because it requires you as a teacher to balance data from one source with information from many other formal and informal measures and observations. There are many reasons for collecting data on student progress, from informing instruction to determining individual differences in progress, reporting and accountability.

Virtually any activity can become an assessment tool. An important aspect of assessment is the notion of self-evaluation because it leads to self-supporting behaviours, both for teachers and students.

 ## Discussion questions and activities

 Points for discussion

1 What types of assessment can teachers access?
2 How has assessment changed over time?

(Continued)

(Continued)

3   Using Google, search for the 'reciprocal teaching' procedure and discuss how you could design a rubric to assess your students' performance.

 Group activities

1   Discuss the importance of setting a goal before an assessment activity.
2   Go to www.readabilityformulas.com/fry-graph-readability-formula.php and assess the readability of a reading passage that children are likely to read. Discuss the pros and cons of using the formula to grade a book or article.
3   In groups, design a cloze procedure and discuss its effective use for the purpose of self-evaluation.
4   Why do you think that the think-aloud protocol enables self-evaluation?
5   In groups of three, discuss how you could use the think-aloud protocol to enhance self-evaluation with the procedure.

Whole-class activity

Divide into groups of about eight and design a rubric to assess a writing activity.

References

Afflerbach, P. (2007). Best practices in literacy assessment. In L. B. Gambrell, L. M. Morrow and M. Pressley (eds), *Best Practices in Literacy Instruction* (3rd edn) (pp. 264–282). New York: The Guilford Press.

Afflerbach, P., Kim, J., Crassas, M. E. and Cho, B. (2011). Best practices in literacy assessment. In L. B. Gambrell and L. M. Morrow (eds), *Best Practices in Literacy Instruction* (4th edn) (pp. 319–340). New York: The Guilford Press.

Alexander, R. (ed.) (2010). *Children, their World, their Education: Final Report and Recommendations of the Alexander 2010 Primary Review.* Oxon: Routledge.

August, D. and Shanahan, T. (eds) (2006). *Developing Literacy in Second-language Learners: Report of the National Literacy Panel on Language Minority Children and Youth.* Malwah, NJ: Erlbaum.

Clay, M. M. (1993). *Reading Recovery.* Portsmouth, NH: Heinemann.

Coccamise, D. and Snyder, L. (2005). Theory and pedagogical practices of text comprehension. *Topics in Language Disorders, 25,* 5–20.

Duke, N. K. and Pearson, P. D. (2002). Effective practices for developing reading comprehension. In A. E. Farstrup and S. J. Samuels (eds), *What Research has to Say about Reading Instruction* (3rd edn) (pp. 205–242). Newark, DE: International Reading Association.

Elley, W. B. (1989). Vocabulary acquisition from listening to stories. *Reading Research Quarterly, 24,* 174–187.

Ericsson, K. A. and Simon, H. A. (1984). *Protocol Analysis: Verbal Reports as Data.* Cambridge, MA: The MIT Press.

Farris, P. J., Fuhler, C. J. and Walther, M. P. (2004). *Teaching Reading: A Balanced Approach for Today's Classrooms*. Boston: McGraw-Hill.

Freebody, P. and Freiberg, J. (2001). Re-discovering practical reading activities in homes and schools. *Journal of Research in Reading*, 24, 222–234.

Gambrell, L. B., Malloy, J. A. and Mazzoni, S. A. (2007). Evidence-based best practice for comprehensive literacy instruction. In L. B. Gambrell, L. M. Morrow and M. Pressley (eds), *Best Practices in Literacy Instruction* (3rd edn) (pp. 11–29). New York: The Guilford Press.

Gersten, R., Fuchs, L. S., Williams, J. P. and Baker, S. (2001). Teaching reading comprehension strategies to students with learning disabilities: A review of research. *Review of Educational Research*, 71, 279–320.

Goodman, K. and Goodman, Y. (1977). Learning about psycholinguistic processes by analysing oral reading. *Harvard Educational Review*, 47, 317–333.

Gunning, T. G. (2003). The role of readability in today's classrooms. *Topics in Language Disorders*, 23, 175–200.

Gunning, T. G. (2010). *Assessing and Correcting Reading and Writing Difficulties* (4th edn). Boston: Allyn & Bacon.

Hattie, J. and Timperley, H. (2007). The power of feedback. *Review of Educational Research*, 77(1), 81–112.

Hay, I. and Woolley, G. (2011). The challenge of reading comprehension. In T. Le, Q. Le and M. Short (eds), *Language and Literacy Education in a Challenging World* (pp. 198–209). New York: Nova Science.

Israel, S. E., Bauserman, K. L. and Block, C. C. (2005). Metacognitive assessment strategies. *Thinking Classroom*, 6(2), 21–28.

Joshi, M. and Aaron, P. G. (2000). The component model of reading: Simple view of reading made a little more complex. *Reading Psychology*, 21, 85–97.

Kintsch, W. (1974). *The Representation of Meaning in Memory*. Hillsdale, NJ: Erlbaum.

Lipson, M. Y. and Wixson, K. K. (2009). *Assessment and Instruction of Reading and Writing Difficulties: An Interactive Approach* (4th edn). Boston: Pearson.

Manset-Williamson, G. and Nelson, J. M. (2005). Balanced, strategic reading instruction for upper-elementary and middle school students with reading disabilities: A comparative study of two approaches. *Learning Disability Quarterly*, 28, 59–74.

National Reading Panel (NRP) (2000). *Teaching Children to Read: Report of the Comprehension Instruction Subgroup to the National Institute of Child Health and Development*. Washington, DC: NICD.

Paris, S. G. and Stahl, S. A. (2005). *Children's Reading Comprehension and Assessment*. Mahwah, NJ: Erlbaum.

Pearson, D. P. and Johnson, D. D. (1978). *Teaching Reading Comprehension*. New York: Holt, Rinehart & Winston.

Pikulski, J. J. and Chard, D. J. (2005). Fluency: Bridge between decoding and reading comprehension. *The Reading Teacher*, 58(6), 510–519.

Pressley, M. (2002). At-risk students: Learning to break through comprehension barriers. In C. Collins Block, L. B. Gambrell and M. Pressley (eds), *Improving Comprehension Instruction* (pp. 354–369). San Francisco: Jossey-Bass.

Reutzel, D. R. (2007). Organising effective literacy instruction: Differentiating instruction to meet the needs of all children. In L. B. Gambrell, L. M. Morrow and M. Pressley (eds), *Best Practices in Literacy Instruction* (3rd edn) (pp. 313–343). New York: The Guilford Press.

Rumelhart, D. E. (1977). Understanding and summarising brief stories. In D. LaBerg and J. Samuels (eds), *Basic Processes in Reading Perception and Comprehension*. Hillsdale, NJ: Erlbaum.

Schunk, D. (2003). Self-efficacy for reading and writing: Influence of modelling, goal setting, and self-evaluation. *Reading and Writing Quarterly*, 19, 159–172.

Schunk, D. H. (2004). *Learning Theories: An Educational Perspective* (4th edn). Saddle River, NJ: Pearson.

Snow, C. E. (2003). Assessment of reading comprehension. In A. P. Sweet and C. E. Snow (eds), *Rethinking Reading Comprehension* (pp. 191–206). New York: The Guilford Press.

Stein, N. L. and Glenn, C. G. (1977). An analysis of story comprehension in elementary school children. In R. O. Freedle (ed.), *Discourse Processing: Multidisciplinary Perspectives* (pp. 53–120). Norwood, NJ: Ablex.

Taylor, W. (1953) 'Cloze procedure': A new tool for measuring readability. *Journalism Quarterly*, 30, 415–433.

Trabasso, T. (1981). On the making of inferences during reading and their recall. In J. T. Guthrie (ed.), *Comprehension and Teaching: Research Reviews* (pp. 56–75). Chicago: International Reading Association.

Trabasso, T. and Sperry, L. L. (1985). Causal relatedness and importance of story events. *Journal of Memory and Language*, 24, 595–611.

Vellutino, F. R., Fletcher, J. M., Snowling, M. J. and Scanlon, D. M. (2004). Specific reading disability (dyslexia): What have we learned in the past four decades? *Journal of Child Psychiatry*, 45, 2–40.

Vygotsky, L. S. (1962). *Thought and Language*. Cambridge, MA: Harvard University Press.

Vygotsky, L. S. (1978). *Mind and Society*. Cambridge, MA: The MIT Press.

Westwood, P. (2001). *Reading and Learning Difficulties: Approaches to Teaching and Assessment*. Camberwell, VIC: ACER Press.

Witt, J. C., Elliott, S. N., Kramer, J. J. and Gresham, F. M. (1994). *Assessment of Children: Fundamental Methods and Practices*. Dubuque, IA: WCB Brown and Benchmark.

Woolley, G. (2011). *Reading Comprehension: Assisting Children with Learning Difficulties*. Dordrecht, The Netherlands: Springer International.

CHAPTER 12

FAMILY AND SCHOOL LITERACY PARTNERSHIPS

Chapter objectives

- To understand literacy learners and their relationships within a modern global and multicultural setting.
- To develop knowledge about the literacy needs of children and how family–school partnerships can increase students' learning outcomes.
- To develop an understanding of cultural sensitivity and how to form home–school literacy partnerships.

Key questions

1. What is meant by the term social capital?
2. How can schools develop social capital for the benefit of their literacy learners?
3. How can schools with diverse and multicultural populations enhance their family literacy programmes?

Key words: cultural diversity, family, home–school partnerships, literacy partnerships, paired reading, support.

Introduction

School systems and policy makers have emphasised the benefits of developing strong home–school literacy partnerships. In general, research shows that greater parental involvement in the education of their children will foster more positive attitudes towards school, improve homework outcomes, reduce absenteeism and enhance literacy development. Effective home–school partnerships develop the social capital of schools and their wider communities by promoting positive home and school cultures that are typified by joint planning, cooperation and the sharing of resources. In particular, family literacy partnerships stimulate personal development among parents by improving the reading outcomes of their children and contribute to professional rewards for principals and school staff. To be effective, schools should: examine and identify current local literacy practices; develop mutual recognition of cultural diversity; identify productive literacy practices and methods; and communicate and disseminate educational information to caregivers.

> The combined evidence supports a clear claim that parent involvement in their children's learning has noteworthy academic benefits for nearly all children. Moreover, when children have mothers with less education, parent involvement exerts an even more powerful influence on children's literacy performance, even eliminating the achievement gap that typically separates the performance of children of low- and high-education mothers (Paratore and Edwards, 2011: 437).

There is a very close correlation between poverty and illiteracy. Often, literacy practices that take place in the classroom have little relevance to many children outside the school environment, particularly for children from lower socio-economic or foreign-language backgrounds (Cairney, 2003). However, many low-income or low-education families do provide rich language experiences in the home but quite often there is a non-alignment with the types of activities that take place regularly in school. This chapter examines these differences and suggests some evidence-based approaches that will enable effective links to be formed between home and school. These links should forge strong literacy partnerships between families and their schools that will be supportive of children as literacy learners and produce positive academic outcomes that will be valued by both the home and the school.

This is not a new idea. Earlier last century, Huey (1908) wrote about the value of parents and caregivers reading at home and its relation to learning literature at school when he wrote: 'It all begins with parents reading with children' (p. 103). Research also supports the importance of the practice of reading at home and the forging of strong links between the home environment and literacy practices that take place in school (Butler, 2010; Cairney, 2003; Hidi and Harackiewicz, 2000).

A demographic shift

In recent years, there have been major shifts in the balance between private and working lives in most OECD countries. There is a trend in the developed world toward individualisation, older parents, smaller families, an ageing population and extended working hours, with a corresponding decrease in the availability of voluntary work. In general, there are more marriage breakdowns, more single-parent families, more blended families and a greater number of mothers participating in both the full-time and part-time workforce (Carter and McGoldrick, 1999). The progression towards globalisation is speeding up connections between cultures and across national boundaries, bringing about a greater acceptance of multiculturalism. This worldwide trend has gained momentum with the introduction of new technologies, easier access to information and the instant flow of communication. With cheaper flights, there is a much greater movement of goods and services; people also move more easily and more often. Increased global employment opportunities and higher levels of migration are contributing to greater ethnic and cultural diversity. In many countries, the proportion of students learning English as their second language has grown dramatically, presenting educators with big challenges (Freebody et al., 2008). While the wealth of most people is generally increasing in developed and developing nations, the gap between rich and poor is becoming ever wider. For example, there is a growing digital divide between homes where children have access to a computer and those where they don't. The consequence of these trends is that many disadvantaged children will not always be provided with the quality of support that is necessary for their ongoing literacy development.

Traditionally, the home has been viewed as the first learning place with parents acknowledged as the first and enduring educators of their children (DEEWR, 2009). However, this view ignores the reality that there are a number of interacting spheres of influence shaping children's learning, such as family, neighbourhood, community institutions and the broader socio-historical context (Alexander, 2010; Schalock, 2004). The ecological model (as seen in Figure 12.1) assumes that children are embedded within complex social and environmental contexts.

The family sphere of influence includes relationships between individuals, parents, caregivers, relatives and friends. Microsystems encompass the individual's involvement with preschool, school, school groups such as classes and sporting groups, other groups and clubs within school and their peer relationships. The macrosystem involves the individual making connections with the wider community such as clubs, sporting and interest groups and faith-based organisations such as churches, mosques and temples. These systems (or spheres of influence) interact with each other in a reciprocal manner, and each will have a profound impact on the learning outcomes of children who are within their sphere of influence (Hollomotz, 2009). Thus, schools should create

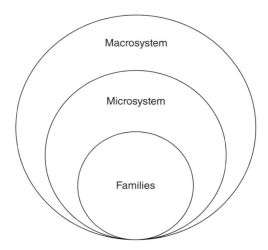

Figure 12.1 The ecological model

Source: Hollomotz, 2009: 104

an environment that interacts with each sphere of influence by supporting parents within the wider community and developing the appropriate communication channels and opportunities to allow this interaction (Veen, 1999).

In England, the Ofsted report (2009) showed that many disadvantaged schools actually beat the odds when it comes to academic attainment, as measured by national testing, showing that it is not necessarily the types of socio-cultural backgrounds that children come from that determine their learning outcomes, but the quality of the educational experiences that parents and schools provide that make the difference. Moreover, the Rose (2009) and Cambridge reports (Alexander, 2010) have asserted that shared responsibility for the education of children between parents, caregivers, education practitioners and other stakeholders will have significant outcomes. For example, children of parents that are highly educated are generally expected to do better in literacy at school but when parents with lower levels of education participate in home–school partnerships the gap is greatly diminished (Dearing et al., 2004).

Other education authorities have also recognised the value of home–school partnerships, for example, in Australia, the Smarter Schools and National Partnerships are a set of agreements between the Commonwealth government and all states and territories to facilitate reforms across six priority areas, one of which is partnerships with parents, schools, businesses and local communities (Butler, 2010). This echoes a widely held belief that effective home–school partnerships are associated with indications of school success, such as more positive attitudes towards school, improved homework outcomes, reduced absenteeism, greater literacy achievement and lower rates of repeating grades (Hoover-Dempsey et al., 2005). What is certain is that the support that families provide to their children at home has the greatest impact on academic achievement (Ofsted, 2009). Another significant Australian educational policy document emphasising this approach is the Melbourne Declaration on Educational Goals for Young Australians (MCEETYA, 2008). This declaration advocates a collaborative approach to supporting children in reaching positive outcomes from birth onwards through involvement and engagement across schools and sectors, individuals and their families. Positive early interventions have also highlighted the need for educators and other professionals to work in concert with children's parents and caregivers (Karoly et al., 2005).

In Britain, the proportion of children living in poverty has widened dramatically and in school these children generally perform poorly compared to their peers (Alexander, 2010). Ideally, parents are expected to become involved at school, but establishing good home–school relations has not been easy. Teachers have often reported low levels of support and follow-up from parents and caregivers (Hoover-Dempsey and Sandler, 1995, 1997). Conversely, many parents have reported that teachers have not always welcomed their involvement at school (Peña, 2001), while not all parents are confident about helping their children at home, particularly with homework and with understanding and using the language of the curriculum (Rose, 2009).

This situation is often compounded by teachers having limited preparation or training in how to effectively involve and engage with families (Hoover-Dempsey et al., 2005). A common belief in many schools is that too many parents have strong anti-school attitudes that may stem from their own experiences of school, and the perception is that some parents are apathetic while some are more openly hostile to educational institutions (Alexander, 2010). Given that parents whose children need the highest level of assistance are often the least likely to engage in school programmes that support their children, there is still some uncertainty as to how to engage in this partnering (Homel et al., 2001). This is a concern within both the UK and Australasian contexts, and different educational authorities have used a variety of approaches in response to the problem (DEEWR, 2009). What is certain is that schools should create an environment that is welcoming and considerate of parents (Veen, 1999).

Parents and other community members can play a significant role in supporting children's learning by being involved in school activities, such as attending school functions, volunteering and participating in decision making. Normally, parents are more predisposed to come to school when their children are performing well and when they perceive that their child's school goes out of its way to make them feel included by providing coffee mornings and other tokens of appreciation (Ofsted, 2009). This interaction is important because schools can be viewed as places that develop a synergy among values, beliefs and preferred behaviours between the home, the school and the wider community. The support given by parents/schools can be at many different levels. Epstein and Connors (1992) have developed a taxonomy that considers six levels of parental involvement:

1. Building home environments that support children's development
2. Supported mechanisms that enable school to inform parents about programmes and children's progress
3. Programmes that enable family involvement at school as volunteers/aides, being an audience for children's performances and taking part in meetings and events
4. Monitoring and assisting children at home in learning activities
5. Involvement in decision making, government and advocacy in school-related organisation
6. Collaboration and involvement in school and community ventures

Family–school literacy partnerships

Positive family–school literacy partnerships contribute to professional rewards for principals and school staff and develop the social and educational capital of parents. The term family literacy is used to describe literacy practices that occur in a family or home context. Family literacy programmes have become one of the key areas of expansion of literacy provision in the USA, Canada, the UK and Australia. It is estimated that there may be over 1000 such programmes across the USA, and family literacy has been gaining momentum in the UK and Australasia (Cairney and Munsie, 1995).

The OECD's Programme for International Student Assessment (PISA) and other recent research show that having books in the home is a major factor leading to success in literacy learning in school and beyond (OECD, 2004). Family literacy programmes support a meaningful relationship whereby there is a sharing of resources between school and home so that learning is enhanced beyond the confines of the classroom. Family–school partnerships can operate for different purposes, such as providing libraries for parents with books, toys, computer hardware and software, language and literacy classes for parents, curriculum information sessions and literacy workshops to enable more effective interactions around homework and other activities at home. Schools should view parents as partners rather than clients. To be effective, schools should: examine and identify current local literacy practices; develop a mutual recognition of cultural diversity; and identify productive literacy practices that are already in operation in the home. It has been shown that parental involvement is closely linked to student academic achievement, to teacher ratings of student competence, student grades and high-stakes test scores (Ofsted, 2009). What is certain is that without the good intentions and efforts of home-school partnerships, many young children will be destined for social and educational disadvantage.

Each family is unique, and it might not be the particular home literacy practices themselves that lead to success or lack of it but rather a complex combination of school and home factors that vary from child to child. For example, having books in the home, or the social and cultural value placed on books, is one of the major factors leading to success in literacy at school (OECD, 2004). There is strong evidence to suggest that communication with children and the encouragement that is given at home contribute to literacy learning outcomes. What is often required is for the school to offer some guidance and support. Family literacy is not something that is done to families, it is something done *with* families to enable them to have greater control over and investment in their children's literacy development (Topping, 1996). In some school districts, parents have reported that their involvement in school had improved their children's attitude towards school and encouraged their learning (Moles, 2000). Moreover, for family literacy partnerships to prosper, emphasis should be placed on friendship and collaboration with the overriding intent of supporting the wellbeing of children (Butler, 2010). School partnership programmes enable parents to be more informed about the kinds of activities their children are involved in, acknowledge that parents are the prime educators of their children and give regular feedback to show how parents' role is central to their children's education and wellbeing (DEST, 2006).

What constitutes a home–school partnership may vary from school to school, from community to community and from one cultural context to another (DEST, 2006). The social, cultural and linguistic diversity of families will affect the learning outcomes of children. Thus, responsive curricula should be developed to build more effective relationships between home and school that are more socially, culturally and linguistically appropriate for the community (Cairney, 2003). Principals have a key role to play by showing leadership and by being visible and available to parents (DEST, 2006). For example, they can invite parents into school by providing a space that they can call their own. In such a space, parent volunteers could be assigned to talk with and offer advice to other parents (Moles, 2000). A community resource centre within a school can also be a venue or an agency for parental self-growth (DEST, 2006). For many families, this type of capacity building is best provided by peers found within the school/parent community. This capacity building will also need to focus on building parental efficacy through developing confidence in parenting and an understanding of the impact parents have on their child's achievement, as well as practical strategies such as how to communicate with teachers and school leaders and how to effectively advocate for their children (Butler, 2010). Parents should be supported and encouraged by unsolicited positive comments from teachers, wherever possible.

Often, the main concern of parents is to help their children with their homework. It is important for teachers to make the curriculum transparent and understandable and to be aware that parents need to be familiar with the language of learning (Butler, 2010). Parents need to be informed about the way things are done in today's classrooms, and enabled to develop the appropriate helping strategies to assist their children. Thus, information sharing with parents in school communities stimulates their awareness, interest and participation.

Home involvement and volunteering at school

A study of parent language and literacy schemes in Australian schools collected data on approximately 260 programmes (Cairney and Munsie, 1995). Many of these programmes placed a great deal of emphasis on parents reading with and to their children at home because there is a strong correlation between consistent home reading and success at school (1995).

The fundamental elements of family literacy learning programmes are the positive language interactions of the child that are guided by a supportive parent or caregiver (Cairney, 2000; Vygotsky, 1962). Once parents begin to interact with their children around reading activities, their children usually respond with eagerness. However, to avoid frustration caregivers need to monitor their children's level of reading difficulty by using reading materials that are at the students' instructional level of difficulty (see Chapter 6) (Miller, 2003). Ideally, reading materials should be suited to students' interests and motivation levels by providing some element of choice of reading material (Hidi and Harackiewicz, 2000). Some guidance from the school may be necessary for choice of books and ease of reading. Further, some training in guided reading techniques by the school is vital because it has been demonstrated that children assisted at home by trained parents generally outperform children assisted by untrained adults (Wasik, 1998a).

In the UK, Hewison and Tizard (1980) conducted a study of a family literacy programme over a two-year period called the Haringey Reading Project in which trained parents were encouraged by the school to listen regularly to children's reading for a short period every day. The researcher found that by the end of the two-year period the participating groups were reading at a significantly higher level than the children in the non-participating groups from the same schools. It was further noted that the differences were sustained three years after the project had finished. Other research has also confirmed the efficacy of family literacy programmes in assisting children to develop improvements in reading and other academic and non-academic areas (Hewison and Tizard, 1980; Morgan and Goldstein, 2004; Nichols, 2000). It is not clear exactly why family literacy programmes are effective but they do provide a sense of belonging, accomplishment and increased motivation (Kemp, 1987b; Woolley, 2011).

Paired reading training programmes

In the USA, there have been a number of other programmes designed to assist parents to more fully support children's early literacy learning. 'Head Start' is one such programme that has been designed to help parents and caregivers to assist in the literacy development of their children (Hindman and Wasik, 2010). Elliott and Hewison (1994) maintained that some parents were more effective than others, due to their superior knowledge about reading. Furthermore, researchers observed that parents who participated in home reading training projects became better informed about reading, the reading process and how to interact with their child in reading tasks.

It has been reported that parents want to be shown how to give better assistance in reading without causing anger, accompanied by an unwillingness to take part in future home reading episodes (Kemp, 1987a, b). Other studies have found that effective home–school literacy programmes are highly structured and involve a high degree of training (Duran and Monereo, 2005; Rohrbeck et al., 2003; Topping, 1998; Wasik, 1998b). Trained parents are generally able to interact more effectively with their children when given appropriate guidance by educational practitioners (McNaughton et al., 1992; Stuart et al., 1998; Topping and Wolfendale, 1995).

Supporting parents requires a range of resources, ongoing guidance and regular feedback (Collins and Matthey, 2001). It is important that the tasks assigned by school for parents to do with their children be consistent with what they can easily and willingly accomplish (Roe and Vukelich, 2001). Parent and sibling satisfaction should be a major indicator in the success of family literacy programmes and be related to the extent to which reading goals are achieved (Fresko and Chen, 1989).

A personalised, responsive relationship-based approach to reading, combined with interesting text and student choice of appropriate material, facilitates reading for students who have struggled for years and have developed a resistance to reading (Cox and Guthrie, 2001; Snow, 2002; Worthy et al., 2002). When children receive informed feedback, they develop positive motivational beliefs and a self-regulating focus (Vollmeyer and Rheinberg, 2005). The interpersonal aspects of tutoring programmes, involving the interaction of parents and students in home and school partnerships, have been recognised as having a positive influence on children's self-confidence and self-efficacy (Cairney and Munsie, 1995; Neuman, 1995).

Vignette 12.1

Burell Park South Infants School is a co-educational school located within a metropolitan area. The school is 20 years old and caters for a predominantly blue-collar workforce but has a large number of single-parent families and approximately 20% have English as their second language. It is a large school with five classes per grade and with an increasing number of families that have both caregivers working. The school has many opportunities for parents to participate in school activities, such as swimming, athletics carnivals and fun days (games) where parents are invited to take part in organising and running some

(Continued)

(Continued)

events. Other parents are invited to run stalls for catering and fundraising and also to hand out awards.

The school also conducts an open day once a year, a grandparents' day, a teddy bears' picnic, a multicultural dress-up and food day, a fancy dress parade (traditional dress), an Easter hat parade, a school fête and other special events. The Parents and Friends group organises many of these activities and also raises funds for community facilities and equipment for the children to use. For example, the group has recently bought an urn and crockery for a meeting room for parents to run English and ethnic cooking classes and topical talks by teachers and community leaders. The room is also used as a drop-in centre for parents to speak to the parent liaison officer who can give advice and relay concerns to the administration.

The school has an open-door policy for parents but does expect that appointments will be arranged ahead of time via email or phone. There are two parent–teacher meetings per year to discuss the children's progress and a parents' evening to share information about procedures and to give advice about homework and other issues.

The school has an extensive classroom literacy programme that supports a well-organised family literacy programme. Each class has an extensive set of levelled and colour-coded readers for children to take home each day. The learning support teacher periodically trains parents during and after school sessions in how to conduct paired reading sessions. The classroom teachers are also trained by the learning support teacher to monitor the programme and to give parents ongoing feedback via a take-home diary and via emails when necessary. The learning support teacher also organises some parents to assist in the early reading intervention programme that gives at-risk students regular extra paired-reading sessions during school time.

The English-as-a-second-language teacher works with the school librarian to develop a bilingual book section to support both L1 and L2 language learning. Other L1 books are donated from home and are supplemented by home-made books with traditional and contemporary stories. The ESL teacher liaises with the classroom teachers to make sure that the reading materials that go home are the most appropriate and progress is monitored regularly.

Questions

1 How was social capital developed within the school community?
2 How did the school promote social capital for the benefit of their literacy learners?
3 How did the school involve diverse and multicultural populations?
4 Do you have any other ideas as to how your future school could support home–school partnerships?

Effective training and supervision

Effective family literacy programmes must be supported by school staff and require specialist teachers to give appropriate training and supervision (Roe and Vukelich, 2001; Vollmeyer and Rheinberg, 2005). Assessment of the programme should be ongoing with specific feedback given to parents and the children's siblings. However, parents and caregivers need explicit information about proven instructional strategies when assisting children with reading at home (McNaughton et al., 1992; Neuman, 1995; Roe and Vukelich, 2001). In terms of helping strategies, *Pause, Prompt and Praise* (McNaughton et al., 1987) has been shown to be effective in New Zealand (Glynn and McNaughton, 1985), Australia (Houghton and Bain, 1993; Houghton and Glynn, 1993) and the UK (McNaughton et al., 1987; Wheldall and Mettem, 1985;). What is certain is that when parents adhere to certain design characteristics, family literacy goals will be achieved when ongoing training and support are provided (Padak and Rasinski, 2004).

Cultural diversity

It has been argued that most programmes have been school-centred and have not considered the valuable contribution made by the home (Cairney, 2000). One of the important things that teachers can do is to understand and acknowledge the cultural diversity and language used in the home. Consequently, schools should set up processes and structures to: (a) examine and study local literacy practices; (b) develop mutual recognition of cultural literacy practices; (c) identify productive literacy processes and methods; and (d) communicate and disseminate educational information (Freebody et al., 1995).

Examine and study local literacy practices

When language-minority students enter school for the first time, they may be confronted by literacy practices that are unfamiliar. This social and cultural mismatch can result in difficulties in communication and modes of interaction within the classroom. This situation can be a significant factor in the ongoing achievement or non-achievement of students at school. However, many low-income and also minority families do offer an environment that enhances literacy development, however these interactions are seldom recognised as valid instances of literacy learning. Schools would do well to promote a broader literacy approach whereby children are encouraged to bring to school literacy practices from their own homes (Woolley, 2010). The culture of your school must reflect the dynamic system of values, beliefs and standards that should be developed through an understanding of the community and its shared values.

Develop mutual recognition of cultural literacy practices

Schools need to develop a strong commitment to students through educational opportunities and programmes that give special attention to language-minority students. Some schools encourage teachers to take on a liaison role by visiting the children's homes before the school year starts: they encourage parents to attend talks by staff about school work and expectations (Ofsted, 2009). When teachers visit homes, they gain a greater knowledge and understanding of a student's background and develop learning experiences based on this information. Parents, and more particularly children, will be empowered in the school context through supportive interactions promoting the notion that all children can achieve at school. Children's literacy skills can be strengthened when they are encouraged to maintain their first language competence at home and at school (Woolley, 2010). Some successful schools also offer English classes or conduct after-school clubs on various issues or topics and investigate other appropriate social communication channels for parents (Veen, 1999). School recognition and support of caregiver/parenting roles play an essential part in nurturing the wellbeing and self-esteem of children.

Identifying productive literacy processes and methods

Well-informed parents foster positive student reading self-concepts and help their children satisfy psychological needs such as relationship, competence and autonomy. The following is a list of effective paired tutoring practices that have been identified in the research literature these three vital elements.

Effective home literacy tutoring practices

Relationship:

- Provide authentic and culturally appropriate and interesting books.
- Ensure that reading sessions are brief, fun, enjoyable and in a place free from other distractions.
- Use semantic-based correction prompts rather than highlighting mistakes.
- Elaborate on the story content by highlighting interesting facts and ideas in the text.

- Explain and discuss unfamiliar words, syntax and punctuation before and after reading.
- Use supportive comments that are not critical.
- Develop support with shared reading goals while encouraging reading independence.
- Share thoughts, experiences and ideas generated from story content.

Competence:

- Use the 'Pause, Prompt and Praise' method for supported reading.
- Emphasise story content and meaning rather than correcting decoding errors.
- Use semantic-based prompts such as re-reading or reading ahead.
- Use repeated readings (see Chapter 6) to promote fluency and familiarity.
- Model reading with expression (see Chapter 6).
- Use cues from the pictures and the context as well as graphophonic cues.
- Avoid interrupting and ignore minor errors that do not change meaning.
- Miscues (mistakes) are not errors but should be regarded as a source of learning.
- Use interesting books to motivate children and encourage reading for pleasure.

Autonomy:

- Give specific and immediate feedback during guided reading sessions.
- Use scaffolding and explicit modelling of comprehension skills.
- Choose books that are at the students' appropriate level of difficulty.
- Promote students' interest and choice of books.
- Generously use specific praise to enhance reading performance and self-efficacy.

Vignette 12.2

Kearney, Fletcher and Dobrenov-Major (2009) investigated learning outcomes for Samoan-Australian students in Logan City. Samoans are the largest and one of the fastest-growing ethnic groups in regional areas of southeast Queensland, including Logan City (Australian Bureau of Statistics, 2003, 2006). Samoan families have a collective or communal orientation that favours group needs and a sense of spiritual relational orientation (Bush et al., 2005; Mafi, 2005). In contrast, mainstream Australian families are more individualistic in that they promote an individual's self-interest and personal privacy while giving less recognition to the needs of those who are outside the immediate family. Kearney et al. (2009) found that teachers initially had a limited understanding

(Continued)

(Continued)

of the non-alignment issues that were found between home/community/church and school. However, they observed that when teachers became more informed and reflective in relation to their practices concerning the nature of the cultural non-alignment, they were able to enact change to their beliefs, dispositions and pedagogy. Thus, effective instruction for children with diverse cultural and linguistic backgrounds demands a coming together of minds between learners and teachers.

Questions

1 What is meant by the term non-alignment?
2 How can schools promote social capital for the benefit of their literacy learners?
3 How can schools with diverse and multicultural populations promote literacy?

Family literacy programmes generally contribute to improved literacy outcomes for many children. Effective family literacy programmes focus on building trusting and collaborative relationships among teachers, families and community members. Information should be provided on what children do in school, including the display of projects, talks given by children and the showing of videos of what they actually do in the classroom. These sessions should encourage open discussion by addressing family needs and showing respect for cultural differences (Butler, 2010; Veen, 1999).

Communicate and disseminate educational information

It must be kept in mind that developing effective, trusting and mutually respectful relationships between school staff and families is not always easy, but family engagement in learning is one of the most under-utilised resources we have for improving children's learning and future opportunities (Butler, 2010). What is needed is for schools and communities to create a collective vision for how home–school partnerships can develop and enrich the social, financial, intellectual and spiritual capital. For this to take place, good communication between the school and the home is essential. This building of a sense of community and identity will not happen overnight but partnership must be built on trust and long-term planning.

Recognition of the role of the family in academic progress must be fostered through consultative decision making and collaboration. It must be emphasised that parents respond better when they believe that their involvement will support their child's education. This will have lasting effects on parental attitudes, particularly in cases where parents' relationship with the school was hostile to begin with (DEST, 2006). A positive school climate is developed when schools have a commitment to develop joint decision-making activities and when they give positive and specific feedback on parent involvement. The role of your school principal in developing positive school climates is particularly important. For example, principals should be seen to visit classrooms on a regular basis and take an interest in students' activities. They should be seen to be promoting parent involvement in many different ways and fostering the professional development of teaching staff. Frequent invitations to parents and good communication will develop trust and empowerment over time (Hoover-Dempsey et al., 2005). For example, some schools have reported good success in employing a school liaison officer. The liaison officer may be employed not only to foster communication between teachers and parents but also to have an input in school policy because they are able to voice the concerns of parents (Blackmore and Hutchinson, 2010).

Conclusion

Family–school partnerships will only succeed if educational leaders and policymakers have a firm commitment that reflects the belief that family–school partnerships will contribute to children's academic success in school. This is also true for teachers, community organisations and parents themselves. However, it is important that partnership endeavours are well designed and implemented carefully. In the past, many administrators and teachers have not viewed parent involvement as central to the school's educational goals and have merely paid lip service to home–school partnerships. When schools take part in a comprehensive programme of parent involvement, it will lead to a change in the culture of the school and improved relationships with homes. If teachers value lifelong learning for all and are keen to support children's learning, they will provide many and varied opportunities for parents and caregivers if they form effective family–school partnerships. Family literacy programmes help children develop better academic outcomes and provide other social and emotional benefits for children. However, for these programmes to be most effective, there needs to be ongoing supervision, guidance and training. In particular, children from minority communities will succeed at school when talents, resources and skills are acknowledged and incorporated into the instructional climate of the classroom. These opportunities can only take place in an atmosphere of mutual respect, trust and friendship, and with a mindset of partnership (DEST, 2006).

Discussion questions and activities

 ### Points for discussion

1 What are some social and cultural factors that impact on literacy?
2 What factors promote/hinder home–school partnerships?
3 What instructional approaches are needed to enhance family literacy programmes?

✝✝✝✝ Group activities

1 Brainstorm and make a list of ways a school could communicate and disseminate educational information among members of the school community, including school staff, students and other community members.
2 Identify ways for teachers and parents to examine their own literacy practices with children.
3 Identify processes and strategies that establish more productive methods to create and maintain partnerships between schools and their communities.
4 Explore ways of enhancing understanding of the differences and similarities between minority homes and school literacy practices among the school community that may lead to more effective mutual recognition of these practices in both sites.

 ### Whole-class activities

1 Develop a family literacy programme – what are the essential elements that this programme should include?
2 You have an open day for parents coming up. What could you promote in the school to develop home–school partnerships?
3 What types of special days or activities could the school promote?
4 What sorts of activities could a parent body run in a school?
5 How can school libraries make a contribution to home–school partnerships in diverse communities?

References

Alexander, R. (ed.) (2010). *Children, their World, their Education: Final Report and Recommendations of the Alexander 2010 Primary Review.* Oxon: Routledge.

Australian Bureau of Statistics (2003). *2001 Census Basic Community Profile: Central District, Logan City.* Canberra: Commonwealth of Australia.

Australian Bureau of Statistics (2006). *2006 Census Quick Stats: Logan City (Statistical Subdivision).* Canberra: Commonwealth of Australia. Available at: www.censusdata.abs.gov.au/ABSNavigation/prenav/ViewData?method=Place%20of%20Usual%20Residence&subaction=1&producttype=QuickStats&areacode=3

0530&action=401&documenttype=Main%20Features&collection=census&textve
rsion=true&breadcrumb=PLD&period=2006&navmapdisplayed=true&
(accessed 17 March 2008).

Blackmore, J. and Hutchinson, K. (2010). Ambivalent relations: The tricky foot-work of parental involvement in school communities. *Professional Voice*, 8(2), 19–26.

Bush, A., Collings, S., Tamasese, K. and Waldegrave, C. (2005). Samoan and psychiatrists' perspectives on the self: Qualitative comparison. *Australian and New Zealand Journal of Psychiatry*, 39, 621–626.

Butler, S. (2010). Family–school partnerships make a difference. *Professional Voice*, 8(2), 11–18.

Cairney, T. (2000). Beyond the classroom walls: The rediscovery of the family and community as partners in education. *Educational Review*, 52, 163–174.

Cairney, T. H. (2003). Literacy within family life. In N. Hall, J. Larson and J. Marsh (eds), *Handbook of Early Childhood Literacy*. London: Sage.

Cairney, T. and Munsie, L. (1995). Parent participation in literacy learning. *The Reading Teacher*, 48, 392–403.

Carter, B. and McGoldrick, M. (eds) (1999). *The Expanded Family Life Cycle: Individual, Family and Social Perspectives*. Boston: Allyn & Bacon.

Collins, L. and Matthey, S. (2001). Helping parents to read with their children: Evaluation of an individual and group reading motivation programme. *Journal of Research in Reading*, 24, 65–81.

Cox, K. and Guthrie, J. T. (2001). Motivational and cognitive contributions to students' amount of reading. *Contemporary Educational Psychology*, 26, 116–131.

Dearing, E., McCartney, K., Weiss, H. B., Kreider, H. and Simkins, S. (2004). The promotive effects of family educational involvement for low-income children's literacy. *Journal of School Psychology*, 42(6), 445–460.

Department of Education, Employment and Workplace Relations (DEEWR), Australian Government (2009). Belonging, Being, and Becoming: The Early Years Learning Framework for Australia. Available at: http://www.coag.gov.au/sites/default/files/early_years_learning_framework.pdf

Department of Education, Science and Training (DEST) (2006). *Family–School Partnerships Project: A Qualitative and Quantitative Study*. Canberra: Australian Government.

Duran, D. and Monereo, C. (2005). Styles and sequences of cooperative interaction in fixed and reciprocal peer tutoring. *Learning and Instruction*, 15, 179–199.

Elliott, J. A. and Hewison, J. (1994). Comprehension and interest in home reading. *British Journal of Educational Psychology*, 64, 203–220.

Epstein, J. L. and Connors, J. (1992). School and family partnerships. In M. Alkin (ed.), *Encyclopedia of Educational Research* (6th edn) (pp. 1139–1151). New York: Macmillan.

Freebody, P., Ludwig, C. and Gunn, S. (1995). *Everyday Literacy Practices in and out of Schools in Low Socio-economic Status Urban Communities: A Descriptive and Interpretive Research Program*. Canberra: DEETYA.

Freebody, P., Maton, K. and Martin, J. R. (2008). Talk, text, and knowledge in cumulative, integrated learning: A response to intellectual challenge. *Australian Journal of Language and Literacy*, 31(2), 188–201.

Fresko, B. and Chen, M. (1989). Ethnic similarity, tutor expertise, and tutor satisfaction in cross-age tutoring. *American Educational Research Journal*, 26, 122–140.

Glynn, T. and McNaughton, S. (1985). The Mangere home and school reading procedures: Continuing research on its effectiveness. *New Zealand Journal of Psychology*, 14, 66–77.

Hewison, J. and Tizard, J. (1980). Parental involvement and reading attainment. *British Journal of Educational Psychology*, 50, 209–215.

Hidi, S. and Harackiewicz, J. M. (2000). Motivating the academically unmotivated: A critical issue for the 21st century. *Review of Educational Research*, 70, 151–179.

Hindman, A. H. and Wasik, B. A. (2010). Head Start families sharing home language and literacy experiences. *NHSA Dialog: A Research-to-Practice Journal for the Early Childhood Field*, 13(2), 112–118.

Hollomotz, A. (2009). Beyond 'vulnerability': An ecological model approach to conceptualising risk of sexual violence against people with learning difficulties. *British Journal of Social Work*, 39(1), 99–112.

Homel, R., Elias, G. and Hay, I. (2001). Developmental prevention in a disadvantaged community. In R. Eckersley, J. Dixon and R. Douglas (eds), *The Social Origins of Health and Well-being: From the Planetary to the Molecular* (pp. 269–279). Melbourne: Cambridge University Press.

Hoover-Dempsey, K. V. and Sandler, H. M. (1995). Parental involvement in children's education: Why does it make a difference? *Teachers College Record*, 97(2), 310–331.

Hoover-Dempsey, K. V. and Sandler, H. M. (1997). Why do parents become involved in their children's education? *Review of Education Research*, 67(1), 3–42.

Hoover-Dempsey, K. V., Walker, J. M. T., Sandler, H. M., Whetsel, D., Green, C. L., Wilkins, A.S., et al. (2005). Why do parents become involved? Research findings and implications. *The Elementary School Journal*, 106(2), 105–130.

Houghton, S. and Bain, A. (1993). Peer tutoring with ESL and below average readers. *Journal of Behavioural Education*, 3, 125–142.

Houghton, S. and Glynn, T. (1993). Peer tutoring of below average secondary school readers using Pause, Prompt and Praise: A successive introduction to tutoring components. *Behaviour Change*, 10, 75–85.

Huey, E. B. (1908). *The Psychology and Pedagogy of Reading*. Cambridge, MA: The MIT Press.

Karoly, L., Kilburn, M. and Cannon, J. (2005). *Early Childhood Interventions: Proven Results, Future Promise*. Santa Monica, CA: RAND.

Kearney, J., Fletcher, M. and Dobrenov-Major, M. (2009). *Improving Literacy Outcomes for Samoan-Australian Students in Logan City*. Canberra: DEEWR.

Kemp, M. (1987a). Parents as teachers of literacy: What more have we learned from them? *Australian Journal of Reading*, 10, 25–31.

Kemp, M. (1987b). *Watching Children Read and Write: Observational Records for Children with Special Needs*. Melbourne: Nelson.

McNaughton, S., Glynn, T. and Robinson, V. (1987). *Pause, Prompt and Praise: Effective Tutoring of Remedial Reading*. Birmingham, UK: Positive Products.

McNaughton, S., Parr, J., Timperley, H. and Robinson, V. (1992). Beginning reading and sending books home to read: A case for fine tuning. *Educational Psychology*, 12, 239–241.

Mafi, S. (2005). *Achieving Better Educational Outcomes for Pacific Islander Young People*. Ipswich, QLD: Education Queensland.

Miller, S. D. (2003). How high- and low-challenge tasks affect motivation and learning: Implications for struggling learners. *Reading and Writing Quarterly*, 19, 39–57.

Ministerial Council on Education, Employment, Training and Youth Affairs (MCEETYA) (2008). *Melbourne Declaration on Educational Goals for Young Australians*. Melbourne: Education Services Australia.

Moles, O. C. (2000). *Reaching all families: Creating family-friendly schools, beginning of the school year activities*. ED Pubs, P.O. Box 1398, Jessup, MD 20794 – 1398. Available at: http://search.proquest.com/docview/62347527?accountid=28745

Morgan, L. and Goldstein, H. (2004). Teaching mothers in low socio-economic status to use decontextualized language during storybook reading. *Journal of Early Intervention*, 26, 235–252.

Neuman, S. B. (1995). Reading together: A community-supported parent tutoring program. *The Reading Teacher*, 49, 120–129.

Nichols, S. (2000). Parental involvement in supporting children with learning difficulties. *Australian Journal of Learning Difficulties*, 5, 23–33.

OECD (2004). *Learning for Tomorrow's World: First Results from PISA 2003*. Paris: OECD.

Ofsted (2009). Twenty Outstanding Primary Schools Excelling Against the Odds. Available at: www.ofsted.gov.uk/resources/twenty-outstanding-primary-schools-excelling-against-odds (accessed 11 October 2011).

Padak, N. and Rasinski, T. (2004). Fast Start: A promising practice for family literacy programs. *Family Literacy Forum*, 3(2), 3–9.

Paratore, J. R. and Edwards, P. A. (2011) Parent-teacher partnerships that make a difference in children's literacy achievement. In L. Mandel Morrow and L. Gambrell (eds) *Best Practices in Literacy Instruction*. New York: The Guilford Press. pp. 436–54.

Peña, D. C. (2001). Parent involvement: Influencing factors and implications. *Journal of Educational Research*, 94, 42–54.

Roe, M. F. and Vukelich, C. (2001). Understanding the gap between the America Reads Program and the tutoring sessions: The nesting of challenges. *Journal of Research in Childhood Education*, 16, 39–52.

Rohrbeck, C. A., Ginsburg-Block, M. D. and Fantuzzo, J. W. (2003). Peer assisted learning with elementary school students: A meta-analytic review. *Journal of Educational Psychology*, 95, 240–257.

Rose, J. (2009). *Independent Review of the Primary Curriculum: Final Report*. Nottingham: DCSF Publications.

Schalock, R. L. (2004). The emerging disability paradigm and its implications for policy and practice. *Journal of Disability Policy Studies*, 14(4), 204–215.

Snow, C. E. (2002). *Reading for Understanding: Toward a Research and Development Program in Reading Comprehension*. Santa Monica, CA: Rand Corp. Available at: www.rand.org/publications/MR/MR1465/ (accessed 12 December 2002).

Stuart, M., Dixon, M., Masterson, J. and Quinlan, P. (1998). Learning to read at home and at school. *British Journal of Educational Psychology*, 68, 3–14.

Topping, K. (1996). The effectiveness of family literacy. In S. Wolfendale and K. Topping (eds), *Family Involvement in Literacy* (pp. 149–163). London: Cassell.

Topping, K. (1998). Effective tutoring in America Reads: A reply to Wasik. *The Reading Teacher*, 52, 42–49.

Topping, K. and Wolfendale, S. (1995). The effectiveness of family literacy programmes. *Reading*, 29, 26–33.

Veen, A. (1999). Research on the relationship between migrant parents and primary schools. In F. Smit, H. Moerel, K. Van der Wolf and P. Sleegers (eds), *Building Bridges between Home and School* (pp. 27–30). Amsterdam: University of Nijmegen.

Vollmeyer, R. and Rheinberg, F. (2005). A surprising effect of feedback on learning. *Learning and Instruction*, 15, 589–602.

Vygotsky, L. S. (1962). *Thought and Language*. Cambridge, MA: Harvard University Press.

Wasik, B. A. (1998a) Volunteer tutoring programs in reading: A review. *Reading Research Quarterly*, 33, 266–292.

Wasik, B. A. (1998b). Using volunteers as reading tutors: Guidelines for successful practices. *The Reading Teacher*, 51, 562–569.

Wheldall, K. and Metten, P. (1985). Behavioural Peer tutoring: training 16-year-old tutors to employ the 'pause, prompt and praise' method with 12-year-old remedial readers. *Educational Psychology*, 5, 27–44.

Woolley, G. (2010). Issues in the identification and ongoing assessment of ESL students with reading difficulties for reading intervention. *Australasian Journal of Learning Difficulties*, 34(2), 119–132.

Woolley, G. (2011). *Reading Comprehension: Assisting Children with Learning Difficulties*. Dordrecht, The Netherlands: Springer International.

Worthy, J., Patterson, E., Salas, R., Prater, S. and Turner, M. (2002). More than just reading: The human factor in reaching resistant readers. *Reading Research and Instruction*, 41, 177–202.

INDEX

Added to a page number 'f' denotes a figure and 't' denotes a table.